"I loved this book! I was engrossed by the sometimes sharp disagreements coupled with the contributors' grace and mutuality. The book was a real page turner in places. For example, I could hardly wait to see what Greg Stier had to say about Fernando Arzola's critique of his primary point. *Youth Ministry in the 21st Century* triggers deep reflection about models and motives and will facilitate advancement of that very kingdom enterprise, youth ministry."

—**Len Kageler**, Nyack College

"Most youth pastors struggle to ever get beneath the day-to-day aspects of youth ministry. But if you want to get to the heart of why and what you do, get this book! The five views expressed allow anyone to explore, compare, and strive to live out a biblically based philosophy of youth ministry. This book belongs on the required reading lists of all youth ministry programs and deserves to be on the shelf of any youth pastor who wants a deeper understanding of where they are, how they got there, and where they might want to go in the future."

—**Allen Pointer**, youth pastor, speaker, trainer, and owner of Point A Coaching

"I have been craving this discussion of youth ministry models with deep theological roots, pointed critiques, and passionate debate on the pros and cons of each view. I predict that *Youth Ministry in the 21st Century* will be a much-needed push beyond the glut of negative statistics about adolescents and their faith into deeper exploration of the theological underpinnings of next-generation ministry and reimagining of effective models of youth ministry. I cannot wait to use this book in my college and seminary classrooms."

—**Danny Mitchell**, youth ministry coordinator, Committee on Discipleship Ministries, Presbyterian Church in America

"As a former youth pastor and Youth For Christ director turned educator, I welcome the critical thinking, assessment, consensus, collaboration, varying perspectives, and even the disagreement found in this book. And while I embrace discussions of theory, this project helpfully transforms theories into the building blocks of ministry practices, skill sets, and practical theology. Whether you have a high youth ministry IQ or you are in youth ministry 101, this book will challenge your thinking."

—**Steve Vandegriff**, Liberty University

# YOUTH MINISTRY

## IN THE 21ST CENTURY

# Youth, Family, and Culture Series

### Chap Clark, series editor

The Youth, Family, and Culture series examines the broad categories involved in studying and caring for the needs of the young and is dedicated to the preparation and vocational strengthening of those who are committed to the spiritual development of adolescents.

# YOUTH MINISTRY

## IN THE 21ST CENTURY

## CENTURY

# FIVE VIEWS

### Chap Clark, Editor

**Baker Academic**

*a division of Baker Publishing Group*
Grand Rapids, Michigan

Published by Baker Academic
a division of Baker Publishing Group
P.O. Box 6287, Grand Rapids, MI 49516-6287
www.bakeracademic.com

Printed in the United States of America

Library of Congress Cataloging-in-Publication Data
Youth ministry in the 21st century : five views / Chap Clark, editor.
     pages cm. — (Youth, family, and culture)
     Includes bibliographical references and index.
     ISBN 978-0-8010-4967-5 (pbk.)
     1. Church work with youth. I. Clark, Chap, 1954– editor. II. Title: Youth ministry in the twenty-first century.
     BV4447.Y5843 2015
     259'.23—dc23                                                          2015007110

15   16   17   18   19   20   21          7   6   5   4   3   2   1

# Contents

Acknowledgments    ix

Introduction: Why This Book?    xi

Introducing the Authors    xix

VIEW ONE:    **Greg Stier**

The Gospel Advancing View of Youth Ministry    3

Responses to the Gospel Advancing View    17

Brian Cosby ✚ Chap Clark ✚ Fernando
Arzola ✚ Ron Hunter ✚ Greg Stier's Response

VIEW TWO:    **Brian Cosby**

The Reformed View of Youth Ministry    37

Responses to the Reformed View    53

Greg Stier ✚ Chap Clark ✚ Fernando Arzola ✚ Ron
Hunter ✚ Brian Cosby's Response

VIEW THREE:    **Chap Clark**

The Adoption View of Youth Ministry    73

Responses to the Adoption View    91

Greg Stier ✚ Brian Cosby ✚ Fernando
Arzola ✚ Ron Hunter ✚ Chap Clark's Response

VIEW FOUR:   **Fernando Arzola**

The Ecclesial View of Youth Ministry   113

Responses to the Ecclesial View   125

Greg Stier ✦ Brian Cosby ✦ Chap Clark ✦ Ron
Hunter ✦ Fernando Arzola's Response

VIEW FIVE:   **Ron Hunter**

The D6 View of Youth Ministry   147

Responses to the D6 View   163

Greg Stier ✦ Brian Cosby ✦ Chap Clark ✦ Fernando
Arzola ✦ Ron Hunter's Response

Afterword: Where from Here?   179

Notes   181

Index   191

# Acknowledgments

**Greg Stier:** Thanks to Jane Dratz for her tireless efforts to make this project. excellent. Her editing skills, insights, and ideas have been a gift from God! I am also deeply grateful to Debbie Bresina, who has been working with me for almost twenty years at Dare 2 Share. Her forthright and wise input into this project, like so many others, has been invaluable.

**Brian Cosby:** I'd like to thank Doug Griffith, Norm Dunkin, and Tim Gwin, who guided me as I wrestled through a means-of-grace and consistently Reformed understanding of ministry in general and youth ministry in particular. Though he doesn't know me, I'd like to thank Voddie Baucham for his theological and exegetical assistance in helping me develop a much more family-supporting approach to my position. Finally, I'd like to thank my wife, Ashley, for her loving support of me over the years as I've engaged to equip the saints for the work of ministry.

**Chap Clark:** Many thanks to the writers in this book, and for all those who keep pushing the edges of youth ministry in the service of the kingdom. And, of course, as always, thanks to Dee, Chap, Rob, Katie, and Ben. You all help me to keep pursuing new views every day!

**Fernando Arzola:** I am grateful to Dr. David Turk and my colleagues at Nyack College for their continued support of my scholarship. To my mother, Aida, and my sister, Rebecca, for their affirmations. To my wife, Jill, for her continued support of my research. To my daughter, Nicole, who has taught me more about adolescent development and youth ministry than any book ever has. To the teens in the Bronx and throughout the New York City area who have kept me honest and youthful in mind and spirit. Finally, special thanks to Chap Clark for his invitation to participate in this endeavor and his encouragement throughout the process.

**Ron Hunter:** Special thanks to Richard Ross, Timothy Paul Jones, Ben Freudenburg, Mark DeVries, Mark Holmen, Brian Haynes, John Trent, Jim Burns, Steven Wright, Tim Kimmel, and Rob Rienow, most of whom lived, wrote about, and taught Deuteronomy 6 before it was called D6. Thanks also to Chap Clark for making this project happen.

# Introduction

### Why This Book?

[Jesus] matters because of what he brought and what he still brings to *ordinary* human beings, living their ordinary lives and coping daily with the surroundings. He promises wholeness for their lives. In sharing our weakness he gives us strength and imparts through his companionship a life that has the quality of eternity.

He comes where we are, and he brings us the life we hunger for. . . . To be the light of life, and to deliver God's life to women and men where they are and as they are, is the secret of the enduring relevance of Jesus.

—Dallas Willard,
*The Divine Conspiracy*

Oh, that we would, that we could, pass excitement for Jesus on to our kids.

—Comment by a father following a
parent meeting on lifelong faith

In 2001 I had the chance to join three other youth ministry leaders to come together to debate in the book *Four Views of Youth Ministry and the Church*: Trinity Evangelical Divinity School's Mark H. Senter III, the editor; Southwestern Baptist's Wesley Black; and Malan Nel, from South Africa. We were invited to define and defend one of four ways of looking at youth ministry, write a brief critique of the other three, and finally have one last word in response to the critiques. The four positions were

> *inclusive congregational* (Nel), where a church "thoroughly integrates its adolescents";
> *preparatory* (Black), seeing youth ministry as preparing "disciples in training";
> *strategic* (Senter), youth ministry as a church-planting strategy; and
> *missional* (Clark), where the emphasis is to focus on evangelism as the primary goal of the ministry.

The initial idea for the book came from an original editor who had asked a couple of us to participate, assigned us the chapters, and instructed us to each do the best job we could to make a distinctive argument in favor of our "view." As the project took shape, the driving theme became to make sure that the boundaries of the view itself framed the central idea, and that the objective was to draw people into debate and ultimately conversation so as to help them to build a comprehensive and integrated model of doing youth ministry. As I subtly noted in the book, the artificial nature of the need for each author to avoid nuance but to make a strong, solid case for his view made for an interesting textbook and dialogue starter but was also somewhat difficult in that each of us occasionally felt overly boxed in regarding what we had written. I, for one, do generally believe in what I wrote about the "missional view of youth ministry," but not without much qualification.

The book has sold well, and continues to do so to this day. I still hear stories of *Four Views of Youth Ministry and the Church* being a helpful resource for churches, and it even remains a textbook in many college and seminary classrooms. I am grateful for the conversation this book has stirred for the past decade and a half, and I am both proud and honored to have been a part of it.

## Why *Youth Ministry in the 21st Century: Five Views*?

As youth ministry has continued to move forward since 2001, with greater emphasis on the many complex issues kids and churches face—like family and parent ministry, dealing with serious crisis and youth at risk, social justice, gender and sexuality, implementing a "practical theology," and missional evangelism—the need for a new conversation has emerged. It is not that the four views themselves have gone away but that the game has changed a great deal since then, and the bar is much higher for us who work with and care for kids in God's name than at any time in recent memory.

It seems to me that what we do not need at this time in youth ministry history is a few more generic models to kick around, to debate their merits, and then set out to create our own contextual way of going about our business. Today in the church, and especially in youth ministry, we are being forced by society and by real people to go deeper and to find more stable theological footing for not only what and how we do our work but also why we do it and where it fits into God's plan for the entire church. Today around the world we are more global, more economically and technologically connected, and arguably more actively invested in the plight of the oppressed, abused, and broken than ever before. At the same time, as a group, Christians have never been under more intellectual attack or more publicly disregarded than we are today. We are also less trusted and considered less relevant than we have been in decades, if not centuries. The rise of the "nones" in United States census data confirms what popular culture has been telling us for several years: that to many of our neighbors, we as a "religious bloc" are at core culturally backward, ignorant, bigoted, and far more concerned with our own agenda and self-protection than we are with even the basic tenets of Jesus. Adding to this societal stereotype, young adults and adolescents are leaving our ranks, and those who still express some level of faith have been described by researchers as having such a shallow understanding of their faith that, as a group, they are "moralistic therapeutic deists."[1] They are also more stressed, and have more expressed struggles, than any generation in recent memory.[2]

Today's youth ministry is in desperate need of a theological, psychosocial, and ecological grounding. We need a fresh trajectory, a new idea. While certainly there are lots of powerful and meaningful ministries, churches, and organizations making a significant impact on the lives of teenagers, there is also a darker underbelly to how difficult it is to maintain the glow of the early years of youth ministry. Few dispute the reality of lengthened adolescence—whether we refer to the newly minted "emerging adult" as a fourth developmental stage (that place between adolescence and adulthood) or believe that adolescence itself is simply extending, in many cases well into the thirties and beyond—the developmental reality of what it means to be a teenager has dramatically changed in the last thirty years. Even the brain MRI studies confirm two things that affect the future of youth ministry: it takes ten years or more today for the adolescent brain to fully develop its adult capacity, and the speed at which it does so is directly linked to the amount and quality of attachments a child/adolescent experiences (which in most cases today are far less than in years gone by).[3] The days of hiring a superstar "youth pastor" and enlisting a few volunteers to run a "quality" youth ministry program on the relational fringe of a church and expecting measurable enthusiasm for a lifelong commitment to Christ and the faith community, much less observable spiritual transformation, have been fading for years if not decades. The larger the church (or organization) and/or the larger the budget, the more capacity for producing the kind of programs that, at least initially, attract kids and demonstrate what looks like health and depth. The evidence, however, is that because even this "success" is located in the developmental center point of an adolescent's journey to maturity, many if not most of them will still need something beyond youth ministry to enable them to find their way to lifelong, mature faith.

Thus this book, which is an attempt to bring together five voices who, while perhaps not representative of all of the major themes in contemporary youth ministry, bring a fundamental way of thinking when it comes to grounding the church's calling to the young. *Youth Ministry in the 21st Century* differs from *Four Views of Youth Ministry and the Church* in our concern not to present a few distinct models of "doing" youth ministry. The authors in this book do not so much advocate for a theoretically distinct model, as helpful as that approach in the original book is; rather, they advocate for their own convictions and perspectives on what ministry to adolescents essentially *is*. Our desire is to offer five relatively unique voices and perspectives on the *basics* and *foundation* of what youth ministry should be about now and in the coming decades. Each author brings years of commitment, writing, leadership, and sponsorship to his perspective. None is asked to soften his perspective or write up his take in such a way as to make for a clean, distinctive, and clear dialogical framework. Each believes that when push comes to shove, his position is preferable and perhaps even simply correct. That is the beauty and the risk of this adventure.

One more point that must be acknowledged at the outset of this project is that the authors do not represent the wide diversity of people who serve the kingdom of God in youth ministry, especially in terms of gender, race, and theological tradition. We know that there are many others who have important and distinct voices and perspectives on these and other positions discussed, and they deserve to be heard. The editorial decision, however, came down to the uniqueness of each of the authors and the followers they represent. Each author has a long, reputable, and, most important, well-known leadership ministry that is reflected in his viewpoint and a global reputation that sets him apart. For the purposes of this book, our hope is that the reader will take this book for what it is, knowing that we realize this is a weakness.

Another and similar point is in answer to the question, Why weren't other popular authors and ministry influencers—in some cases far more well-known, like Kara Powell and Doug Fields—asked to participate? The issue related to choosing the authors of this book had to do with how their views represent a theoretical, and theological, foundation on which youth ministry strategy and practice could flow. Kara Powell, my close friend and long-term colleague at Fuller Theological Seminary, is not only one of the recently recognized "Most Influential Women" by *Christianity Today* but, as the executive director of the Fuller Youth Institute, is also a gifted and prolific author and speaker. Her writing and work, however, at least in the last few years, has focused less on a detailed description of the theological foundations of youth ministry than on the essential elements of what it means for a Christian community to nurture lifelong faith in adolescents, primarily through the *Sticky Faith* body of work.[4] Kara and her team, of which I am a part, work with and represent the faculty members at Fuller's three schools who research and study family and youth issues—everything from youth at risk to urban trauma to the leadership realities affecting congregational change. This is all extremely valuable and helpful work for the church and parachurch. For the purposes of this book, Fuller Youth Institute's work could be a useful resource and strategy to any of the views expressed.

Doug Fields, arguably the prototypical youth ministry leader who has had the greatest influence on the field, is also noticeably absent (as are so many others too numerous to mention).[5] *Purpose Driven Youth Ministry* is one of the most comprehensive books on youth ministry programming ever written. It is based on the theological premise that there are five "purposes" of the church, and therefore of youth ministry, and that we must then structure our programs to fulfill those purposes. It can be argued that many if not most people who actually employ *Purpose Driven Youth Ministry* (PDYM) use it as less of a *theology* of ministry than a *structural philosophy* of how to do Christian ministry. PDYM (and other related materials) is, without a doubt, the cleanest, most easily applicable and direct manual on putting together a youth ministry program. For our purposes in *Youth Ministry in the 21st Century*, however, we were looking for emerging foundational assumptions that would drive the implementation of PDYM or *Sticky Faith*.

There is no doubt that in terms of their contribution to youth ministry, both *Purpose Driven Youth Ministry* and *Sticky Faith* have changed the way youth ministry is strategized. The beauty of both of these authors, books, and programs is their flexibility (thus the multiple languages they have been translated into). Any one of our five views can easily use either of these books and strategies to create a program and implement it. Perhaps a way to consider the difference is to see PDYM and *Sticky Faith* as containers or shells, or an operating system within which different foundational philosophical and theological systems can work like different programs on a phone or tablet. Almost anyone who has a solid handle on what they want to pass on (the discipleship classes in PDYM, for example, or parent training in *Sticky Faith*) and who has staff and a church willing to incarnate themselves with kids can be greatly helped by either. So a Pentecostal, a Roman Catholic, one of Brian Cosby's "orthodox Reformed" followers (see his chapter), student leadership devotees, and even communities that aren't Christian can and are using PDYM and *Sticky Faith*. Thus we have chosen to focus on those perspectives that were so foundational that they could fit either of these strategies.

## Getting the Most Out of *Youth Ministry in the 21st Century*

Our hope is that you will engage the perspectives and issues raised here to examine more deeply what youth ministry is in your context and what it should be. Our intent is to give you a clear and compelling apologetic for each of our views and to defend their basic tenets even as we attempt to respond to and at times "correct" one another. This idea is not to stake our claims in such a way that we would enlist followers to walk with us in lock step but rather to engage the conversation regarding where the church needs to go in the future concerning our love for and ministry to the young in the future. It is possible, perhaps even probable, that you may forge your own way by combining one, two, or several of the views into your theological map.

We also hope you engage this book in a group. We as authors are convinced that our best work is done when we collaborate, push against others, and work to integrate insights that the Lord may wish to sharpen through our willingness to listen and speak to one another. We believe that is true for every person, especially for those in leadership.

We have added a web-based element to this journey as well. Baker Academic, in partnership with Fuller Theological Seminary, has created a website dedicated to this book, www.youthministry.fuller.edu. This site will not be limited to this book but will also include the forthcoming *Adoptive Youth Ministry: Integrating Emerging Generations into the Family of Faith* and other books and topics that move us to think differently about youth ministry. In addition, the website will offer several videos related to *21st Century Youth Ministry: Five Views* as well as other youth ministry topics.

So grab a few friends and hash out the pros and cons of each view. Argue (kindly) as you formulate your own viewpoint. And allow yourself to be critical not just of our words but of your own convictions, assumptions, and history. Perhaps out of this churches and organizations will grow in how they think about ministry as we move deeper into the twenty-first century. This is our overall goal. And perhaps also more kids will know that Jesus Christ and the kingdom of God are their calling and vocation and that the body of Christ is the family that God has given to them as they grow in his likeness for his sake and glory. That is, at the end of the day, the reason for all of this. We thank you for joining in on the conversation.

# Introducing the Authors

Five authors, five views of youth ministry in the twenty-first century. In order not to give preference to any author, as editor (Chap Clark) I made the decision to not put our articles in alphabetical order, because I would be first. I then thought maybe we would go with the first name, but for such an illustrious group of leaders that seemed a bit too informal. I finally decided to go the biblical route and cast lots (or actually, to draw out of a hat!). Thus the authors listed here are not in alphabetical order, but in order of the articles they have written.

**Greg Stier** is founder and president of Dare 2 Share Ministries, a ministry that equips teenagers to share their faith relationally. Greg has spoken to and trained over a million teens and youth leaders in the last twenty years. A former pastor, church planter, and youth leader, Greg is the author of fifteen books. He has been married to his wife, Debbie, for twenty-two years. They have two children.

**Brian Cosby** (PhD, Australian College of Theology) is the author of a number of books, including *Giving Up Gimmicks: Reclaiming Youth Ministry from an Entertainment Culture* and *Rebels Rescued: A Student's Guide to Reformed Theology*. He has served in youth ministry for over a decade and currently pastors Wayside Presbyterian Church (PCA) in Signal Mountain, Tennessee.

**Chap Clark** (PhD, University of Denver) is professor and chair of Youth, Family, and Culture at Fuller Theological Seminary. Chap was on the Young Life Staff for fifteen years, has been a senior pastor, was the vice provost at Fuller for several years, served as senior editor for *Youthworker Journal* for eight years, and is president of ParenTeen, a nonprofit organization that provides parenting, culture, and family seminars and consulting. He has written or coauthored over twenty books. He has been married for thirty-five years to Dee. They have three grown children and live in Gig Harbor, Washington.

**Fernando Arzola** (PhD, Fordham University) is dean of the College of Arts and Sciences and associate professor of religion at Nyack College. He is the author of *Evangelical Christian Education: Mid-Twentieth-Century Foundational Texts*; *Exploring Worship: Catholic, Evangelical and Orthodox Perspectives*; and *Toward a Prophetic Youth Ministry: Theory and Praxis in Urban Context*; and coauthor of *Foundations for Excellence*. He founded the Urban Family Empowerment Center, a holistic community center in the Bronx. He is married to Jill and has a college-age daughter, Nicole.

**Ron Hunter** is the executive director and CEO of Randall House and the publisher of D6 Curriculum, and serves as the D6 Conference Director. He regularly speaks at various conferences and consults for ministry and business organizations. Ron has written numerous articles for various Christian magazines and coauthored *Toy Box Leadership*. He graduated from Welch College and earned his MPA from the University of Colorado, and is in his final stages of earning his PhD from Dallas Baptist University. He married his college sweetheart, Pamela, and they have two children in college, Michael and Lauren.

# Greg Stier

# The Gospel Advancing View
# of Youth Ministry

'm convinced that Jesus was a youth leader. Before you shake your head
in disagreement, think about this. Most rabbis at his time engaged their
disciples to follow them when they were in their teenage years.[1]

There also seems to be scriptural support for this radical assertion. Two
relatively unknown Bible passages, one in the Old Testament and one in the
New, indirectly point toward the likelihood that most of the disciples were
teenagers when they began to follow Jesus.

In Matthew 17:24–27 we read,

> After Jesus and his disciples arrived in Capernaum, the collectors of the two-
> drachma temple tax came to Peter and asked, "Doesn't your teacher pay the
> temple tax?"
>
> "Yes, he does," he replied.
>
> When Peter came into the house, Jesus was the first to speak. "What do you
> think, Simon?" he asked. "From whom do the kings of the earth collect duty
> and taxes—from their own children or from others?"
>
> "From others," Peter answered.
>
> "Then the children are exempt," Jesus said to him. "But so that we may not
> cause offense, go to the lake and throw out your line. Take the first fish you
> catch; open its mouth and you will find a four-drachma coin. Take it and give
> it to them for my tax and yours."

This passage gets more interesting because all of his disciples arrived in
Capernaum, but only Peter and Jesus seem to have paid the temple tax. When
you cross-reference this passage with Exodus 30:14, you can see the youth

ministry implications: "All who cross over, those twenty years old or more, are to give an offering to the Lord."

All the disciples were there. Only Peter and Jesus paid. The temple tax is only for those twenty years old or older. If I'm reading this right, then Jesus was a youth leader with one adult sponsor (and one really rotten kid named Judas). He had a small youth ministry budget and no youth room. But with that small youth group, he changed the world.

The question is, how? The answer is clear.

But before we dive into the answer, you may be thinking something like, "Well, that was Jesus. Sure, he could take a group of teenagers who smelled of fish and turn them into world changers. After all he was the Son of God."

I'm sure his disciples assumed the same. After Jesus was gone, things would go back to normal because, after all, Jesus was God in the flesh. But Jesus reminded them as he reminds us in John 14:12, "Very truly I tell you, whoever believes in me will do the works I have been doing, and they will do even greater things than these, because I am going to the Father."

Jesus is telling us that you and I can drive the same basic model that he did with his small youth group and do even greater things! Why? Because now Jesus is working from the inside out! Through the Holy Spirit, Jesus himself is advancing his kingdom through each of us, including those involved in youth ministry—both the adults, paid and volunteer, and the believing students.

The question arises that, if this is the case, then why aren't youth ministries seeing the same results? I believe the answer lies not in complexity but in simplicity.

The modern youth ministry model has largely abandoned the focus of Jesus and delivers, instead, a series of competing programs. We have exchanged mission for meetings. We have separated evangelism and discipleship. We have turned outreach into a program instead of a lifestyle.

What I'm about to share with you is not original with me or the ministry I lead, Dare 2 Share. It is a cutting-edge, highly relevant ministry philosophy that's two thousand years old. It's what I call a Gospel Advancing Ministry. It's what we see in the Gospels and what we read about in the book of Acts.

It's a messy approach that embraces the bad, the broken, and the bullied. But it's an approach that truly transforms teenagers not into "good church kids" but into world changers.

When the religious crowds criticized Jesus for going into the house of a notorious sinner, he gave us a peek behind the curtain of what drove him. He simply responded, "For the Son of Man came to seek and to save the lost" (Luke 19:10).

At the core of the heart of Jesus is a desperate search-and-rescue mission for the lost. This was the lens through which he trained his disciples. His earthly ministry with his followers was basically a three-and-a-half-year mission trip laced with teaching and training meetings along the way.

Toward the end of that mission trip, Jesus connected his mission and the mission of his disciples in what is commonly called "the Great Commission." (I call it "the Cause" because teenagers are into causes, and the term "Great Commission" doesn't quite connect with them.)[2] He told them, "All authority in heaven and on earth has been given to me. Therefore go and make disciples of all nations, baptizing them in the name of the Father and of the Son and of the Holy Spirit, and teaching them to obey everything I have commanded you. And surely I am with you always, to the very end of the age" (Matt. 28:18–20).

If we really want teenagers to be like Jesus, then we must cultivate in them a driving passion to reach the lost. And, as we begin to unpack this ministry approach, I believe you'll agree that cultivating this passion in believing students not only brings lost souls into the kingdom, but leads to discipleship acceleration in their own hearts and lives.

Again, the goal here is not more evangelistic programs but nurturing teenagers to live and give the gospel in word and deed in their spheres of influence. When reaching non-Christians with the gospel becomes a primary passion of their hearts, transformation is triggered on a whole host of spiritual development levels.

It was a Gospel Advancing Ministry that transformed my life from the inside out when I was a teenager. I'll never forget the first time I attended the youth group known as "Youth Ranch."

I could tell right away that this youth group was different. Over a hundred urban, suburban, and rural teenagers were tightly packed into a poorly decorated youth room, interacting and laughing. The conversations were not normal; they centered on Jesus—sharing Jesus and growing in Jesus. And cliques (although I'm sure there were some) didn't dominate the atmosphere.

Teens of different ethnicities and socioeconomic backgrounds were talking to each other. I could pick out the student leaders in the room. They were driving the conversations, introducing newcomers around, and influencing the emotional and spiritual thermostat in the room.

I immediately felt right at home.

And feeling at home wasn't something I was used to, not even at home. I never knew my biological father, and my mom was, in many ways, like the woman at the well. She had been married at least four times—maybe more. But none of those men was my biological father. No, I was the result of a short-term relationship with a guy she met at a party.

I always wondered why my mom looked at me with those eyes of guilt. Often, my tough, inner-city mother (who was known for her proficiency in fist-fighting) would burst into tears when she talked to me. Later, my grandma filled me in on the backstory. My mom had driven from Denver to Boston to have an illegal abortion when she found out she was pregnant with me. My grandparents convinced her to come back and have the kid. Mom never knew that I knew . . . not even up to the day that she died.

I was raised "American poor" in a high crime area of Denver—in apartments and trailer parks, on a single-parent income, by a mom too proud for government assistance. I was scared and scarred during my childhood. My mom and five uncles had a reputation for violence, and I'd witnessed too much of it by the time I was barely in elementary school.

But this Youth Ranch youth group in the suburbs reached out to the city and was used by God to reach my entire family for Jesus Christ. Eventually aunts, uncles, cousins, my mom, and my half-brother, Doug, were transformed by the amazing good news of Jesus Christ. All because of one Gospel Advancing church that had an amazing Gospel Advancing student ministry.

At the end of the day, like every other teenager, what I really needed was security and significance. This security comes from the message that nothing can separate us from the love of God (Rom. 8:39). It was this gospel reality that helped me realize that I didn't need an earthly father because I had a heavenly one. And my new Father would never leave me nor forsake me. This youth ministry provided mentors in my life who became my spiritual fathers and mothers. They poured into me and told me again and again that I was lavishly loved by God. This theological security that burst forth from the gospel saved me from a floundering, wasted, and potentially crime-ridden life.

But this Gospel Advancing student ministry didn't stop there. The people there gave me significance, as well. I had a purpose, a mission, and a cause to live for. They relentlessly drove home the urgency of reaching other teenagers with the gospel. They trained us how to live it and how to give it. They challenged us to engage in gospel conversations everywhere we went.

As a young teenager, I stepped out and initiated a Bible study for my neighborhood friends, whom I had the privilege of leading to Christ. This didn't come naturally to me, but I was inspired and equipped by my youth leaders. We all were.

Over the years, that youth group exploded to literally hundreds in attendance weekly. The vast majority of us had put our faith in Jesus as a result of the youth group's outreach efforts. And a primary focus of those efforts was equipping us teenagers to share Jesus with our friends, disciple the new believers, and equip them to do the same.

To be honest, it wasn't as complicated as you might think.

They had one purpose: to energize a generation to evangelize their world. Discipleship shook out from there. Their premise was that teenagers could change the world, and in the process, their own hearts would be transformed by a deeper and deeper relationship with Jesus. In other words, as teenagers advanced the gospel externally into their community, the gospel would also advance internally, deeper into their hearts.

As I search the New Testament, I see this same ministry philosophy on full display in the life of Jesus and his followers. And as a youth leader and church planter, I've seen it work. That's why it forms the basis for the youth ministry model I train youth leaders in all across the country.

## The Benefit of a Gospel Advancing Ministry Model

Unfortunately, in the twenty-first-century youth ministry context, discipleship has been relegated to a meeting where some sort of information is exchanged between the youth leader and the attending teenagers. Stories are told. Blanks are filled. And, if you look at the statistics, not much sticks.[3]

Why? Because we have failed to capture the heart of Jesus's desperate quest to reach the lost! We have communicated to our young people that the Christian life is about more meetings. Go to camp (meeting). Go to youth group (meeting). Go to small group (meeting). Go to church (meeting).

Yes, Jesus had meetings, but they were in the midst of an ongoing mission. He taught his disciples as he took them from town to town preaching the gospel of the kingdom. He debriefed, shared insights, and interpreted parables as he prepared his small youth group for evangelistic action. By the time he was finished, they were leading the charge for the evangelistic outreaches, and he was coaching them. This was the essence of Jesus's discipleship process.

I'll never forget when I was a middle school youth leader at a small Baptist church in Arvada, Colorado. My first Sunday was rough. The twenty or so middle schoolers had their arms folded and their lips curled in snarls. These kids were twelve and thirteen years old but already hardened little legalists who knew the answers and endured the meetings.

I had a full hour and fifteen minutes with them. I had no games or music planned. It was just me and my little lesson on evangelism. I was done in twenty minutes. They looked at each other when I declared the lesson was over with "this-guy's-never-gonna-make-it" expressions. They knew that fifty-five minutes were still on the clock.

From that point on the conversation went something like this.

"Okay, I'm done with my lesson. But we're just getting started."

Confused looks all around.

I continued, "The Bible says, 'Be doers of the word and not hearers only,' so now we're going to go and do what we just learned."

More confused looks.

"We're going to go into the neighborhood around the church and go door to door. We're going to tell people who we are, ask them how we can serve them (raking leaves, cleaning windows, etc.) and see if we can pray for them. Then we're going to seek to engage them in gospel conversations. If they are open to talking, then we'll talk with them. If they're not, we'll wish them a great day and move on."

One teen shot his trembling hand up and said, "We can't do this because we're in Sunday school."

I shot back, "Yeah, we're in Sunday *school*. During school you take field trips, and that's what we're gonna do!"

One kid blurted out, "I'll get in trouble with my parents."

I responded, "No, I'll get in trouble with your parents. But I only get paid $100 a month, so I don't care if I get fired. We are doing this!"

And we did. And those trembling teenagers came back as heroic, story-telling, high-fiving evangelists. That marked a turning point in the youth group as evangelistic action became the driving force in everything we did. I would train them in the process. We prayed together. We rejoiced together. And at times we wept together over those who rejected Jesus.

I'm not saying we should quit youth group twenty minutes in and go evangelizing the neighborhood. But I am saying that when we lead the way for evangelism personally and equip teenagers to do the same, it accelerates the discipleship process faster than just about anything.

## What a Tim Keller Tweet Taught Me about Teenagers

During one of his Q & A sessions, Tim Keller sent out an insightful tweet about students: "Teenagers have more information about God than they have experience of him. Get them in places where they have to rely on God."[4]

Of course, social justice and service projects accomplish this goal. Mission trips do this too. There's nothing like getting teenagers away from the mainland, away from technology, and putting a brick and a trowel in their hands to do some work in an impoverished part of the world. But I propose that there is *nothing* like relational evangelism to put teenagers in a position where they are forced to rely on God.

If you give the average teenager a choice to go to the Amazon to build a mud hut for the poor while fighting off hungry pythons or going to their school cafeteria and dropping the "J Bomb" on a group of their friends, most teenagers would pick the pythons. Why? Because the average teenager would rather risk getting choked by a giant snake than getting choked out of their social circle!

This very real, very visceral risk causes teenagers to count the cost of following Jesus. Yes, salvation is a free gift, but growing in grace is accelerated when their faith is stretched and they learn to joyfully risk everything in service to the King.

This is exactly what James was writing about in James 2:21–22: "Was not our father Abraham considered righteous for what he did when he offered his son Isaac on the altar? You see that his faith and his actions were working together, and his faith was made complete by what he did."

According to Genesis 15:6, Abraham was declared righteous when he believed God's promise. More than two decades later, he put that faith to the test by his willingness to sacrifice Isaac on the altar. "His faith and his actions were working together," and as a result his faith was matured (the word "complete" in the Greek means mature as the result of a growing process).

What does that have to do with teenagers, evangelism, and discipleship? When teenagers are willing to sacrifice what means most to them—for many, what their peers think of them—their faith and actions work together, and they are spiritually matured by that process of sacrifice.

The bottom line is that if we are serious about teenagers spiritually maturing, then we'll want to get them sharing their faith as quickly as possible.

### The Vital Elements of a Gospel Advancing Ministry

1. Equip teenagers for relational evangelism.

For teenagers to develop a lifestyle of evangelism, they need to be equipped to share their faith. This includes knowing how to naturally bring up the gospel, explain it clearly, tie in their story, and navigate various responses to the gospel. They also need to learn how to ask great questions and listen deeply to others.

Of course, this takes time, prayer, patience, and coaching. And more than anything, it takes youth leaders who are modeling evangelism personally for their students on a consistent basis.

2. Share stories, stories, and more stories.

Storytelling is the fuel of movements both big and small. What makes the book of Acts so exciting to read? All the stories of transformed lives and heroic evangelism! As teenagers share stories in youth group and youth leaders share stories in their talks, teenagers begin to see risk-taking, relational evangelism as truly transformational. As stories of evangelistic efforts begin to bear fruit and groups grow with new disciples, a Holy Spirit synergy develops; stories keep evangelism front and center, new believers share the good news with their unreached circles of friends, and excitement builds.

Of course, this process is messy. Of course, these new teenagers bring all their baggage into the group. Of course, there will be those who look at a Gospel Advancing Ministry with distain or cynicism. But, just like in the book of Acts, the momentum of changed lives overcomes all the negatives. The focus shifts from fun and games to mission and purpose.

3. Give the gospel relentlessly in youth group meetings.

Somebody once asked Charles Spurgeon what his preaching style was. His response was, "I take my text and I make a beeline for the cross."[5]

The apostle Paul said it this way in 1 Corinthians 2:2, "For I resolved to know nothing while I was with you except Jesus Christ and him crucified." Teenagers, both saved and unsaved, need to hear the gospel. Of course, this message can save the unbeliever, but it also serves to sanctify the believer.

Seasoned youth leader David Hertweck put it this way: "The message of the Gospel is not something that is solely necessary at the beginning of a teenager's faith journey; it is their faithful companion every step of the way. We never graduate from the truth of the Gospel, rather we cling to it and allow it to bring about more and more change in our lives."[6]

Why do you think Jesus left communion as a regular ordinance for the church? As a reminder that we need to continually be impacted by the message of the shed blood and broken body of Christ! The gospel's message is simple yet profound. As we plumb its depths, it saves the unbeliever, sanctifies the believer, and supercharges the Christian's mission to reach the lost.

When Jesus told his disciples to "go and make disciples," he was challenging them to take the good news "wide" (to the ends of the earth). When he mandated that they teach these new disciples to "obey everything I have commanded you," he was directing them to go deep.

This philosophy takes teenagers deeper into their relationship with God as they are going wider in their outreach to the lost. The deep feeds the wide, and the wide feeds the deep. (See fig. 1.1.) Of course, the deep side entails theological training as well as spiritual disciplines as central to building the student into a fully matured follower of Jesus.

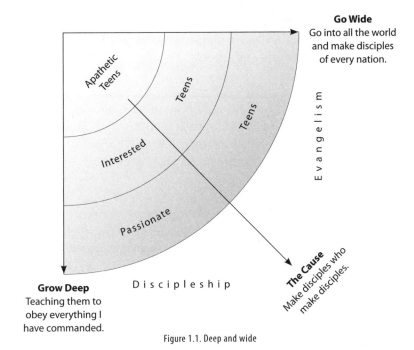

Figure 1.1. Deep and wide

## 4. Start with the 10 percent.

A Rensselaer Polytechnic Institute article titled "Minority Rules: Scientists Discover Tipping Point for the Spread of Ideas" noted the following interesting sociological phenomenon: "Scientists at Rensselaer Polytechnic Institute have found that when just 10 percent of the population holds an unshakable belief, their belief will always be adopted by the majority of the society."[7]

Have you ever wondered why Jesus poured so much into twelve young men? It's because he was getting them fully committed toward an "unshakable" set of beliefs. When he ascended and they scattered, they took this message with them everywhere they went. They were willing to die horrible deaths because of these beliefs.

As a result of Jesus focusing on the 10 percent instead of the masses, he multiplied his efforts long after he ascended into heaven.

In the same way, when youth leaders focus their efforts on getting the most willing students ready to go deep and wide, they can multiply their efforts with the other teenagers in the group. A Gospel Advancing Ministry model requires a handful of highly committed students who are willing to help the youth leader reach other students. Being a student leader is more than just setting up chairs for youth group; it's about filling those chairs with teenagers who are being reached for Christ.

Just like Jesus, youth leaders should minister to everyone but pour their lives into those teenagers who are willing to go all in for Christ and his cause. They will help reach the other teenagers.

5. Gospelize everything.

To truly build a Gospel Advancing Ministry model, nothing can be separated from the gospel. If we do a car wash fundraiser, we must figure out how to use it to effectively spread the gospel. If we do a service project, we must tie the gospel in. If we take teenagers on a mission trip—you guessed it—we gospelize it!

Our social justice efforts should ooze Jesus and be done in a more holistic way than the world's. When we give a hungry person a piece of bread, we must give them the Bread of Life as well. When we give a thirsty person water, we must give them the Living Water too. When we build someone a house on earth, we build them one in heaven as well.

If we want teenagers to truly reach out to the lost and love their neighbors as they love themselves, we must coach them on how to provide physical provisions for temporal needs, along with spiritual provisions for eternal needs.

6. Make prayer a big, big deal.

The importance of prayer in this whole process cannot be overemphasized. Isn't it interesting that Jesus was always escaping ministry opportunities to pray? He prayed for his disciples and for us (John 17:15–21). He prayed for God's glory to be magnified and God's kingdom to be advanced (Matt. 6:9–10). He prayed for strength to stand strong (Matt. 26:36–46). In the same way, we must pray, and we must mobilize teenagers to pray.

The thought of a Gospel Advancing Ministry model intimidates some. Or their first inclination may be to nitpick it apart and say, "Yeah, but . . ." or "Wait now . . ." or whatever. But I find that many times, hovering beneath these responses is a genuine conviction that this was Jesus's and the early disciples' model, though it may be quickly followed by a real fear of the implications for their life and ministry.

If the thought of building this brand of youth ministry overwhelms us, we must let it drive us to our knees in prayer. The same Jesus who said, "Go and make disciples" also said, "And surely I am with you always, to the very end of the age" (Matt. 28:19–20).

We need to pray. We need to help students learn how to pray. We need to have regular prayer meetings and put more prayer into our regular meetings. When true intercessory prayer becomes the engine and not the caboose of youth ministry strategies, we will see momentum in ways we never expected.

## What Kind of Adult Involvement Is Necessary?

1. Adult sponsors who model it.

The heart of the average teenager longs for authenticity in the adults who minister to them. They can sense the adults who are the real deal and the ones who are not. Their "attitude barometer" is on all the time.

The adults who are modeling a Gospel Advancing lifestyle will have the biggest impact on teenagers, especially if they *don't* have the gift of evangelism. Those adults with the gift of evangelism (like me) can sometimes freak teens out. We tell crazy stories of axe-wielding murderers we've led to Christ, and they cheer and clap their hands and then think to themselves, "Are you crazy? I would never do that."

But when a "normal" adult who strives and struggles to live a lifestyle of evangelism models a Gospel Advancing approach to life, students are filled with courage. They know that if those kinds of adults can do it, then maybe they can too.

Of course, this means that we need to equip adult sponsors to share their faith relationally as well. As we equip and consistently encourage them, we'll see more and more traction and impact on teens.

2. Parents who coach it.

The believing parents of teenagers in a youth group should consider themselves coaches in this whole process. Some teens need to be coached to get off the bench and get into the game of evangelism. Others need to be coached to stop tackling so hard in their apologetics or to run a little harder in their evangelistic initiative.

One of the simple ways to do this is to email three or four open-ended questions to parents every week based on the lesson content, questions that are designed to engage in real conversation. These should include at least one question that leans toward evangelism. For instance, if a lesson was on sexual purity, questions might include:

- Why is it so challenging to stay sexually pure as a teenager in this culture?
- How do you think sexual promiscuity negatively impacts the teenagers engaged in it at your school?
- How does choosing to abstain give you an opportunity to share your faith?

As youth leaders provide open-ended questions week in and week out and parents become accustomed to talking with their teenagers about spiritual things, parents will become increasingly equipped to take the primary role of discipler in the lives of their teenagers.

3. Church leaders who embrace it.

There is nothing like evangelism to rock the proverbial boat. When a youth leader starts bringing "those kinds of kids" into their youth ministry, the worries and whispers start. Before they know it, they're in an emergency elders meeting talking about their position and whether they're the right fit for the church.

That's why it's vitally important to get key church leaders on board with this strategy. Youth leaders must pray that God will grant them favor (and keep praying), then share their vision for Gospel Advancing Ministry with the board members and senior pastor.

Unfortunately, I've seen youth leaders who exercised this model get fired, even when they sought church leadership support in the right way. So it is a risk. But it's a risk that's worth taking to reach the next generation.

### Unique Differences for Ages and Stages of Development

Obviously, engaging teenagers in this model takes wisdom and strategy for every age and developmental stage. I think of it like a sport. There are amateurs, rookies, and pros.

The goal is to move younger teenagers from amateurs to rookies when it comes to evangelism. Developmentally, less mature students are typically better suited to more concrete, structured training. For example, they can learn the raw truths of the gospel message and basic ways to initiate gospel conversation. The less mature they are, the more coaching they generally need. Unleash the wrong fired-up seventh grader with a handful of Gospels of John, and he'll end up on a chair in the mall cop's office. (I know, because I was that seventh grader!)

More developmentally mature teenagers can move from rookie to pro as their more abstract, critical-thinking skills further develop. They can learn basic apologetics and the art of listening deeply to others, so that the Holy Spirit can help them find pathways into their friends' souls to effectively share the gospel with them. In this stage, they move from gospel presentations to give-and-take spiritual conversations. And they move beyond making converts to making disciples who in turn make disciples. This is the final developmental phase—that of coach. Young adults can move into this "multiplier" role and help other teenagers learn to share their faith effectively.

## Final Thoughts

When evangelism becomes the driver in the youth ministry paradigm, discipleship will flow out in ways we never imagined. The kingdom of God will advance both inwardly into the hearts of teenagers and outwardly into the heart of the community. And, to be honest, youth ministry is way more fun and way more rewarding when lives are being transformed.

Yes, we can and should have meetings. Let's keep having dodgeball tournaments, pizza parties, and lock-ins. Let's worship loud and play hard. Let's exegete, teach, and ask hard questions. But let's gospelize it all. "I am not ashamed of the gospel, because it is the power of God that brings salvation to everyone who believes: first to the Jew, then to the Gentile" (Rom. 1:16).

# Responses to the Gospel
# Advancing View

✚ **Brian Cosby**

Greg, your "Gospel Advancing" approach is clear, bold, and intriguing. For the sake of organizing my response to your position, I'd like to offer what I see as some very positive aspects of your chapter and then some areas of disagreement and constructive criticism.

### Positives of the Gospel Advancing View

Broaching the topic of evangelism among Christians typically causes many to blush, squirm, and reel with embarrassment—that they haven't evangelized enough. I constantly sense a feeling a shame and guilt when this topic gets brought up. But you have described this call and mission (or "cause" as you put it) in a very inspiring, uplifting, and exciting way. Thank you!

You do a great job in pointing out that teenagers (or any Christian, for that matter) actually grow spiritually as they boldly share the gospel. This is a point often missed. God uses the mission of the church in forming and transforming his people more and more into the image of Christ. One of the many ways this happens, as you describe it, is by being forced to depend on God. This dependence empowers a greater fellowship with God and a greater desire to grow in a deeper knowledge of him and his Word.

Another thing I really like about your chapter, Greg, is your "10 percent" discussion—how reaching 10 percent of a population or culture affects the whole. I can see this working in the local church or with students. And you

17

rightly point to the example of Jesus in choosing twelve ordinary guys to pour his life into. In turn, those twelve had a widespread impact, which would eventually lead to millions and millions of believers all over the world. While it might seem counterintuitive to pour into a select few, it actually has a greater impact in the long run. Excellent discussion.

Finally, I love your criticism of modern youth ministry, namely, that "we have turned outreach into a program instead of a lifestyle." It's easy to organize a program—it's measurable and oftentimes predictable—*unlike* a lifestyle! The switch from program-oriented to lifestyle-oriented mission and outreach can be costly to a youth pastor's job, as you point out. But this is certainly Jesus's example. Your chapter was refreshing, convicting, and encouraging all at the same time.

### My Concerns with the Gospel Advancing View

While you have many helpful thoughts, I must disagree with a number of your observations and conclusions, meant here (of course) as constructive criticism.

1. Was Jesus a "youth minister," as you suggest? Well, maybe. While they didn't have to pay the tax, they were still "grown up" by today's standards. In fact, people then were considered to come into manhood or womanhood around the age of thirteen. Many teenagers married and had families. Thus it's not a direct comparison to today's youth minister and youth. In this sense, it would be anachronistic to call Jesus a youth minister.

2. While evangelism is certainly an important aspect of ministry, it's *one* aspect of many. Your view, therefore, seems to be biblically *un*balanced. What do I mean? While evangelism is certainly what we see in the historical narrative passages in the Gospels and the book of Acts, there are also plenty of other areas of the Christian faith that we see throughout the pages of the New Testament: discipleship, church life, family life, church-state relationship, vocation, qualified elders and deacons, marriage, taking care of widows on the church rolls, caring for those in the household of faith, corporate worship, tithes/offerings, and all of the "one another" passages. All of these are important in forming youth because they are all part of the counsel of God.

Other than a few seemingly passing references to other books in the Bible, your focus is on the narrative descriptions rather than prescriptions. As you put it, "It's what we see in the Gospels and what we read about in the book of Acts." While we should learn by example and possibly even wear a WWJD bracelet, we should also pay careful attention to the commands and instruction from the entire New Testament. These, in turn, form a balanced approach with shepherding youth.

3. Another thought I have in reading your article is the overemphasis on getting youth to become "heroic, story-telling, high-fiving evangelists." If I had to summarize your chapter, it would be this: get youth to be radical, revolutionary, world-changing heroes for Jesus! But isn't Jesus the real Hero? What about the simple, faithful, plodding-along believer? Is every kid called to be a world changer? Does this really match up with the variety of gifts we find in Scripture? Is it wrong, as Paul writes, "to aspire to live quietly, and to mind your own affairs, and to work with your hands" (1 Thess. 4:11 ESV)? While we should seek to advance the gospel where we live, work, and play—as well as in focused local and foreign missions—the Christian life involves so much more, and so should youth ministry. I don't think our goal is to get "teenagers to change the world." I think our goal is to get teenagers to glorify and enjoy God forever by faithfully planting and watering the gospel through his Word, prayer, sacrament, worship, service, evangelism, and community. God changes the world through his appointed means, and he uses us to accomplish his mission.

4. Is Jesus really on a "desperate" search to seek and save the lost? Obviously, he came to seek and save the lost. But you mention his *desperation* a couple of times. It portrays Jesus as being frantic, without full control, desperately trying to get people to join his team. But this isn't the Jesus we encounter in Scripture. He's the Lord of the universe; he will build his church, and the gates of hell will not prevail against it (Matt. 16:18). He even explains why some reject him: "You do not believe because you are not among my sheep. My sheep hear my voice, and I know them, and they follow me. I give them eternal life, and they will never perish" (John 10:26–28 ESV). He exudes confidence, not desperation.

5. What about the centrality of parents, families, and the offices of elders and deacons in the local church? Other than a quick note about parents being their kids' "coaches" (where's *that* in the Bible?), this is at best secondary in this model. Because your focus is on seeing the *example* of Jesus's evangelism, this model doesn't take into account the plethora of passages dealing with family or the ordained leadership in the local church. This should be central to *any* ministry, youth ministry included.

6. What's *God's* role in evangelism? How does God save and sanctify his people? Your chapter came across with a low view of sin and a low view of God. Sin is sin. As much as we would like to twist it to be something more palatable in the realm of psychotherapy (brokenness, mistakes, etc.), the issues you describe still come back to humanity's rebellion against the holy and sovereign God. Moreover, in a chapter focused almost solely on evangelism, it would have been nice to see how salvation comes about. How does God's mission relate to our responsibility in evangelism?

7. You almost seem to pit a model of evangelism against the local church. Yes, the church "meets" together, and this "meeting" is not bad or unbiblical. It is part of the Christian life, as we see throughout the New Testament. Should we teach and lead youth to worship together and be discipled through a variety of means (evangelism included)? Of course. Should a youth pastor work closely with qualified church leaders (i.e., Acts 6; 1 Tim. 3; Titus 1; 1 Pet. 5) and parents to equip (young) saints for the work of ministry (Eph. 4)? Absolutely. Yet these are not really part of your model.

8. Finally, if your emphasis is on evangelism and seeing people come to saving faith, where's the praise and gratitude for God for saving people in the first place? Rather than praise the "heroism" of me or you or any youth, we should praise God and thank him for his grace and mercy. God uses the verbal witness of the gospel to save sinners (Rom. 10:17). But he gets the glory. I'm not suggesting that you believe otherwise; it was simply disappointing to see this entirely missed in a model driven by evangelism.

Overall, and I say this with affection, although I appreciate many aspects of your chapter and approach, it seems to me rather biblically unbalanced and devoid of God's supernatural work in regenerating souls. It also seems devoid of the primary responsibilities of the local church, parents, and God-appointed elders and deacons. In other words, you make a wonderful case for Christians being engaged in evangelism—and rightly so—but miss a holistic approach to youth ministry in the process.

## ✚ Chap Clark

"We've exchanged mission for meetings. We have separated evangelism and discipleship. We have turned outreach into a program instead of a lifestyle." In these few words, Greg Stier summarizes what drives this model. His passionate (is there any other word to describe this thoughtful, articulate evangelist and his chapter?) commitment to those who do not know Christ and his plea for God's people to see their role in verbal proclamation of the good news is infectious. I hesitate to respond because to even hint that I might be critical of this single-minded missional zeal seems to violate the very foundation of Jesus's call to his disciples, the original apostles, as well as the fifteen-year-olds in Denver. That said, because for many years I have so appreciated Greg's faithful commitment to encouraging young people to care about others, and especially those outside the faith, I do believe that there may perhaps be a few thoughts that could strengthen the foundation and practice of this model.

I begin with a few issues where I agree with you, Greg, and believe that your perspective is helpful in developing a solidly theological ministry emphasis. Following this, I will offer three thoughts for rethinking how this impassioned plea to a lifestyle of evangelism relates to the church as the body of Christ and its mission to the world. In closing, I will try to bring these two together.

### *Where "Gospel Advancing Ministry" Is an Important Component of Any Youth Ministry Strategy*

1. As a seminary professor, one of the most important roles I play is to help students and church leaders be cautious in how they interpret and especially proclaim Scripture. In framing your model on what is usually called the Great Commission (although this is a label attributed to biblical editors and is not found anywhere in the actual biblical text), you begin with Matthew 28:18, "All authority in heaven and on earth has been given to me," as opposed to where most people start, "Go and make disciples" (v. 19). To affirm that all ministry flows from the authority of Jesus Christ, as you do, is vital to any biblical model of ministry. John 6:28–29: "What must we do to do the works God requires?" Jesus answered, "The work of God is this: to believe (Greek, *pisteuo*, "trust") in the one he has sent." To know, love, trust, and follow Jesus Christ, who has all the authority, is the call of the church. I appreciate how you have grounded your model on this truth.

2. In describing your own faith journey, you affirm the familial aspect of the church that nurtured you and your family ("This youth ministry provided mentors in my life who became my spiritual fathers and mothers"), referring to these relationships as the arbiters of your "theological security." Your zeal for mission grew and has been nurtured out of the family of God surrounding you (and your family), guiding you, and grounding you in a safe community. As is obvious from my chapter, I too believe that participating in God's adoptive calling is where all ministry should be focused toward those who feel somewhat disenfranchised, which, in the case of youth ministry, is every young person in our midst.

3. While you earlier decry meetings "replacing" mission, you then later state that meetings have their place and are helpful as a means to mission ("Jesus had meetings," and "we can and should have meetings"). You do not advocate diminishing or eliminating more-or-less typical youth ministry programs and even "fun" ("Let's keep having dodgeball tournaments, pizza parties, and lock-ins. Let's worship loud and play hard. Let's exegete, teach, and ask hard questions"), but rather you seek to bring mission to the forefront. You recognize that to "make disciples" we must build bridges where teenagers can

trust adults and develop a core understanding of our young. This is the aspect of youth ministry that I believe is so often mislabeled as merely superficial "entertainment," and it remains a vital component of ministry to and for our young in today's atomized church and society.

4. You experienced, were raised up, and were trained in a conviction that is similar to mine, where "I once was lost and now am found" became the mantra for using all of what I have received so that others might also be found. (I was a Young Life product and have some of the same DNA that you express in your chapter.) I not only understand where your model comes from experientially, but I resonate with your passion, especially in relation to a youth ministry landscape that sometimes seems to be more about keeping kids "healthy" and "happy" than encouraging them to be participants in the work of God. Without question, all believers need teaching and encouragement to care about those who do not know the story of God's love in Christ.

5. I so appreciate your final emphasis on prayer as the driver and the source of insight for doing what you describe as God's mission to evangelize the world. Prayer is, as you rightly point out, central to our lives as believers, both personally and corporately (what you call the "engine and not the caboose").

I not only align with you in each of these points, but as I described them, I wholeheartedly agree with you. I do, however, wonder whether there are aspects to your model that have either not been as carefully considered or factored in. Or perhaps they have not yet crossed your radar screen. As I consider your model as expressed in the chapter, and as I also apply and broaden your perspective to those who have a similar view of the role of youth ministry (as in the "student leadership" movement) in nurturing the young toward a solid, lifelong, and communal trust in God, I offer these thoughts to you.

### Where I Wonder about the "Gospel Advancing Ministry" Model

1. My greatest issue with not only this model for youth ministry but also others that seek to set free young people to use their gifts in ministry is that there is often too limited awareness of the developmental place and needs of today's young.[1] Some say we ask too little of kids, and that that is the biggest problem with today's adolescents and therefore youth ministry (e.g., Robert Epstein, *Teen 2.0*, and the Harris brothers, *Do Hard Things*). My take is that while there is truth in this perspective on one level—the young are neither empowered nor expected to "make a difference"—there is an important aspect to this that is often overlooked. The systemic erosion of adult investment and involvement in the lives of children and adolescents over the past several decades (what is known as "social capital") has handicapped adolescents to

the point where they simply have not received enough training, experience, guidance, or support to be internally prepared for adult-like responsibilities. Adolescents may be functionally capable of "sharing the gospel," but do they have the social awareness they need to be consistent "salt and light" (Matt. 5) with those they seek to reach? Do they have the mature internal mechanisms for ferreting out their own motives or insecurities in a way that would allow for the kind of individualistic leadership being asked of them? And, most important, taking into consideration the research that demonstrates that early (eleven- to fourteen-year-old) and middle (fourteen- to twenty-year-old) adolescents have such a need for adult approval and blessing, could it be that what we think is personal conviction and commitment is actually adaptation to the expectation of the adults around them?[2]

When it comes to youth ministry primarily as evangelism, where young people are encouraged to (alone, at least implicitly) "risk everything in service to the King," we are subjecting them to a developmentally untenable choice: either they risk their relationship to the church, youth group, and youth pastor as their leader and their "spiritual father or mother" or they deny the church pressure and continue on their own to navigate the complex social nature of their lives. I tend to think this model may, for most kids, discount their level of developmental insight and health and could therefore hurt them down the road. Even the examples you cite are adults—from Abraham to Martin Luther and Charles Spurgeon.[3] You do say that "the less mature they are, the more coaching they will generally need," and yet you limit this "coaching" to guidance on how to be more effective as an evangelist, not on what it means to grow up into maturity as a man or woman of God. That must be our chief concern: not simply making them better, "world changing" evangelists but helping them to become whole people who know and love Jesus Christ, care for people without mixed motives that may get in the way of Spirit-driven evangelism and discipleship, and live out the kingdom of God in how they respond to and live alongside others. Then Spirit-driven evangelism will naturally pour out of them.

2. You ground your model on "the Great Commission" but do not mention what seems to me to be two equally as great if not more pointed commissions: "Peace be with you! As the Father has sent me, I am sending you" (John 20:21) and "You will be my witnesses" (Acts 1:8). To be witnesses, especially when being "sent" as Jesus was sent, encompasses so much more than verbal proclamation. In Matthew 25:31–46, the image of the sheep and the goats, what you tend to refer to as "social justice," is actually a prerequisite for receiving the "inheritance" of God's kingdom. There is no mention in this passage, or in many if not most of the others related to how we are to treat

people (i.e., Sermon on the Mount, Matthew 5–7; the good Samaritan, Luke 10:25–37), of making an effort to "gospelize everything" (your point #6). I fear that in the attempt to emphasize evangelism (or more accurately, verbal proclamation), you place this above what is unfortunately often referred to, as you do, as "social justice." Theologically, there is no such distinction, for neither the "greatest commandments" (Matt. 22:37–40) nor the "one command" (John 15:9–17) even hint at the necessity to "gospelize everything" the way you describe it.

The *last* thing I want to do is dampen your enthusiasm and passion for calling the church to care about the lost. And in your model there is a nod in the direction of "serving," but clearly this is presented as a means to an end, to "seek to engage them in gospel conversations." The danger of not allowing for the simple act of visiting prisoners or feeding the hungry *as an expression of the gospel itself* is to make too light of something so central to the Scriptures. As N. T. Wright puts it, "In terms that the author of Acts might have used, when the church is living out the kingdom of God, the word of God will spread powerfully and do its own work."[4] "Social justice" and verbal proclamation together form biblical evangelism. They are inseparable; neither is the means to the other.

3. Lastly, the goal of the model, it seems to me, is lacking in a theological terminus (or *telos*), or even a long-term motivating force for the young disciple. "The bottom line is that if we are serious about teenagers spiritually maturing, then we'll want to get them sharing their faith as quickly as possible." To equate "sharing their faith" with what it means to grow into healthy adulthood in Christ seems to put the cart before the horse. "Sharing" as a "witness" comes out of experience, failure, received and embraced mercy, and reflection, and theologically it is an organic expression of maturity (again, see Matt. 25: "When did we see you . . . and feed you?"). The goal of ministry to the young is to create an environment where the inner development of identity in Christ, alignment with Jesus Christ and his kingdom (see Paul's final years in Acts 28:30–31), and lifelong connection to the body of Christ as a cared-for yet not-quite-developed participant in God's work in the world, *including but not limited to* verbally "sharing their faith," is the call of youth ministry.

In closing, I agree with your foundational passion and commitment to the lost. Yet without the investment of adults who are committed to the long-term spiritual and developmental health of the adolescent (which you do affirm) and without the careful eye of the full range of God's call to the believer (John 20:21 and Matt. 25, in addition to Matt. 28), we may easily end up creating great evangelists for the short term who eventually outgrow—or worse, crash out of—their commitment to Jesus Christ along the way. Yes, let us provide opportunities that honor each young person's developmental journey as we teach them to serve in God's kingdom, but let us always remember that we first must create the environment where they can flourish as called men and women without being expected to be "world changers." To be a "world changer" is simply not the point of lifelong discipleship. For it is God who is changing the world, and we are his loved and set-free sent ones who follow him together as salt and light (Matt. 5:13–16).

## ✚ Fernando Arzola

Greg's suggestion that Jesus was a youth leader is quite interesting. His connection between Matthew 17:24–27 and Exodus 30:14 makes for a thought-provoking discussion. If this is accurate, it changes our perspective of the disciples and underscores the truly revolutionary concept: that Christianity was birthed and spread by the lives of young people.

This upends many of our presuppositions about the ages of the disciples. Pragmatically speaking, it makes sense. Much of the travels of the disciples with Jesus would have required people who were able to abandon their lives—at least for a three-year stretch. It's reasonable to infer that younger people were more able to do this. Many historic and contemporary revolutionary movements were started by young, idealistic people who did abandon their lives for a cause for which they were passionate. And this might be no different.

Greg then suggests that Jesus's "small group youth ministry" strategy may serve as a model for us today. I appreciate Greg's insight that part of the problem of contemporary youth ministry lies "not in complexity, but in simplicity." That is, many youth ministries seem to focus more, he argues, on delivering a series of programs instead of simply focusing on Jesus. This has not been my experience, however. Most youth ministries programs *do* focus on Christ and *don't* offer sufficient other programs other than Bible study and worship.

In my book *Toward a Prophetic Youth Ministry: Theory and Praxis in Urban Context*, I suggest that most youth ministries actually fall in the "Traditional Youth Ministry" paradigm. I then suggest a "Prophetic Youth Ministry" paradigm, providing a menu of programs. The rationale is that teens have a myriad of issues with which they can use support. To focus solely on "spiritual" matters is what makes some youth ministry programs irrelevant and dualistic. Adolescents are wrestling with emotional, hormonal, sexual, biological, and social issues. I propose a more holistic paradigm and programming beyond Gospel Advancing Ministry.[5]

Nevertheless, I think Greg is on to something here! I believe the complexity he laments comes with the barrage of perspectives related to theology, worship, and spirituality in today's Christian culture. And yes, there are too many meaningless programs. The simplicity I recommend is, yes, focus on Christ—but not necessarily simply on evangelism. While I hear him talk about discipleship, Gospel Advancing Ministry seems to be evangelistic specific.

I recommend the simplicity of spiritual disciplines. These time-tested and classic disciplines provide teens with tangible expressions of the spiritual life. I think evangelism and Bible study is too narrow.

Two of my favorite books that address spirituality, spiritual disciplines, and spiritual formation for youth and young adults are *Presence-Centered Youth Ministry* by Mike King and *Ancient-Future Evangelism* by Robert Webber.[6]

Greg argues that we have exchanged the focus on Jesus for delivering a series of programs. Fair enough. However, he then suggests "a ministry model" that seems to me to be one big evangelism program. Doesn't this undermine the very thing he is critiquing?

He also states that his program transforms teenagers "not into good kids, but into world changers." But what does this mean? Don't we want our teens to be good kids? And what's a "world changer"? In my experience, most teens who grow up spiritually mature live out a simple faith through their spheres of influence—their families, friends, work, communities, and churches. Perhaps if we think of "world changers" as "thinking globally and acting locally," then I agree with this.

Jesus's time here was certainly more than a mission trip. He was offering a way of life, a way of engaging creation, a way of understanding the law, a way of interacting with others, a way of living more deeply in God, a way of being more deeply human.

Greg says that at the heart of Jesus is a desperate search and rescue for the lost. I agree. But this is not all. Again, to make this the central point makes the Gospel Advancing Ministry Model just another evangelism ministry to me. And while evangelism is certainly an essential aspect of the faith, to make this the driving force seems to me to overemphasize the conversion of people rather than the love of people for the sake of their being human. Jesus didn't evangelize. He accepted people, loved people, created community for people (especially broken people), and invited people to join him in this way and life. Isn't the fullness of life the heart of Jesus? To help people become more fully human? To help draw people closer to God?

I am overwhelmed by your personal testimony. Thank you, Greg, for your vulnerability and honesty. I think that your experience with Youth Ranch demonstrates that the fullness of the support you received reflected the fullness of the faith beyond evangelism—fellowship, mentorship, discipleship, and service. But most important, they provided you with love and community. This, I believe, is the heart of twenty-first-century youth ministry—a non-judgmental, inclusive community of love and support, a community where the stories of Christ are for lifting up, inspiring, and self-reflection. Even the language of "reaching the lost" smells musty to many, and it is certainly not common language for a twenty-first-century youth ministry.

I have to confess, I'm not a huge fan of the Gospel Advancing strategy for youth ministry; at least not in the traditional sense. It seems to smack of the old "fire and brimstone" approach that, I believe, is one reason why so many teens eventually leave the church. It tends to feel more like an imposition to accept a formula rather than an invitation into a deeper way of life. It tends to encourage counting heads during altar calls instead of going more deeply in the faith. It seems to breed the kind of faith that Robert Webber calls "a mile-wide and an inch deep." I mean, are we not all lost in some way? Is not the evangelist as much a sinner in need of mercy? I am reminded of Brennan Manning's words, "God loves us just as we are, not as we should be."[7] This is what grace is all about, at least to me.

However, the concept of being transformed by developing a deeper relationship with Jesus certainly resonates with me. I think this happens primarily through love, by providing a loving Christian community, and through the simplicity of spiritual disciplines. Hopefully, this brings one deeper into Christlikeness.

I am reminded of the classic 1960s hymn "They Will Know We Are Christians by Our Love." Greg suggests (or doesn't suggest) the possibility of quitting the group after twenty minutes to evangelize the neighborhood. I like the idea of taking teens out of the classroom and into the streets. But I would recommend more community service activities that do not necessarily require verbally proclaiming the gospel in the neighborhood. I am reminded of Francis of Assisi, who is quoted as saying, "Preach the Gospel at all times, and when necessary, use words." I think people will better absorb the gospel more through our actions than our words.

But Greg is correct that teens would rather go to the Amazon to build huts and fight pythons than evangelize friends in the cafeteria. But why would teens want to evangelize friends in the cafeteria with their words? Is it not more effective for their friends to see the light of Christ in the teens through their actions? Here is where I think helping teens develop social awareness and consciousness, which in itself is every bit as much an aspect of Christian witness as verbal proclamation, is essential. It helps them to develop a more holistic faith perspective.

## ✚ Ron Hunter

Greg's "Gospel Advancing Ministry" advocates for teens sharing their faith as a way to strengthen their walk and obey the call of Christ. Listen to some of his profound statements from his chapter of this book. Amid the highly programmed youth ministry, the "answer lies not in complexity but in simplicity." Greg goes on to say, "We have turned outreach into a program instead of lifestyle." Greg teaches teens how to rake leaves and clean windows to create an opportunity to share the gospel. The power of the Gospel Advancing Ministry is that it teaches teens beyond the classroom. In this lab-like, hands-on way, the youth minister walks teens step by step through how to share their faith. The difference between Greg's model and more typical youth ministry programs occurs when leaders get the youth out into the world to share their faith and serve within the community.

Greg suggests the youth leader embrace the bullied, broken, and, yes, even the bad kids. He quickly admits the goal is not to create kids who act good but rather to transform teens into world changers. Focusing on behavioral outcomes generates conformers more than believers. In the same paragraph, he uses the word "transform," suggesting a youth-centric approach over a method-centric focus. While he advocates a Gospel Advancing Ministry, the efforts described emphasize the transformation of the teen more than the goal of how many were won to Christ. I really value how his approach downplays performance and emphasizes the teen's transformation into confident, Christ-following, Christ-sharing believers.

The event-driven mentality that expects certain meetings to capture the hearts of teenagers has failed, according to Greg. He further shows the inadequacy of the meetings-based discipleship such as camp, youth group, small group, and church itself. The failure of such experiences comes from the lack of sustainability outside a "Christian environment." The need exists for both discipleship and sharing to be part of the teen's everyday life. To accomplish a lifestyle like this, it helps to have the youth pastor and parent working together so the church and home provide consistency for the family.

The combination of evangelizing and social justice, according to Greg, moves a teenager further along in their faith and stand for Christ. Hearts often soften as people receive acts of service done in the love Christ taught. Caring for people prepares the heart for planting the seed of the gospel. Christ repeatedly modeled serving a physical need followed by a straightforward invitation to follow him. An act of service prepares both parties, the one serving and the one being served, for a deeper conversation. Greg shows how the teen lives out James's call to works that reflect one's faith. Acts of service help remove selfish tendencies. The continued diminishing of selfishness brings more confidence to share his or her faith with less regard for one's standing within the peer group.

Anytime a youth leader wishes to teach acts of service, he or she can share the power of how Jesus served people's physical needs and connected with them personally. Jesus had a mission, but the mission was people. Christ's model of feeding, healing, filling a need, or just affirming them helped remove their barriers to hearing the most important message of their lives.

Greg's steps to adult involvement sound a lot like the D6 approach to youth ministry; adults modeling it, parents who coach it, and church leaders who train and embrace it. The concern I have with the remainder of his chapter is how Greg talks as if the youth leader is the only active leader in the teenagers' lives. He just spelled out the universal principles of parental influence that constitute the major portion of the formula for shaping a child and teen's worldview. However, the youth leader has limited opportunities to spend time with the group and even less in one-on-one mentoring situations. Enlisting the help of parents increases the long-term effectiveness of Greg's approach. Youth leaders could involve parents regularly in the training and community outreach.

When a person reads about the lack of spiritual parental influence in Greg's childhood, one could easily understand why his first impulse is not to include parents in this Gospel Advancing Ministry. He hints at the impact the other adults can make but does not develop the possibilities of what this combination could look like. As the power of 10 percent of teens following a Gospel Advancing Ministry can influence the entire youth group, imagine the impact of 10 percent of the parents joining their teenagers. If the teens need to find ways to be comfortable with their faith around other teens in their school, moms and dads need to consistently find ways to implement their faith alongside their own teenagers.

A key motivating factor for getting teens out sharing their faith is also getting them to rely on God. One of the most poignant realities described by Greg was when he showed how teens would rather deal with the hazards of the Amazon and build mud huts than share their faith in their school cafeteria. He argues correctly, "The average teenager would rather risk getting choked by a giant snake than getting choked out of their social circle." This observation is one of the most insightful and accurate statements describing teenage fears. When the teens share their faith, they immediately possess an incentive to live consistently in front of their peers.

Greg suggests that when teenagers adopt the lifestyle of sharing their faith and the gospel with their peers, it accelerates the discipleship process in their own lives. Does sharing automatically generate maturity in discipleship? I would like to hear more about the process of discipleship that comes from sharing the gospel. When describing the Youth Ranch youth group, he reports that "discipleship shook out from there [evangelization]"—but how? While he acknowledges the value of discipleship, the scale dramatically leans toward sharing the gospel. Paradoxically, those who emphasize discipleship rarely engage in any form of evangelism. The Great Commission passage most often quoted from Matthew suggests a cycle of reaching and teaching. Teaching grounds the new believers. While there is no waiting period to share one's newfound faith, the need to grow deeper in Scripture will help as one shares the gospel. Most people concentrate on the evangelistic side of this passage, but this is to miss half of the command.

We have all seen strong evangelistic churches who constantly win people but whose attendance fails to keep pace with the number of new converts. The proverbial back door of the church exists in the absence of discipleship. The Matthew 28 passage speaks as much about discipleship when it says, "make disciples," "teaching them to obey what I have commanded you." One should teach new believers, including teenagers, to share the faith while also helping them to know and thereby gently and respectfully (1 Pet. 3:15) explain their faith. One of the best ways to balance teaching teens how to advance the gospel to their peers is also to teach them and their parents how to defend the existence of God and the validity of Scripture and other doctrines. A growing number of churches provide mission trips for families instead of just the teens. By getting the whole family dedicated to a cause, evangelism, missions, discipleship, service, and other ministries strengthen the family and the body of believers within the church.

This approach falls short if the youth minister possesses any inhibitions over sharing the gospel. To be clear, there are no exemptions for Christians to avoid the Great Commission. What happens when you find a youth minister who lacks Greg's passion and fails to be obedient in evangelizing others? Kids tend to live stale, insular Christian lives. People dismiss this responsibility by saying, "Witnessing or evangelizing is just not my strength or gift." I agree with Greg's approach that teaching, modeling, and facilitating ways for teenagers to share their faith will strengthen them as long as they are simultaneously being discipled.

Greg, in the middle of the section, you discuss seven vital elements for the Gospel Advancing Ministry. These practical steps help others adopt your approach. It is always energizing when a writer takes the concepts beyond theory into practicality and shows the reader how to implement the ideas, principles, and teaching. All of the elements are vital, but two provide the fundamental connection to people: equipping teens for relational connection and sharing stories. How would you suggest training teens to be relational when their God-given bent or talent is toward tasks instead of people? Most every personality inventory categorizes people into two major subsets, those who are relational and those who are task oriented. It does not mean that each cannot possess secondary abilities in the other set, but that the other set does not come as naturally. Since this is trainable, what do you recommend to youth ministers to help the task-oriented teens become more relational and tell stories in the same compelling way that you do?

The reader understands that Greg is suggesting a balance of the need for meetings with dodgeball, pizza, and other fun activities with more substantive experiences and discussions. Greg even talks about teaching prayer and having specific prayer meetings with the teenagers. What I would like to see is more on the fourth vital element. There is little described about going deep in discipleship; rather, the whole section features going wider by sharing one's faith. I get the sense Greg acknowledges the need for discipleship, but it just did not get much attention in this chapter. Spending a page or more on discipleship would further strengthen what is already a very good chapter.

## ✚ Greg Stier's Response

Thank you all for your thoughtful insights. It's always a little intimidating having "wicked smart" people critically analyze a ministry model you are passionate about and pouring your heart into. Chap, Brian, Fred, and Ron, your encouragements filled my soul with joy, and your criticisms made me think.

For me, youth ministry is an intriguing, exciting, and at times daunting venture. We all want to see students grow in Christ *and* go into their world to make disciples.

That's one thing that really stood out to me across all your critiques of the Gospel Advancing Ministry model. I don't think I emphasized the "grow" part as much as I should have. Instead, I emphasized the "go" part (after all, I am an evangelist!).

But, having been a church planter and preaching pastor in the past as well as the father of a teenager in the present, I can say that I am fully convinced that all believers need to grow *and* go. Brian, you wrote, "While evangelism is certainly what we see in the historical narrative passages in the Gospels and the book of Acts, there are also plenty of other areas of the Christian faith that we see throughout the pages of the New Testament," and then you listed several. I agree. There are so many different areas that we must help teenagers grow in to become fruitful disciples of Christ.

My contention underlying the emphasis on evangelism is that teenagers "grow as they go." I'm convinced that when young people are engaging their peers with the love and message of Jesus, they pray more, gather in church more, worship more, and study God's Word more. For me, Brian, it's context. The church that reached me took me through systematic theology while sending me into the harvest fields. I read my first systematic theology book when I was fifteen because my church challenged me to. The reason I read it was because of the urgency of the mission before me.

And it was a good reminder to emphasize the glory of God in this whole endeavor. I live by the motto attributed to St. Ignatius, *Ad majorem Dei gloriam inque hominum salutem* ("For the greater glory of God and salvation of humanity"). God is the hero of the story. He is the hero of my story. I fully agree with you on that point.

Chap, thanks for the reminder as well that "the systemic erosion of adult investment and involvement in the lives of children and adolescents over the past several decades (what is known as 'social capital') has handicapped adolescents to the point where they simply have not received enough training, experience, guidance, or support to be internally prepared for adult-like responsibilities." I agree that teenagers need adults to pour the love and knowledge of Jesus Christ into their lives to give them that encouragement, support, and training when it comes to living the gospel and sharing it. Your adoption model of youth ministry does a wonderful job demonstrating this. I guess where you and I may differ is when it comes to whether they can be given the "adult responsibility" of making disciples.

It was that very responsibility (in the context of adults who cared for, discipled, prayed for, and encouraged me) that transformed me as a teenager. I've seen this calling, this cause, give teenagers a sense of purpose for their Christian lives that pulled them out of the muck of their self-absorption like nothing else could. I believe hurt teenagers can actually find healing as they take others to the hospital. But, to your excellent point, they need to be nurtured, loved, and poured into in the process. Thanks for reminding me of that, Chap!

The teen years, as we all know, are years of learning, excitement, and adventure. Why not tap into that adolescent boldness and point it toward advancing the mission and message of Jesus? I'm convinced that's what Jesus did with his young disciples. We can too!

Fred, regarding the Gospel Advancing model, you wrote, "It seems to smack of the old 'fire and brimstone' approach which, I believe, is one reason why so many teens eventually leave the church." Fred, that's the last thing I want. Your words remind me to unpack this more clearly in the future as I share the Gospel Advancing Ministry model with others.

When I refer to evangelism, I'm not talking about stapling gospel tracts to people's foreheads and bullhorn bullying them into the kingdom. I'm referring to teenagers loving the unreached, building relationships with them, and sharing the good news of the hope that we have in Jesus. I constantly coach teenagers to "engage, don't enrage" when it comes to reaching their peers with the gospel. Your words reminded me of the need to truly clarify what I mean by evangelism. And you are right in saying that some of the terminology may smell a little "musty." But, however we phrase it, we need to get our teenagers serious about sharing the good news of Jesus in their communities and contexts.

You also mentioned, "Perhaps if we think of 'world changers' as 'thinking globally and acting locally,' then I agree with this." Yes, that's what I mean. Actually, I would go a step further and say, "Act globally and act locally." Our teenagers need a global view as well as a local one. They need to work in the soup kitchen and on the mission field—all the while advancing the gospel, of course!

Ron, you critiqued, "What I would like to see is more on the fourth vital element. There is little described about going deep in discipleship; rather, the whole section features going wider by sharing one's faith." To be honest, the only reason I didn't dive deeper into this point is that the vast majority of the teen curriculum out there (to a greater or lesser degree) focuses on teenagers growing deeper in their faith. But I agree that this "deep and wide" emphasis deserves its own page (or chapter)! Teenagers need to grow deeper. I also agree that, ideally, parents are the key driver when it comes to helping teenagers grow deep and wide.

One point I may not have emphasized enough in my chapter is what I mean by the term "Gospel Advancing." As teenagers advance the gospel externally, it advances deeper into their own hearts. As they share it externally, they own it more and more internally. As they speak the good news to others, they are reminded of all Jesus sacrificed for them and learn to more fully embrace a life of knowing, loving, and serving him out of deep gratitude for this greatest gift of all.

My hope and prayer is that all of our chapters click together like building blocks. I pray along with my friend Chap that youth ministries spiritually adopt these teenagers into their churches so they can be ministered to on the deepest level. I pray along with Brian that teenagers become grounded in prayer, fellowship, discipleship, and the sacraments as they all keep their eyes on the King to bring him the glory that he deserves. I pray with Fred that we help build into teenagers a view of the church that erupts from the idea that we are all "one, holy, catholic, and apostolic church" on mission, both locally and globally. I pray with my friend Ron that moms and dads can be called back to their "D6" mission of being the primary spiritual coach in the lives of their teenagers. And finally I pray that that final piece (maybe the wheels) clicks on to enable youth ministries to mobilize their teenagers to advance the good news of Jesus in their Jerusalem, Judea, Samaria, and to the uttermost parts of the earth!

Thanks again, guys. This has been an exciting journey!

# Brian Cosby

# The Reformed View
# of Youth Ministry

T hat God is sovereign over all history, events, cultures, and our salvation is foundational to a consistent biblical theology in general and a theology of youth ministry in particular. God has not only declared the end from the beginning (Isa. 46:10), but he has also brought those decrees to fruition in time and space (Acts 4:28; 17:26). At his command, he created all things *ex nihilo* so that he might receive all glory and honor, "for from him and through him and to him are all things" (Rom. 11:36). Nothing happens outside his control, power, or wisdom. Not even a sparrow falls to the ground apart from his sovereign will (Matt. 10:29).

This is the God we worship and serve. Unlike a weak, impotent, therapeutic *theos*,[1] the true and living God reigns as one self-sufficient, complete in himself as the Triune God from all eternity. He chooses to use us in his mission on the earth not because he *needs* us but because he *loves* us and takes delight in his adopted children.

Youth ministries today often (unknowingly) emphasize what I call Home Depot Theology—"You can do it; God can help"—as if Jesus were standing outside in the cold just begging for a chance to come in and take the wheel! God is not your copilot. He is *El Shaddai*, God-Almighty, "who works all things according to the counsel of his will" (Eph. 1:11 ESV). Even when biting sheep or well-intentioned dragons in the church intend you harm,[2] God overrules it all so that *all things* work together for good for those who love God and are called according to his purpose (Rom. 8:28; cf. Gen. 50:20). God will continue to make a great name for himself, and he uses the various ministries of the church—including youth ministry—to do it.

## Consistently Reformed

Most evangelical youth leaders today would agree on a majority of youth ministry goals and concepts. Many would even agree on accepted icebreakers, worship music, and whether it's okay to have a nose ring. However, we need to make some clear distinctions between a *consistently Reformed* youth ministry—which I believe to be the biblical approach—and other views, some of which are represented in this book.

I use the word "consistently" to clarify the reality that some self-professing "Reformed" youth ministries are so *in name only*. That is, while they affirm the various doctrines of grace as understood by the Reformed community since the Protestant Reformation,[3] those doctrines do not inform or shape the approach or practice of their day-to-day ministry. In what follows, I want to present *both* a Reformed youth ministry approach *and* one that is consistently expressed in daily ministry.[4]

Wayne Rice, cofounder of Youth Specialties, has argued for a "reinvention" of youth ministry (again) by reaffirming parental responsibility, seeing the youth pastor as a legitimate *pastor*, and emphasizing the local church among other things.[5] These are all worthy ideals, but *how* do you make disciples of Jesus Christ? What *kind* of "Christian community" should we be striving toward? Should we encourage local church involvement, or are parachurch programs (e.g., Young Life) sufficient? Is youth ministry—as we often think of it today—even biblical? Behind these questions are concerns about the foundational *theological approach* that shapes the content and method. The answers to these questions provide the distinctions among the various views of youth ministry.

As noted, in using the term "Reformed" in this view of youth ministry, I am specifically affirming the distinctive theological doctrines as exposited by the Protestant Reformers and post-Reformers of the sixteenth and seventeenth centuries. However, it would be anachronistic to talk about "Reformed youth ministry" *in* the sixteenth and seventeenth centuries, as we understand the concept and practice of youth ministry today. Then, as it *should* be now, parents (especially fathers) held primary responsibility in bringing their children up "in the discipline and instruction of the Lord" (Eph. 6:4 ESV). Christian parents—in submission to and under the teaching of ordained church leaders—catechized their children, taught their children the Scriptures, and disciplined their children when they sat in their house, when they walked by the way, and when they went to bed each night (cf. Deut. 6:7).

While I wholeheartedly affirm the appropriate responsibilities of parents and the local church integrated as a unified effort in discipling youth,[6] I *also* want to present in the pages that follow a clear perspective of youth ministry that conscientiously affirms a consistently Reformed *methodology* as expressed in the historic "means of grace." God sovereignly uses various means to both save and sanctify his elect; particularly, the ministry of the Word, prayer, sacraments (baptism and the Lord's Supper), service, and gospel community.

Some of these "means" might seem similar to the well-known "purposes" as outlined in Doug Fields's *Purpose Driven Youth Ministry*,[7] but they are different in both approach and content, as we shall see. The same is true of what are often referred to as "spiritual disciplines." While Fields's "purposes" or various spiritual disciplines are similar to the means of grace—historically understood—they differ over the theological approach and implementation within a youth ministry context. We'll come back to this later. But for now, we need to understand *why* this view of youth ministry is needed today against the backdrop of youth and church ministry culture.

## Why Entertainment Hasn't Worked

Depending on how you interpret teens' "commitment" to church or the Christian faith in the first place, between 50 percent and 88 percent of those teens are leaving the church by the end of their first year in college.[8] Other research, however, has shown that this departure from the church happens *before* they hit college; college is simply the release point of freedom from the faith of their parents.[9] The drive to elevate experience over biblical teaching and ministry within a youth ministry context has caused youth leaders to spend through the roof on fog machines, circulating lights, dueling DJs, and artistic backgrounds. While the numbers of teens leaving the church are staggering, youth ministries across the nation continue to pack in more and more pizza parties and video games to keep youth coming back—thinking that somehow their lives will be changed.[10]

In the September 2010 issue of *World* magazine, Janie Cheaney argues that the "youth group is often seen as a way to keep kids off the streets."[11] If we can just get them into a church, that'll fix the problem. While going to church is certainly a good thing, it's what happens *in* those church settings that makes the difference (or not). The irony that Cheaney points out is that in an age where teenagers are busier than ever with sports, Scouts, math clubs, and homework, they are at the same time "bored" and purposeless. They are living from one pleasure high to the next, hoping to find that which will satisfy their wandering souls. But, as apologist Ravi Zacharias once noted, "The loneliest moment in life is when you have just experienced that which you thought would deliver the ultimate, and it has let you down."[12] No wonder the number one fear of American teenagers is "to be alone"; they've been let down over and over by the entertainment-driven culture that promises continual happiness and fulfillment.

But they've also been let down because of the entertainment-driven *church*. Indeed, many of the problems we observe in youth ministry are simply a microcosm of the church at large.[13] Kenda Creasy Dean in *Almost Christian* argues, "The religiosity of American teenagers must be read primarily as a reflection of their parents' religious devotion (or lack thereof) and, by extension, that of their congregations."[14] And what is the majority report for these American teenagers? Dean says, "Three out of four American teenagers claim to be Christians, and most are affiliated with a religious organization—but only about half consider it very important, and fewer than half actually practice their faith as a regular part of their lives."[15] So what should we *do* about this sociological-religious problem of American teenagers?

This is where the importance of *method* comes to the forefront. How do we get these bored, purposeless, yet (self-professing) "religious" teens not only into the church but also into a sustainable, Christ-treasuring faith? Many churches have turned to competing with the world to woo and attract them by all sorts of gimmicks and giveaways. (I recently heard of a large church in the Atlanta area giving away iPods to the first one hundred youth at a lock-in!) But is this the method that God has given us to draw young people into a relationship with him, or are we supplanting the God-ordained means by which *he* does that work of saving and sanctifying?

Rather ironically—considering these trends—I have witnessed an increasing interest in the Bible, theology, and prayer from students within my own denomination (Presbyterian Church in America) and those either involved in other churches or no church at all. Youth find it refreshing when a church is honest about what they believe and why they believe it—*even* the "offensive" elements of their theology. They've seen how the American Dream has left their parents and the "boomers" empty and still dreaming. Entertainment simply hasn't provided meaning or answers to the ever-seeking hearts of America's youth.

The authors of *Sticky Faith* also confirm this desire among teenagers in their research. When they asked post–youth group students what they wanted to see more of in their high school youth ministries, they answered (in order of priority): (1) time for deep conversation; (2) mission trips; (3) service projects; (4) accountability; and (5) one-on-one time with leaders.[16] Note what's *not* included in this list: more video games, a louder "praise and worship" band, Chubby Bunny, and so on.

Several years ago, I attended a parachurch organization's weekly youth "Ignite" meeting (or some similar name), which was invariably filled with all sorts of entertaining gimmicks. I could have guessed the rationale: "We only do these things to get them in the door," the speaker explained. "Then (and get this) we tell them about Jesus." Sneaky.

If you are thinking about charting this course of a "do-whatever-it-takes" approach to ministry and worship, please consider this maxim: *you keep them by how you attract them.* If youth are coming to your church because of your funny, light-hearted stories, you'd better not stop, because they will leave. If you've attracted teenagers to your ministry through your blue-haired rock star worship leader, you'd better not let him go. Ironically, those who have told me that they do these stunts only to get people in the door *never stop.* What begins as an evangelism tactic quickly becomes a regular *method* of ministry.

Although most youth workers will deny promoting an entertainment-driven youth ministry, they end up promoting it on a *functional* level. They will affirm that Scripture's method of ministry is "sufficient," but functionally implement methods that would be foreign to the biblical authors. We need consistency.

So what's the alternative? If it's not entertainment or sneaky attempts to woo teenage attenders, what does the Bible affirm as the correct view of youth ministry? Before we answer that question (by outlining a consistently Reformed approach to youth ministry through the historic means of grace) one other principle needs to be explained: *faithfulness to God is always more important than success in ministry.*

## Faithfulness over Success

If there's anything a youth pastor knows—even after only a few months in ministry—it is that fatigue and feelings of burnout often come with the task. The constant pressure from parents, youth, church leaders, the senior pastor, and families can wear a minister out very quickly. Moreover, there is the continual expectation to meet certain number standards. The most frequent question I get in ministry is, "How many?" It sometimes becomes a plague and burden—driving you to either be prideful (wow, I attracted a ton of youth tonight!) or despairing (nobody came . . . and nobody will come next week either). It's no wonder that the average youth minister stays in one location less than eighteen months![17]

Kent and Barbara Hughes, in *Liberating Ministry from the Success Syndrome*, rightly argue that it is always better to be faithful to the Lord than successful in ministry.[18] Being "faithful" to God in ministry means maintaining an approach that is consistent with what is practiced, and both approach and practice being informed and affirmed by Scripture. Success-oriented ministry, on the other hand, will necessarily fall into pragmatism—"whatever works best"—and will lead to a number of problematic conclusions: a preoccupation with inventing the most attractive show and experience on earth, a constant fear of failure, a focus on celebrity worship leaders or skit guys, and an elevation of fashionable (i.e., Christ-less) Christianity over truth.

When you realize that our task is to simply be *faithful* to God rather than *successful* in ministry, you will have an overwhelming sense of freedom and joy. As an alternative to the entertainment and success-driven models, I maintain that the "how to" of being faithful in youth ministry—indeed, in *all* ministry—is demonstrated through the means of grace; particularly, ministry of the Bible, prayer, the administration of the sacraments in worship, service, and gospel community. In other words, our task is to plant and water the gospel of Jesus Christ—while *God* gives the growth (1 Cor. 3:7)! Not only is this the biblical model given by Christ and witnessed in the early church, but it remains, I believe, the most faithful and Christ-centered approach to youth ministry today.

The remainder of this chapter will seek to provide both the *content* of the means of grace as well as how to incorporate that content into a holistic means-of-grace *methodology*. It is my hope and prayer that whether you are a minister, seminary student, youth volunteer, or parent, this will be a helpful guide to starting and continuing a vibrant and spiritually rich ministry with youth.

### Theology of the Means of Grace

We've already noted 1 Corinthians 3:7 as a great insight into understanding the means of grace. But the idea is scattered throughout Scripture. We find all five of these "means" together, for example, in Acts 2:42–47. The early disciples "devoted" themselves to five things: the Word, fellowship, the Lord's Supper, prayer, and service. The result: "And the Lord added to their number day by day those who were being saved" (v. 47 ESV). In Acts 13:48, the gentiles—on hearing the preaching of Paul and Barnabas in Antioch in Pisidia—"began rejoicing and glorifying the word of the Lord, and as many as were appointed to eternal life believed" (Acts 13:48 ESV). They preached; God saved.

The Westminster Larger Catechism (1647) asks, "What are the outward means whereby Christ communicates to us the benefits of his mediation?" Answer: "The outward and ordinary means whereby Christ communicates to his church the benefits of his mediation are all his ordinances; especially the word, sacraments, and prayer; all which are made effectual to the elect for their salvation" (Q. 154).

The London Baptist Confession of Faith (1689) likewise maintains, "The grace of faith . . . is increased and strengthened by the work of the Spirit through the ministry of the Word, and also by the administration of baptism and the Lord's Supper, prayer, and other means appointed by God" (14.1). In other words, God has provided the ordinary means by which he both saves and sanctifies his people. Robert Reymond comments that these means are instruments not of *common* grace but of *special* grace.[19] That is, they are made effectual in the lives of believers through God's saving, redemptive grace and not through his common grace given to all men and women everywhere (Matt. 5:45).

The means of grace do not "work" *ex opere operato*, as Roman Catholic theology contends;[20] they do not function like a magical formula of cause and effect. For example, preaching God's Word does not *necessarily* mean that every unbeliever who listens will surely come to saving faith, and neither does it mean that every Christian will surely grow in his or her faith that day. Rather, our sovereign God works in and through the means of grace *as he sees fit* for the building up of his church.

We shouldn't miss the fact that these are means *of grace*: means of undeserved favor by God. As sinners, we deserve the wages of sin—death (Rom. 6:23)—but God, being rich in mercy, made us alive together with Christ (Eph. 2:4–5) *through* the various means of his appointment. These are the means God has called us to supply as a blueprint of biblical methodology in youth ministry. In other words, God's Word, prayer, the administration of the sacraments, service, and gospel community all provide a God-glorifying and biblical method of making young disciples of Jesus Christ.

But let's get practical. Just because I mention five "means" as the right methodology for ushering teenagers into the green pastures of God's transformative grace does not mean that the *application* of each of these is biblical and God honoring, which is why I am stressing the word "consistently." So what would a *consistently* Reformed, means-of-grace approach actually look like in these five areas?

## Ministry of the Word

First, the ministry of the Bible—preaching, teaching, and reading—is the *primary* means by which God saves and sanctifies youth. Whether Scripture is infused into large-group teaching, small-group discipleship, or individual Scripture memory and meditation, the Spirit of God attends the Word of God to produce new life in the people of God.

Historically, Protestant churches have affirmed the centrality of the Word in both worship and ministry, and for good reason: "Faith comes from hearing, and hearing through the word of Christ" (Rom. 10:17). We are born again by the Spirit through the "living and enduring word of God" (1 Pet. 1:3, 23). If you want young sinners saved and sanctified, you will be dedicated to the ministry of the Word.

By using the phrase "ministry of the Word," I am affirming the faithful and correct exposition and use of the Word. This is why I wholeheartedly encourage preparation for the ministry, whether in seminary or some other rigorous practical education where one learns Hebrew, Greek, theology, biblical content, hermeneutics, church history, and the like. God's call on your life doesn't come as an "ordination package" sent to your doorstep for only $19.95 (plus shipping and handling). Instead of filling your time learning the seven keys to building Your Best Life Now or Becoming a Better You, learn the contents, fundamental unity, and faithful application of the Bible.

If faith comes through hearing the Word of God—as a gift by the power of the Holy Spirit—why do we think that faith will come through some other unbiblical means when God has already ordained the method? Do we not trust the sufficiency of God in his Word? As much as I may like to think that a heart-moving story about my past would bring a teen to faith, it is *God* working through the ministry of his revealed Word who saves souls. Again, we plant and water the gospel, and the Lord gives the growth (1 Cor. 3:7).

There are several practical ways you can lead a Word-infused youth ministry. Perhaps most important, preaching during Lord's-Day worship should hold a central place in the week for your youth. Hughes Oliphant Old writes that, for the Reformers, "the sermon was an act of worship, the fruit of prayer, a work of God's Spirit in the body of Christ; it was the doxological witness to the grace of God in Christ."[21] Preaching is the foundational means of grace in the corporate worship of God. If you are a youth pastor or youth volunteer, you might not be the one preaching each Sunday. However, you can build up the corporate worship of God and the hearing of his Word preached in your weekly ministry to youth. This can be done simply by teaching them about worship, encouraging youth to *prepare* to hear the Word preached, or by being an example—living out your own appreciation, anticipation, and joy for Lord's-Day worship.

Other practical ways to lead a means-of-grace approach through the ministry of the Word might include: (1) regular teaching of the Bible in large groups and small groups, (2) encouraging families to read and study the Bible together, and (3) encouraging youth to memorize and meditate on the Scriptures. Don't succumb to cheap entertainment in your youth ministry—even in the name of "fellowship"—rather, lead them in content-rich ministry grounded in the faithful exposition of Scripture. Lead them to memorize and meditate on it *by doing it yourself!* The ministry of the Word is a means of God's grace by which he both saves and sanctifies youth.

## Prayer

You probably remember exactly where you were on Tuesday morning, September 11, 2001. The reports and images of planes crashing into the World Trade Center sent the nation into fearful shock. If you were in ministry at the time, you probably also remember what happened the following Sunday. Churches across the country witnessed one of the largest—if not *the* largest—day of attendance in history. Services were packed with confused, frightened, and inquiring souls asking the most basic questions of life: "How could a loving God let this happen?" and "Is there really life beyond the grave?" At the same time, the president and government officials called on the nation to pray for the victims and their families.

While prayer is certainly necessary and appropriate in the midst of suffering and pain, our nation has taught teenagers over the years that we really don't need God *until* tragedy hits. In the end, America's school of prayer has educated our youth that God is nothing more than a divine bellhop—devoid of sovereign control over the day-to-day events in our lives (e.g., suffering). In this paradigm, God can only comfort us and help us out when we experience difficulty.

Moreover, prayer oftentimes gets left in the dust of American pragmatism—time at work, with family, at school, or playing golf brings more reward and productivity than time in prayer. And so prayer is sifted through the "not-enough-time" grate. Whatever the case may be, prayer has been sidelined in the Christian life, and our youth are experiencing the devastating effects.

What is the teen's response to this? David Kinnaman, president of the Barna Group, has witnessed in his research a steady decline over the last twelve years of "born again" teenagers claiming to pray at least once a day. In a generation imbued with social networking sites, he notes, "Talking with God may be losing out to Facebook."[22] Teenagers prize experience, honesty, and relationship, and our world is teaching them that those things can be found—in their truest form—from a culture of entertainment and pleasure.

The world, the flesh, and the devil have their sights set on preventing you and your youth ministry from being saturated with biblical prayer. Why? Because it is a means of grace by which God empowers, comforts, strengthens, sanctifies, and nurtures his people to grow in a stronger relationship with him. Through prayer, we become strangers of this world and imitators of Christ, and *that's* not on Satan's agenda!

So how can you lead a prayer-filled youth ministry? First, and this *should* seem obvious, pray (or have a youth pray) as you start and end times of teaching or worship. Not only does this help focus minds and hearts on God, it conveys the truth that you are an instrument of the *true* Teacher, the Holy Spirit. When you open in prayer, you call attention to God's holy presence among the assembly.

Second, break up into small prayer groups during youth group or Sunday school from time to time. This doesn't have to be every Sunday or youth group, but it should be regularly planned. It might also be appropriate to divide the groups by gender so that those in the group will have less distraction (go figure!). This can also happen in small groups, where it's a good idea to have an adult leader or parent to help guide the youth as they pray.

Third, have seasons of prayer, particularly during periods of fasting. We want to pray and fast so as to be changed through the journey. We want to see spiritual fruit spring forth from a heart of greater faith. Isaiah exhorts us, "If you pour yourself out for the hungry and satisfy the desire of the afflicted, then shall your light rise in the darkness and your gloom be as the noonday. And the Lord will guide you continually and satisfy your desire in scorched places" (Isa. 58:10–11).

Fourth, encourage your youth leadership to pray together regularly for the youth, for you as their leader, for the church, and for God to be glorified in your ministry. If you are at a church where youth volunteers are few and far between, don't worry. You're not alone! You may begin by pulling *one* semiconcerned parent along with you and slowly build that core group of praying shepherds.

Finally, as a youth leader or parent in youth ministry, you will be called on to pray in times of crises or emergency. This is one of the greatest privileges and responsibilities of a youth worker. From rushing to the hospital due to an injury to hearing of a death in the family, offering sincere and compassionate prayer on behalf of your youth is not only an example of ministry; it is actual and effective ministry. God uses our prayers to accomplish his sovereign purposes.

## The Sacraments

The sacraments of baptism and the Lord's Supper are also means of God's transformative grace.[23] But unfortunately, like the ministry of the Word and prayer, the sacraments enjoy little thought or understanding in the average pew, much less among America's youth. The fundamental question we are faced with is simple: If God's promises in the gospel are true and life changing, and if God communicates those promises and seals them in baptism and the Lord's Supper, then why have they taken such a backseat role in the life of the church today?

If you are a youth pastor or youth leader, you can have a profound impact on the lives of your youth by highlighting the importance of celebrating the sacraments. Not only can you teach about their meaning and institution, but you can also prepare and encourage youth to participate in and reflect on the life and death of Jesus through these means of grace.

John Calvin defined a sacrament as "a testimony of divine grace toward us, confirmed by an outward sign."[24] Echoing Augustine, he taught that a sacrament is "a visible form of an invisible grace."[25] That we call the sacraments "signs" and "seals" of God's *covenant of grace* is very important. They communicate the bound relationship we enjoy with God through our union with Christ and point to the continuity of God's unfolding revelation in his Word. This covenant extends throughout the Old and New Testaments as an organic relationship that finds its fulfillment in Christ Jesus. In the New Testament, however, the sign of this covenant changed from the bloody sign of circumcision (fulfilled through the shed blood of Christ) to the universal sign of cleansing, water baptism (cf. Col. 2:11–12). Likewise, in instituting the Lord's Supper, Jesus took the Old Testament feast of Passover and infused it with new meaning in himself. The sacraments, then, are a means by which God visibly presents and applies his covenantal grace to his people.

### Baptism

What are some specific ways to integrate baptism into a means-of-grace youth ministry? First, you can *teach* the biblical significance of baptism to your youth. Many times, we assume youth know what baptism symbolizes. But I have found that, when asked, youth have a very hard time articulating the meaning of baptism. And if they don't understand what it signifies or seals, then it will be very difficult for their minds and hearts to be engaged when they witness a baptism in worship.

Second, press home the need to see this holy pledge find its full fruition in *communing membership* at a local church—whether the teenager was baptized as an infant or simply hasn't become a communing member yet. According to the Barna Group, American Protestants have witnessed a 22 percent drop in church attendance from 1998 to 2008 in families with children under the age of eighteen. A bigger picture revealed that, at the end of that same period, only 15 percent of American adults were members in a Protestant church.[26] More than ever, teenagers in America are not being taught the need for commitment to a church body, the need for submitting oneself to the discipline of the church, or the benefits of taking part in the overall direction of the church through voting, nominating, or potentially serving as a leader in the church one day.

Third, you can teach youth how to improve on their own baptisms—even as they witness a baptism—by calling on the Lord to create in them a pure heart, sprinkled clean by the inward baptism of the Holy Spirit (cf. Ps. 51:10; John 3:5; Gal. 3:27). Ask them to examine whether their hearts have been buried with Christ in baptism and raised to walk in the newness of life (cf. Rom. 6:4).

### The Lord's Supper

When believers partake of the Lord's Supper, they partake of Christ's body and blood really, truly, and *spiritually*.[27] The Lord's Supper builds up and nourishes the believer in his or her faith and seals our union with Christ, ushering us unto his banqueting table of divine love. Thus, it's more than merely memorializing Christ's death. We do that, but we also commune with Christ by participating in his body and blood through faith (1 Cor. 10:16).

There are several ways you can incorporate the Lord's Supper into your ministry with youth. First, you can teach the doctrine, theology, and application of the Lord's Supper on a regular basis, whether in a series on it or sprinkled in your weekly lessons.

Second, the Lord's Supper can be used as a call to repentance and faith. Not long ago, I had a friend tell me that as he was fencing the table one Sunday,[28] a middle-aged man stood up in the middle of the congregation and walked toward him. This man, weeping over his sin, had a tremendous desire to take the bread and wine after hearing of the finished work of Christ on his behalf. He received salvation that day through the preached gospel and the *visible* gospel portrayed in the sacrament of the Lord's Supper.

Third, you can incorporate this means of grace by encouraging participation in worship, where the Lord's Supper is administered. There, youth tangibly experience the gospel message by tasting and seeing that the Lord is good (Ps. 34:8). It also points us to that great day when we gather around the marriage supper of the Lamb as a pure and spotless bride (Rev. 19:9), at which point the sacrament of the Lord's Supper will then fade into the reality of the Lamb's celebration.

God has appointed baptism and the Lord's Supper to strengthen his people, young and old. If God has seen fit to ordain these sacraments as means of communicating his grace, then we should be dedicated to supplying their meaning (through teaching) and use (in worship) in our ministry with youth.

## Gospel-Motivated Service

Few other expressions of faith are more central to the Christian life than being poured out in humble ministry to others, especially among the poor, the sick, the outcast, and the unsaved. The irony is that while we give our hearts, minds, money, time, and strength to benefit others' needs, God fills us with joyful satisfaction. *Service is a means of grace whereby God grows our faith, extends our love, and brings us joy and peace.* Entertainment-oriented, success-driven youth ministries that don't equip and lead youth in works of ministry and service fail to provide them with a biblical model of Christian living. When we are at our end—physically, emotionally, and spiritually—we are enabled to commune with Jesus afresh and be filled with his Spirit.

One way to lead your youth in a ministry of service is by providing them a model of servant leadership—one that leads from the front, *inspiring* youth to join in the vision and mission you call them to. It shows them that you are willing to live out what you teach. It guides them in the "how-to's" of serving others with gospel motivation, even as you look to the Great Servant.

A second way to equip and lead your youth in the work of ministry is by teaching both biblical truth and cultural awareness. Biblical truth consists of theology, historical confessions, knowledge of the Bible, and God's instructions for holy living. Biblical truth centers on the gospel of Jesus Christ and calls us to respond to that gospel with faith, humility, love, and obedience. In addition, teaching cultural awareness provides knowledge of the context in which they serve.

Third, we can lead our youth in the work of ministry and service by prayerfully serving *together*. Taking youth to a hospice center or a homeless shelter, for example, may be very difficult to experience, but it will equip them for future service in similar contexts. You can do projects within your church body (e.g., serving the widows, the elderly, or the disabled), the surrounding community, or to the ends of the earth! Serving can be done individually, in discipleship groups, or as a large group. It can be done with parents or with friends. Whatever the case may be, it usually requires some amount of intentional leadership to organize, teach, and guide the youth.

Another way to serve is by evangelism or going on mission trips. This may seem rather obvious for some of you, but it is surprising how few churches encourage individual evangelism or participate in local and foreign missions. One of the most amazing things I hear from youth who go on mission trips is that *they* are the ones who have been impacted most by going and serving—more so than those to whom they ministered! If you've been on a mission trip, you probably have experienced the same because serving is a means of God's grace whereby he grows our faith and extends our love for him and for others.

By serving, God satisfies us with his love and stretches our faith in his daily provision for our lives. Giving and being poured out in service for others is but an echo of the sacrificial love of Jesus, who came to serve and to give his life as a ransom for many (Mark 10:45).

### Gospel Community

In my opinion, the idea of a "youth group" is a relatively new concept. Over the last fifty years or so, the growth of youth groups in America can be traced proportionally to the decline and breakdown of the family. In many respects, the modern-day youth minister is a result of the failure within the home to bring children up in the nurture and admonition of the Lord (Eph. 6:4). However, my view is that since our nation has become more and more secularized, there is an ever-increasing need for the existence of some aspect of youth ministry within the local church.

For an increasing number of teenagers today, the church is not just *another* place to receive biblical guidance and instruction; it is the *only* place to receive biblical guidance and instruction. There, in the community of faith, youth from unbelieving homes find a plethora of spiritual fathers, mothers, aunts, and uncles.

Gospel "community," however, might be confusing, especially with so many parachurch "communities" in existence. While parachurch ministries have their place, they are not the God-ordained institution here on earth called to equip the saints for the work of ministry. Indeed, you would be hard pressed to make any case *from the Bible* for "para"-church ministries. Although many of these ministries see the assimilation of youth into the local church as their goal, I would venture to say (from my experience over the years) that most are content to let *their* ministry be the "church."

Parachurch ministries cannot provide youth with the necessary means of grace that God has given his church. They cannot support (1) weekly preaching in worship, (2) multigenerational discipleship and service, (3) the call and blessing of the sacraments, (4) the privileges and responsibilities associated with church membership, (5) the command to conduct or be under church discipline, or (6) spiritual and physical oversight by the God-ordained elders and deacons. In addition, they often leave youth confused over the significance and importance of Lord's-Day worship. If a teenager's "church" is on Tuesday morning before school, the fourth commandment soon dissolves in the Petri dish of first-period chemistry. But God has graciously provided his people with a community through which he transforms our minds and hearts and redirects our worship toward himself. That community, in the Scriptures, is called the *church*.

Gospel community is both *sound* and *safe*. By "sound," I'm talking specifically about promoting and enjoying sound theology and biblical doctrine. Any community that neglects a growing understanding of God, the nature of humanity, salvation, Christ, the covenant, the role of the Holy Spirit, and other similar doctrines cannot grow in spiritual maturity. Sound theology that centers on God in his Word will necessarily embrace the sovereignty, majesty, and power of our triune and personal God. It will behold the wonder of his grace in drawing sinners to himself through the effectual application of the work of Christ by the Holy Spirit. In other words, sound theology is Christ-centered, God-exalting, and gospel-focused, and it leads to *sound community*.

But gospel community is also a *safe* community. By "safe," I'm not talking about creating an ivory tower in isolation from the unbelieving world, and neither am I talking about the desire to remain untouched by the brokenness, disease, and misery of the suffering around and among us. The "safe" community I'm alluding to involves the safety and security of knowing that our identity, righteousness, and acceptance are all fully secured by our union with Christ—in *him* there now is no condemnation (Rom. 8:1)! We can rest assured that nothing will suddenly make us spiritual orphans again. We have been bought at a price (1 Cor. 6:20), sealed by the Spirit (Eph. 1:13), and adopted as sons and daughters of God Almighty (Gal. 4:5). You have an unwavering security in a God who will never leave you nor forsake you (Heb. 13:5).

Christian growth happens within the context of a believing community. In his book *Puritan Reformed Spirituality*, Joel Beeke writes, "Growth in piety is impossible apart from the church, for piety is fostered by the communion of saints."[29] The opposite life, one of isolation, will lead to the reverse: "A Christian life lived in isolation from other believers will be defective; usually such a believer will remain spiritually immature."[30]

In addition to the various practical applications of "community"—such as discipleship groups and youth events—I would suggest integrating your youth with older members of the congregation: visiting them, serving them, and praying together. The beauty of the body of Christ is that it is multigenerational, transcultural, and made up of different backgrounds, races, tribes, peoples, and languages. As much as your youth ministry might seem to form its own community, it is necessary to integrate that community within the larger community of the local church.

From beginning to end, this Triune God has called out a communion of saints that will one day join together in heavenly worship. As J. C. Ryle says, "Yet a little while and you shall see a congregation that shall never break up, and a Sabbath that shall never end."[31] But even now, we get a taste of heaven in worship. Jon Payne writes in his book *In the Splendor of Holiness*, "When Christians gather to worship God on the Lord's Day, they take part in the most meaningful, significant, and wonderful activity possible."[32] Worship according to God's Word combines the heart and mind and ushers them into an awestruck wonder of the majesty, beauty, and grace of God in Christ Jesus.

The communal life we enjoy is but a reflection of the *imago Dei* stamped on humanity, the roots of which are found in the eternal community of the Trinity. The gradual transformation that takes place in the church will find its full expression when Jesus "will transform our lowly body to be like his glorious body" (Phil. 3:21 ESV).

God has already provided both the *content* and *method* of biblical youth ministry. These means of grace, as we've seen, should inform how we go about drawing young men and women into the church and into a life of faith. While many youth remain disillusioned by the gimmicks and fog of an entertainment-driven world of empty pleasure, let us preach Christ crucified to our youth and display *him* as the all-satisfying Savior that he is. With all my heart, I plead with you not to be tempted with success, professionalism, or the fading fads of our self-centered culture. Rather, strive to faithfully feed his young sheep through the means of grace that God has already provided his church and "let us leave the elementary doctrine of Christ and go on to maturity. . . . And this we will do if God permits" (Heb. 6:1, 3).

# Responses to the Reformed View

✚ Greg Stier

I really appreciate Brian Cosby's back-to-the–New Testament approach to building a biblical youth ministry model. I share his supposition that the widely accepted entertainment-focused youth ministry model is watering down our efforts to keep teenagers integrated into the church post–high school graduation. If youth group is just a fun time to keep teenagers off the streets while sprinkling a little "Jesus dust" on them in the process, then, of course, why wouldn't they evacuate the church after (or even before) they graduate?

And I fully agree with his focus on Acts 2:42–47, which makes it clear that "God's Word, prayer, the administration of the sacraments, service, and gospel community all provide a God-glorifying and biblical method of making young disciples of Jesus Christ."

This "go deep" approach is necessary for teenagers to understand, embrace, and own their faith for the long haul. Teens need to learn biblical theology, embrace the sacraments, engage in service, and immerse themselves in community. These are all part of the foundation youth leaders must build for them in the youth ministry context. But if not combined with a "go wide," Gospel Advancing drive, it can quickly turn a youth group into a small group.

Brian correctly notes the importance of engaging teenagers in evangelism and mission. But Jesus's commissioning of his young disciples to "go and make disciples" in Matthew 28:19 was not merely part of a process. It was the purpose!

Making disciples who make disciples was the driver of the early church's efforts throughout the book of Acts. Evangelism is not a mere spoke on a wheel to building a biblical model of youth ministry. It is the engine itself. Jesus himself said, "For the Son of Man came to seek and to save the lost" (Luke 19:10). When we follow him, his primary mission becomes our primary mission.

While far too many youth groups have veered away from these basics and become entertainment driven, it doesn't mean that we should jerk the steering wheel and do a 180-degree turnaround. We don't want youth group meetings to look like a liturgical service held in a medieval castle. Does an emphasis on taking teens both deeper into their relationship with God and wider into the world with the good news of Jesus mean we can never play games or have fun? I say no!

If anyone has a reason to laugh and have fun, it should be Christians. Joy was one of the distinguishing marks of the early believers: "They worshiped together at the Temple each day, met in homes for the Lord's Supper, and shared their meals with great joy and generosity all the while praising God and enjoying the goodwill of all the people. And each day the Lord added to their fellowship those who were being saved" (Acts 2:42–47 NLT).

As long as fun and games don't distract youth leaders from truly engaging their teens in growing deeper and going wider, then why not? After all, they are teenagers, and a dodgeball game or pizza party won't derail a kingdom-advancing ministry.

Jesus's missional call to go make disciples who make disciples is radical, revolutionary, dynamic, life-changing, scary, stretching, countercultural, energizing, and Gospel Advancing. Let's take them deep and wide, and let's have a ton of fun in the process!

## Chap Clark

Thank you, Brian, for this thorough and thoughtful article. Your commitment to the care and nurture of the young is evident, and your desire for them to come to know and follow the Savior is clear. Even in your most stinging critiques of strategies and methods of reaching out, there is no doubt that your motive is for Jesus Christ and his kingdom. Your article is "thick" (a favorite word for practical theologians) and loaded with Scripture references. Your plea for faithfulness over against success is a helpful reminder of what so easily ensnares, and your critique of the guise of "professionalism" as opposed to faithful preparation is an important reminder for those who sense a call into vocational youth ministry.

I also want to affirm, without qualification, that I fully agree that our theological convictions must be the driving mechanism for our approach to passing on faith from one generation to the next. At Fuller Theological Seminary, where I am on the faculty, we have noticed a trend that has now taken over—there are now more "nondenominational" students who attend the largest fully accredited seminary than any other denomination. Even three years ago, this was not the case. But over the past few years it's become evident that, as so many have reported, denominations that have defined American Protestantism for centuries are on the ropes.[1] And with this decline of historically oriented, steeped-in-tradition denominations is a similar decline in loyalty to a particular theological tradition. Thus today we see churches springing up across the country that are functionally theological hybrids. This has not only also been the trend in youth ministry as well, but especially over the last few decades this has been a consistent rally cry for many in youth ministry leadership (e.g., speakers and writers) who decry the "rigidity" of denominational—and by default theological—boundaries. Given this climate, then, there is much to commend in your article, which makes the case for a return to a well-formulated and highly codified theological tradition. Not only do you plead for theological grounding, your single-focused apologetic is to your version of "orthodox Reformed" Christianity. To those who share this perspective, this article will sing like a Glasgow boys' choir. To those who do not, or, as in the case with many of the "nondenominationals" who read this, there may be some serious dissonance.

That said, and especially for those who do not find themselves readily drawn to Cosby's interpretation of youth ministry (I'm not sure how many Young Life staff or Purpose Driven folks are still reading, but hang in there!), it is worth repeating: there is much here that the entire youth ministry community needs to consider. Language and rhetoric aside, in this article Brian Cosby makes a strong case for deepening especially the core content of the gospel message. So as I begin this response, I will first examine the boundaries of the Reformed model, followed by a few thoughts that caused me to question how to pull off this model.

### The Language and Boundaries of the Reformed Model

You have so loaded up this article, Brian, that to give a two-thousand-word response is difficult indeed! On every page there was something I underlined either because I felt like it was a needed point to be heard or something I wanted to explore further, and usually both. In sum, then, my overall concern, likely shared by many readers, is with the overt boundaries offered by the single theological framework you use. Frankly, I'm not sure that you need to limit this to the Reformed tradition; you have a great amount to say to all of us.

Specifically, I wonder if you might reconsider your proposed methodology of youth ministry residing synonymously with the notion of the "means of grace." As you point out, the "means of grace" (even in the title of the article) is a core concept in Reformed theology. One definition you give is the means "by which *he* [God] does that work of saving and sanctifying," specifically through the "ministry of the Bible, prayer, the administration of the sacraments in worship, service, and gospel community." Interestingly, the two basic texts you use to support the distinction between "methods" that are unbiblical and the historic Reformed "means of grace" as a *model* for youth ministry do not say everything that you seem to be taking from them. For example, 1 Corinthians 3:7, your grounding text, does say that we plant and water but God does the growing, but in the context, planting and watering are clearly metaphors for the doing of ministry as opposed to the specificity of the method for doing ministry. Then, in Acts 2:42–47, what one could argue is hermeneutically a description of what took place, you lock into a code and create a fixed "method"/model for the church for all situations and for all of time, when we really have no idea how they went about their way (method) of *doing* the work of ministry (e.g., was communion delivered as a normal part of the dinnertime meal? Clearly, in Scripture, we simply do not know). Yet it is at this point that you venture into a theological rationale from Reformed documents to affirm that "means" of grace and "methods" of ministry are essentially synonymous. This gets you into what I see as unnecessarily divisive hot water. Your basic affirmations are so good, but the implicit defensiveness in your argument may overshadow them.

My concern here is that someone from a Wesleyan, Orthodox, Roman Catholic, or "nondenominational" background could do precisely do what you do—grab a few verses, cite their own historical documents and a handful of their theological thinkers, and make their case—and would end up with a somewhat different "method" for ministry. To equate the "means" of how God grows individuals and his people with the methods we use to plant and water is, I believe, untenable. I don't disagree, per se, as I believe that these things are all valuable and important aspects to our role in growth. Yet I do not see the connection between how one goes about planting and watering and how God uses what Reformed theology refers to as the "means of grace." Consider a volunteer Young Life leader, for instance, who happens to be Presbyterian, building a friendship with a disinterested teenager or a disabled child without a closed-set agenda in the name of Christ. As the friendship grows and God moves that adolescent toward trust in Christ, the method and outcome are no different than when Paul and Barnabas were in Antioch (Acts 13:44–48). The method of what you call parachurch, after all, has a rich ecclesial history and is modeled after Paul's planting and watering (method) and God's grace (means).

### What the Reformed Model Doesn't Discuss

In many ways, for any person who seeks to faithfully lead young people into a vibrant, lifelong, and communally experienced faith, this article is hard to argue with. The basic theological framework of the historic "means of grace" has several different labels, depending on theological tradition (whether one is aware of the historic tradition driving their own perspective of such "means" as the Bible, Lord's table, etc., is beside the point). This article, then, with some flexibility in the language, offers a broad and rich perspective on any youth ministry strategy.

In addition to wondering about translating the basic concepts of your argument, Brian, there are three foundational issues that I felt are either inadequately addressed or ignored altogether. First, while there is a very brief mention of developmental differences in the last section of the article, there is little recognition that developmentally, adolescents are in so many ways unique from adults, even young adults. Second, and related, there is no acknowledgment of the fairly robust research that suggests that adolescents do not by default trust adults. And third, there is an assumption that "if we build orthodox Reformed youth ministry, they will come," yet without any substantive appreciation for how difficult it is for a church or individual to actually pull off what you recommend as the "method" of offering the "means."

#### DEVELOPMENTAL REALITIES OF EARLY AND MID-ADOLESCENTS

My initial concern is how developmental differences between the early, middle, and late adolescent (or emerging adult) affect how messages and data are received, stored, and employed, especially in terms of the brain and the social environment. It seems to me that to disparage those people and programs who spend a great amount of time on affect, the relational and social environment, and other noncognitive methods to reach young people denies the generational and developmental gulf between adults and today's young, even young adults. For early adolescents, for example, who have the basic brain capacity of children and are in the process of "pruning" what they have stored as they are seeking to prepare for adult abstract brain function,[2] being able to take in the highly abstract concepts of the Reformed model is difficult at best. I do not believe that you, Brian, would be opposed to translating, or even contextualizing, to a specific age or population, but the way you state that the method is embedded within the "means of grace" makes me wonder how one would actually go about this.

### The Need to Build Trust with Kids

Second, and related to this, my concern is how growing up in today's performance- and individualistically oriented society has caused mid-adolescents to lack trust in adults and adult-controlled settings, and how this fact therefore makes this article, from what I have studied and witnessed, nearly impossible to pull off *without* some amount of "bells and whistles." It is one thing to simply dismiss "Ignite" or Young Life for being "entertainment driven"; it is quite another to assume that young people are, in essence, clamoring for adults in a church to "teach the historic truths of the Christian faith." It makes me wonder how you have personally handled those who feign disinterest (or actually are bored)? Do you propose simply teaching those who want to be taught and move on from those who seem to not care? Is it important to first build a bridge of trust?

With due respect to Ravi Zacharias, I'm not sure where the idea came from that the reason why the "number one fear of American teenagers is 'to be alone'" is that "they've been let down over and over by the entertainment-driven culture that promises continual happiness and fulfillment." I don't know of any research, data, or even anecdotal support for this reasoning. There is, on the other hand, a great deal of research pointing to the reality that the reason young people feel "let down" is due to the collision of two powerful forces that all American young people face: a highly complex series of performance expectations calling for their full attention and loyalty, and a measurably exponential decrease in the necessary social capital to live up to the demands. I refer to this as "systemic abandonment."[3] Kids are lonely because there are so few who are present for and with them without an agenda. So overcoming the lack of trust in a culture that has failed to provide them with what every generation before them has received—an adult community who walks alongside of them[4]—is a necessary prerequisite for any young person to allow him- or herself to be subject to the level of catechetical instruction you propose.

### What Modes of Delivering the "Method" Should One Use?

Lastly, while you equate "means" with "method," you did little with making the method something one could actually do apart from a few suggestions like "encouraging youth to memorize Scripture." If one were to attempt to implement this "method" on the ground, hoping for "here's how you do this" types of delivery examples, they would be in trouble. I could conceptually see in your article that the method is tied in with the "means," but your use of the term "method" does not seem to easily answer those sticky pragmatic questions like "When?" "Who?" and "How?" I do understand that in seven thousand words there is only so much you could say, but, while you did touch on this, I found it to be lacking in the connection to the actual day-to-day delivery.

In sum, I agree that the basic elements that you refer to as "Reformed" are important and even vital ingredients to teaching the truths of the faith to anyone, including the young. I am also moved by your convictions, especially theological. I personally am not quite satisfied that the delivery methods, or the developmental and sociologically contextual questions, are addressed in the article. It seems to me that a youth ministry could be greatly strengthened by employing the essence of your argument for their content—but that the content could be implemented and delivered by a choir of relationally committed adults who are willing to receive and adopt young people into the local body of the church while throwing cream pies and singing worship songs before they teach. Ah, describe that combination, and then you've really got something!

## Fernando Arzola

There is little more important for adolescents (and for all of us) than to be assured of God's grace. Teens are swimming in a life of ever-evolving technology, thought, and insecurities. And they are bombarded with messages at a rate that was unheard of even ten years ago. Therefore, I welcome Brian's emphasis on the great traditions of the church, the sacraments, the ministry of the Word, prayer, service, and community. These are pillars that have stood the test of time and continue to uphold the church in its various forms.

Brian argues that entertainment-driven youth ministry hasn't worked. I agree. For those who come from an "altar call" tradition, they may disagree, as success is often related to external matters such as attendance, responses, and excitement. I think what Brian is emphasizing is internal matters such as reflection, depth, and inner passion.

He also underscores a very challenging dilemma. On the one hand, the ultimate purpose of the Christian faith is what he identifies as a "sustainable, Christ-treasuring faith." However, I believe we not only want individual "sustainable" faith, but we also want teens connected with the institutional church, the local congregation. There lies the rub. His use of the *Sticky Faith* research underscores teens' desire to go deeper in the faith through conversations, service, and relationships with leaders. These help to nurture adolescents' spirituality.

Brian is also on point when he emphasizes that the use of entertainment as an evangelistic hook will ultimately become a functional method. But let us not become too quick to judge. This functional approach may be no different than a church using a large professional choir singing traditional hymns. The musical genres may be different, but is not the approach the same? What *is* important is honest faithfulness. And Brian holds all our feet to the fire when he argues that while the theological "content-talk" may sound different from how most people in youth ministry teach, the ministerial "functional-walk" seems to be the same. If it walks like a duck, and talks like a duck . . .

I appreciate Brian's development of the "means of grace." In my years of youth ministry experience, when I heard the term "grace" being used, it generally referred to God's free and unmerited favor; rarely was it used in reference to its means—the Word, fellowship, the Lord's Supper, prayer, and service. These are tangible ways of experiencing God's grace, which help to strengthen and build up the church. This challenges youth ministry leaders to ask, "What methods do I/we use to help our teens experience the means of God's grace?"

In the second part of the chapter, Brian provides both theological and practical insights. The insistence of focusing on the ministry of the Word over and against testimonials is valid. While there is a place to hear the stories of how people's lives have been transformed, when this replaces biblical preaching, we lose out on being transformed ourselves. It's easier to hear about the work of others than to do the inner work ourselves.

Prayer does seem to have fallen by the wayside for teens. The notion of spending time with God is essential, and one we take for granted; however, like all spiritual disciplines, it does require discipline. But the stillness of prayer seems to be a challenge for adolescents (and for all of us). We are all so distracted from the things of this world that it is difficult to be connected to the Spirit. Henri Nouwen poignantly yearns,

> Why, O Lord, is it so hard for me to keep my heart directed toward you? Why do the many little things I want to do, and the many people I know, keep crowding my mind, even during the hours that I am totally free to be with you and you alone? Why does my mind wander off in so many directions, and why does my heart desire the things that lead me astray? Are you not enough for me? Do I keep doubting your love and care, your mercy and grace? Do I keep wondering, in the center of my being, whether you will give me all I need if I just keep my eyes on you?
>
> Please accept my distractions, my fatigue, my irritations, and my faithless wanderings. You know me more deeply and fully than I know myself. You love me with a greater love than I can love myself. You even offer me more than I can

desire. Look at me, see me in all my misery and inner confusion, and let me sense your presence in the midst of my turmoil. All I can do is show myself to you. Yet, I am afraid to do so. I am afraid that you will reject me. But I know—with the knowledge of faith—that you desire to give me your love. The only thing you ask of me is not to hide from you, not to run away in despair, not to act as if you were a relentless despot.

Take my tired body, my confused mind, and my restless soul into your arms and give me rest, simple quiet rest. Do I ask too much too soon? I should not worry about that. You will let me know. Come, Lord Jesus, come. Amen.[5]

Some youth ministries tend to be disconnected from the congregation, particularly on Sundays. Perhaps the thinking is that the "adult service" is not relevant to teens. Whatever the case may be, one of the greatest losses of the means of grace is when teens do not participate in the celebration of the sacraments or ordinances. The Lord's Supper in particular is a means of grace that not only strengthens the individual believer but brings together the beloved community. The mystery of God is incomprehensible, and the celebration of the Lord's Supper makes this mystery more incarnational, tangible, and immanent among us. By receiving the bread and cup, it embodies in us our union with Christ.

Thomas Oden argues in *Life in the Spirit*, "Because intentionally instituted by the Lord, there can be no church without a fitting sacramental life. . . . Where there is no one baptized, there is no church. Where the farewell meal is uncelebrated, one has no right to expect the true church."[6]

The Last Supper, particularly as expressed in the Gospel of John, leads us to the model for servant leadership; as Christ washed the feet of the disciples, we are called to wash the feet of others. Yet I'm not sure what Brian means by "gospel-motivated" service. How is this different from "service"?

He then uses the term "gospel community" to emphasize its church/congregational context, which is different from parachurch ministries. I have mixed feelings here. I do agree that the church is the "God-ordained institution here on earth called to equip the saints for the work of ministry." However, do not parachurch ministries do this as well? And often do they not do a better job? How many of our youth and church leaders come from or were trained by parachurch ministries? While I appreciate his critique, I do believe that most people in ministry seek to also "equip the saints for ministry."

One area I would critique is that Brian, I believe, is too quick to dismiss the insights that the label Moralistic Therapeutic Deism can give. That is, its popularity seems to reflect a real yearning from adolescents who have perhaps been pushed away or confused by the competing theologies that have been marketed by the church—and frequently by contemporary American youth ministry. And while respected leaders may sometimes struggle with this perspective, I think it provides us real and deep insights into the hearts of adolescents.

Finally, his desire and passion to present a "consistently Reformed youth ministry" is admirable. However, Reformed denominations are diminishing as quickly as many others, so there must be something amiss. As I read Brian's well-written chapter, I kept thinking that while I may debate the pros and cons of a "Reformed" youth ministry perspective, I do agree with Brian 100 percent on emphasizing God's grace. This, I believe, is what needs to be emphasized by more and more youth ministries across the denominational spectrum.

## ✚ Ron Hunter

How refreshing to read how Brian emphasizes matters of substance. This chapter covers many excellent points and correctly separates general methods from methods rooted in theology. The past couple of decades of analysis show that more churches relied less on substantive methodology and more on a pragmatic approach to evangelism and discipleship. Brian calls for a "consistently Reformed" methodology, which he describes as ministry with the Word, service, ordinances, and gospel ministry through grace. I am thankful for the attention given to realigning youth ministry purpose with a profundity of teaching. Brian, I admire the thoroughness of your section.

I read many notable and well-articulated statements in this chapter, such as how culture has created bored, purposeless teenagers "living from one pleasure high to the next, hoping to find that which will satisfy their wandering souls." In a media-driven age, the difficultly is seen when youth pastors are constantly vying for focused attention. Some churches with larger budgets create a fairly high standard for smaller ones. More so than ever, children's pastors feel they must offer a Disney-like experience, and youth pastors need a full-on, multisensory approach in this screen-driven culture. I will definitely differ here with Brian because I think these methods of engaging teens should be used, but with the type of depth Brian writes about and Christ expects. Brian offers the maxim, "You keep them by how you attract them." This expression implies the "only" attraction is lights, bands, and games when it could be the combination of such along with serious Bible study and presentation of the gospel of Christ.

An old saying reflects the sentiment of this chapter: methods are many, principles are few; methods often change, but principles never do. Brian's premise calls youth leaders to use a principled approach, and he highly criticizes methods, especially the "fluffy" or "entertaining" methods. But the methods used and the content taught sit on two distinct planes and in two different categories. Methods can transmit depth or fluff. It can be dangerous when entertaining methods are not accompanied by deeper teachings within the faith, but if the entertainment is accompanied by a depth of teaching, one can be less critical. Brian helpfully clarified that methods should not be confused with objectives, but I think he goes too far in moving all nonsubstantive methods to the unscrupulous category.

Brian discusses burnout, fatigue, and pressure felt by youth pastors under the high pastoral and parental expectations. What he does not say is the philosophy he promotes reinforces the "hired-gun" or "superhero" approach to youth ministry, where the entire weight rests on the youth pastor. While staff members and parents should feel equal responsibility for all goals set for the youth pastor, sadly, in these situations, they don't. Never confuse blame with accountability. In contrast, the team approach tackles the problem together and holds each party accountable to help correct the small problems before they become big problems. The pressure cooker of high business-like expectations has claimed many youth pastors who no longer serve the church or Christ.

Brian is to be commended for how he elevates the sufficiency of God's Word. Youth pastors should teach the sufficiency of Scripture so teens learn to examine life's decisions by the matrix of God's principles rather than career economics, zip codes, or type of handbag. Parents need to help their teen do the same. Breakthroughs emerge when the parents' goals for their teens cease to be financial success or the appearance of success in life but rather to learn and follow God's will God's way.

Brian, like Greg, calls for teenagers to focus outward beyond themselves in service and ministry to others. He describes servant leadership in solid terms of leaders modeling service to the point that the teens, as followers, begin serving. Brian calls Christ the "Great Servant" and indicates that the gospel functions as the motivation. Teens who focus more on helping others will find a natural growth in their own lives simply in the preparation to serve.

A cautionary point I would emphasize is that youth ministers should not create a world that makes teens feel the youth group is the only place where they can be discipled. You should teach the teens how to dig out the truths of Scripture on their own away from the lights, drums, and even the youth pastor. You do not want parents feeling like they cannot compete with how their kids view the youth pastor or youth worship center. Teen worship should enable the teen and the parents to live out their faith and walk just as strongly when not at church.

I think there is misplaced blame regarding why substantive issues have taken a back seat to what you describe as a merely entertainment methodology. Around the mid-1970s and early '80s, parachurch organizations began to present curriculum alternatives in place of the traditional, stale, and outdated resources of denominational publishers who had grown complacent relying on denominational loyalty to sustain their business. I know this because I was a part of a team that did this until we recognized our responsibility to meet needs with depth and excellence. The new parachurch publishers earned customers with customer service, stronger applications within lessons, and excellence in design. The problem with parachurch publishers stemmed from their desire to appeal to all denominations, therefore representing none of their distinctives. Often such an approach can lack depth and certainly does not help reinforce the core theology of one's ecclesial identity. The quality of the design and entertainment value drew many users. In contrast, some denominational publishers' depth of content lacked this excellence, resulting in the loss of many of their customers. Excellence without depth or depth without excellence ultimately cheats the end user.

Another point of Brian's that I think needs clarification is his discussion of success versus faithfulness. One can have success while pursuing faithfulness, but one must desire faithfulness over success. To state it a bit more clearly, success is not the antithesis of faithfulness. Some confuse success with excellence. The suggestion of excellence as only a pragmatic philosophy fails to recognize that everything Christ did on earth contained both excellence and substance. Even before Christ performed miracles, he knew people were going to follow him for the "signs and wonders." Christ cared about people's physical condition and performed miraculous acts, which engaged the crowds at a seemingly more shallow level before going deeper. Christ was the master at deploying both method and content.

Brian's subsection titled "Faithfulness over Success" implies one is exclusive from the other. Do note that success is not to be equated to excellence. Above I discussed excellence as an approach, but success is an outcome of winning or achieving. An alternative title could have introduced the motive behind the two nouns (faithfulness over success) and suggested that neither of them alone should tip the scale. Brian could have given a qualifier of motivation to show how faithfulness is the goal, and while success should be desired, only faithfulness is required. Youth pastors can only control one of the two; faithfulness is within their ability, while success has other factors of determination. While in Scripture God always calls his people to faithfulness, he does not consistently call us to be unsuccessful. Yes, he called Jeremiah to be faithful knowing his preaching and prophecy would fail to change Judah as it approached its own demise. Yet his call to Abraham was given to bear fruit. We should desire faithfulness before success, but often success can be a barometer for the depth of our faithfulness.

There seems to be a negative sentiment toward youth pastors with a large ministry or signs of success that they must have compromised solid teaching. Brian, I am not sure you are saying this or that you are totally against the types of methods you describe. I would call for a precision of wording on this matter, as some may read this and equate the use of such tools as evil. This very well may be the same misunderstanding some get when they misquote how money is the root of all evil rather than the "love of money." The distinguishing factor is motive. A youth pastor can use special lighting, a praise band, or special events to complement the depth of teaching; they are not all mutually exclusive.

I truly loved Brian's approach to core teachings as the framework on which all other areas are built. My favorite points within this section included citing Wayne Rice calling for parental responsibility. I think Wayne wisely knows that the task of the youth minister is about multiplying efforts to accomplish ministry. The insight of Kenda Creasy Dean that the religious devotional barometer of teenagers can be measured by their parents' level reminds us of the need for ministers to partner with parents. We know parents shape the worldview of teenagers in areas of politics, sports, ethics, authority, and, yes, their view of God. Youth pastors can greatly influence the teenager by helping shape the parents' worldview. Parents, even with minimal confidence, sharing their faith and values with their teens becomes a spiritual multiplier of the youth pastor's efforts. Both Moses and Christ reached more people at a deeper level by delegating and partnering with other leaders whom they developed to accomplish more. Youth pastors could call on all parents, knowing they will get help from the same ones who help shape the rest of the teenager's world.

Brian, you quoted Ephesians 6:4 and Deuteronomy 6:7, both showing that God always intended the primary influence to be parents, and you affirmed the responsibility of the parents. What would it look like for the youth pastor to teach the same consistency by using the Word, service, ordinances, and gospel ministry to both students and parents? At the very least, the youth pastor could seek to have a concerted effort by other staff members teaching this in tandem. Imagine, as an illustration, teaching Scripture as being like a tandem bike, with parents and kids working together, trading off who steers up front and who encourages by pedaling from the rear. At first dads and moms do the steering, but when the student gets older, he or she should take the handlebars while mom or dad pedal in support. The most effective energy spent by youth ministers would be helping dads and moms connect spiritually with their kids. Brian cited Dean as saying the teens' faith is weak because their parents' faith (and therefore the congregation's) is weak. Would you rather have one faucet in your home filtered for safe drinking or have the whole house safe? Teach every person, teens and parents, the depth of Scripture, the understanding of God, and the sacrifice and redeeming power of Christ. Then the Living Water will flow from all and overflow into others.

Brian's section discusses the ordinances of communion and baptism, which have deep and careful teaching connected to each. All teens should know what each symbolizes as well as the doctrines of salvation and the cross. You could also add the teaching, even without calling it an ordinance as some do, of the washing of the saints' feet. The model Jesus gave could be observed with the youth minister teaching Brian's key element of serving others with humility. Even if not participated in by all teens within a service, the act could be demonstrated and taught. A number of denominations use this act in conjunction with the Lord's Supper, showing how they went together on the eve of Christ's crucifixion.

As one of the diverse set of readers of this book, I would be remiss not to caution against the unnecessary doctrinal polarization of this section. Brian, you laid out a strong case for substance over form as a means to reach teenagers, but you may have needlessly prompted some to skip past your section with the use of "Reformed." I admire how you are being true to your doctrine, but I think your chapter could have easily been addressed to both Arminian/Wesleyans as well as the Reformed/Calvinists. Studies have shown a smaller percentage of the pastors from mainline denominations consider themselves Reformed/Calvinist. When asked, an equal number of Southern Baptist Convention pastors indicated their congregations reflected either an Arminian view (30 percent) or a Calvinist view (30 percent).[7] By opening this up to a broader label, you potentially double your audience without compromising your intent. Your wisdom would be welcomed beyond the Reformed churches. Your admonition works in both circles, and we all need to teach more substantively in ways that draw teens to Christ and keep them following in their faith.

Thanks for reminding us of the core issues. Teens and young adults today desire depth from the church. The surface-level worship and inconsistency within one's life contributes to many walking away from church. This chapter reminds everyone, with abundant grace, not to neglect the Word, service, ordinances, and gospel ministry.

## ✠ Brian Cosby's Response

### *To Greg Stier*

I love your passion and vision, Greg. Thanks for your input and feedback! Just a few items of response. You seem to suggest that my impression of youth ministry or the Christian life is joyless and never fun. How far from the truth! I'm all for having fun; I'm just against entertainment as the primary method of getting people into the church, which describes more than a few youth ministry programs (as I'm sure you would agree!).

Yes, you are correct that we are at a point of disagreement over the evangelism issue. While I believe that evangelism and missions is certainly necessary and a significant calling in our lives, Scripture teaches that it is but one aspect of many. Those of us who are married are also called to be loving husbands and wives, child-instructing parents, faithful elders who shepherd the *already-saved* flock of God, and the list goes on and on. Evangelism doesn't drive these callings. Certainly faith comes by hearing the Word, and sharing the good news of Jesus is what God has called us to. But this monolithic, narrow view of youth ministry downplays the rich abundance of the multifaceted life of following Jesus.

### *To Chap Clark*

Great points, Chap—thank you. With precision, you pick out my equating "methods" with "means," which is certainly a goal (albeit *with* qualifications!). You believe that connecting these in the manner in which I've done it is "untenable" with regard to Scripture. That's understandable, but let me explain further.

In my chapter, I'm trying to get at the answer to this question: What are the methods (or means) that God has called us to in his Word with regard to youth ministry? We would be agreed on much of the *content*, I'm sure. But in thinking through methods as *means*, I'm specifically talking about being engaged in ministry with an eye toward *God's* sovereign grace in saving and sanctifying his people. My preaching, for example, doesn't save. God saves. But he uses my preaching as a *means* of saving. Preaching is a method, therefore, of reaching the lost, but it's also a means by which God saves the lost. Similarly, does prayer change things? No, God does. But he uses prayer to do it. Prayer is a means by which God works in and through his people.

You are correct in that I am not opposed to contextualizing the message in age-appropriate ways. And you are also correct that I should have made more than a passing comment about this. I guess I assumed this to be the case, and so I didn't spend any ink working this out. Good point.

If you are taking my comment about the number one fear of teenagers as "being alone" to be attributed to Ravi Zacharias, then I should have said that differently. That poll came from other sources and primary research. What I was intending to communicate is that youth feel a sense of being let down when they thought something would bring satisfaction and it doesn't. It brings a sense of discouragement and disillusionment. For example, if a teenager believed that the act of premarital sex with her boyfriend would bring security and closeness only to be rejected after the fact, it would cause incredible loneliness. That's the point I was trying to make.

The trust issue is interesting. All of us—teenagers included—have a harder time trusting someone just because of their position or status, thanks in part to the television reporting constantly displaying the faults and moral failures of those in positions of authority. This was a very small aspect (a passing comment) in my article, but that's what I was getting at.

Good point on the fact that I didn't get very specific with practical "how-to" examples. That's what I tried to do in my book! It's hard to argue my position in seven thousand words *and* give a host of examples of what it might look like. But I concede that I should have given a few more. Point well taken. Thanks again for your insights!

### To Fernando Arzola

You are very encouraging and gracious; thanks for taking it easy on me! I'm glad you can appreciate a focus on God's grace in youth ministry—both in its content and method.

You asked about the distinction between "service" and *gospel-motivated* service. The difference lies, as you might guess, in the specific motivation. All sorts of people around the world give themselves to so-called "good works" of service: the man in Peru handing out food, the doctor in China serving the outcast and sick, the woman in Moldova helping people grow their own food. But without faith, their service doesn't please God. Paul writes in Romans 8:7, "The mind governed by the flesh is hostile to God." The writer of Hebrews agrees: "Without faith it is impossible to please God" (Heb. 11:6). *Gospel-motivated* service would be that service rendered in light of God-given faith as a response to the gospel—service that is pleasing to the Lord.

You question my critique of parachurch youth groups, and that is understandable. They do seem to "work," but I'm sure you would agree that we're not after pragmatism but faithfulness to God and his Word. Parachurch youth ministries *that usurp the weekly ministry of the local church* are not the God-established institution on earth called "to equip the saints for the work of ministry" (Eph. 4:12 ESV), the "pillar and buttress of the truth" (1 Tim. 3:15 ESV), the bride and body of Christ (Eph. 5:23–27; Rom. 12:5) of which God has given overseers (Acts 20:28), and directives on worship and ministry (1 Cor. 14:26–40). Indeed, it's hard to find *any* biblical support for a "parachurch" youth group that usurps the local church.

For some reason, you seem to think that I dismiss the research of Christian Smith in the Moralistic Therapeutic Deism (MTD) findings. But I actually appreciate the research of MTD! Perhaps the confusion is that I'm sad at what they uncovered in their research.

Finally, you write, "Reformed denominations are diminishing as many others, so there must be something amiss." That might be true of some, but the denomination that I am a minister in—the Presbyterian Church in America (PCA)—is one of the fastest-growing denominations in the nation. At the time of writing this response, the latest PCA report (from 2013) noted growth in both the number of churches and members.

I really do appreciate your kindness and graciousness. Thank you for your reaffirmation of the means of grace in youth ministry and your input. I'm very grateful!

### To Ron Hunter

Thank you very much for your feedback and input, Ron. Just a few quick thoughts. You argue that we can have both entertainment *and* substantive content, which is true. I'm all for having fun. But the point I'm making is that entertainment relegates the substantive items (Word, prayer, sacraments, worship, service, community) to the periphery. Moreover, can you really make a case for entertainment-driven youth ministry from the Bible? As a seminary-educated pastor, I surely can't do it!

You differ over my separation of faithfulness and success, calling it a "flawed comparison." That's understandable. I love to see success, truly, but I'm *called* to faithfulness because God is the One who gives the success (cf. 1 Cor. 3:7). You note that I believe that excellence is simply a pragmatic philosophy that should be dismissed. I don't remember ever saying that anywhere in my chapter. We should absolutely strive for excellence in the things that God has given us to do. Our approach, however, is not toward being the most successful but rather being faithful to God.

You write, "A cautionary point I would emphasize is that youth ministers should not create a world that makes teens feel that the youth group is the only place where they can be discipled." I actually fully agree 100 percent with that statement, so I'm not sure what I said that led you to believe I think otherwise.

Finally, you question my use of "Reformed." I understand that I would probably have a bigger audience if I didn't use the term, but it accurately describes what I'm trying to do. I'm stressing the sovereign grace of God in youth ministry, *not* humanity's goodness that somehow overcomes their dead-in-sin plight and their ability to become children of God through self-will. If it is *God* who saves and sanctifies (and it is!), then what are we called to do? The answer is to avail ourselves to the means by which *he* grows us by his grace. Thus, I'm offering a consistent view that dovetails God's sovereignty in salvation and sanctification with our responsibility of planting and watering the gospel. I do appreciate your emphasis on the family, as that is a great burden of my own heart. I give a hearty "amen" to you!

# Chap Clark

# The Adoption View of Youth Ministry

The success of youth ministry in this country is an illusion. Very little youth ministry has a lasting impact on students. I believe we're no more effective today reaching young people with the gospel than we've ever been. . . . So let's be honest. Youth ministry as an experiment has failed. If we want to see the church survive, we need to rethink youth ministry. What does that mean? I don't have a clue. But my hunch is that if we want to see young people have a faith that lasts, then we have to completely change the way we do youth ministry in America. I wonder if any of us has the courage to try.

—Mike Yaconelli, "The Failure of Youth Ministry," *Youthworker Journal*, May 2003

I have an apology to make. In my rush to make deadline my last column communicated the wrong message. What I thought I said and what many people read were two quite different things. I was hoping to throw some cold water on the high profile ministries out there that give the impression they're attracting gazillions of young people to their ministries and changing the lives of gazillions more. I was trying to level the playing field by introducing a dose of reality. . . . What most of you read was, "Youth ministry is worthless, useless, and not worth doing." I apologize. The last thing I want to do is discourage youth workers. What I intended (and didn't accomplish) was to un-intimidate those youth workers who were discouraged because of all the "successful" ministries who were implying results different from the rest of us. . . . Maybe

we don't need a revolution in youth ministry; maybe what we need
is what we've always needed—a few adults who are willing to follow God's call to love young people into the kingdom of God no
matter what the result.

—Mike Yaconelli, "An Apology,"
*Youthworker Journal*, July 2003. Mike
Yaconelli died in October 2003.

Around the time Mike was writing those articles, a local teacher started
a small group. Three young men in their senior year of high school,
fresh off camp where they together committed their lives to Christ,
started meeting weekly with their middle-aged volunteer. They came to read
their Bibles, share their struggles, and pray in support of one another. All three
were good friends at school, active in youth group, played football together,
and knew and liked their adult leader. For two of them, faith was a new thing,
and they were excited to learn and grow. The third, raised in the church,
had less overt enthusiasm but still was drawn in by his friends' excitement.
Each one became active in church attendance, served as a student leader, and
even led younger students. When they were together, going deeply after their
faith, sometimes the conversation was passionate, sometimes it felt stiff, and
occasionally it just fell flat, but for most of the year the power seemed to be
simply in the meeting. Each guy knew that they were cared for, and that when
they met, something always good happened.

In spring, as they prepared to graduate and as life got busy, they stopped
coming to the youth ministry programs but tried to keep the group together.
That summer and through the next fall, they attempted to meet monthly,
but it was rare when all four were able to come. The leader tried to stay in
touch and connected, but because each one had gone a different way, it was
not only less convenient to gather but seemed to be less desired. Soon the
group stopped altogether, and soon the leader took on a new small group of
incoming freshmen to "pour his life into."

A few years later, the one who was raised in the church stopped coming
to services as well—"I have to work . . ." was his reply when asked. Another
started attending a Bible study at his new college. The third became a middle-
school leader for a local parachurch organization while attending community
college and working. Today, the one raised in the church attends now and then,
but comes alone and sits in the back with his girlfriend, leaving immediately
after the service is over. Neither of the others stayed involved in a church or
ministry. They have simply drifted away. One, when asked via Facebook how

he was doing in his faith, simply replied, "That was all great in high school, but I haven't thought about God in quite a while." End of conversation.

What became of these three? They were sincere about and invested in their faith. Each one prayed, served, and sought to make Christ Lord of every aspect of his life. One was an outspoken evangelist, and the other two were quieter but not afraid to talk to anyone who was interested. They were known at school for their faith, and people gave them space to live their Christian lives and yet remain socially connected. Their growth was visible and real. Yet around the time they began to look beyond the routine and expectations of high school life, and shortly thereafter, they seemed to see their faith journey as a part of a bygone era as opposed to a radical change of vocation. While Jesus still mattered, at least verbally, for a few years following graduation, the impact their faith had on their choices and lifestyles slowly began to dissipate. Within two to three years after graduation, active engagement in faith, and especially the faith community, had become a thing of the past.

For so many young people, this is their story—perhaps even the majority. There are various academic studies and market research groups that have tried to get at the scope of the issue, yet one thing is clear from all of them: even for those who were active in church or church-related discipleship ministries, by the time they move into their twenties, the faith they once saw as vital and experienced as vibrant became for most of them relegated to the narrative of a stage of life gone by. And there is no current evidence that they will come back when they "stabilize" (meaning, find a meaningful job, get married, and have children). The trends of past decades cannot possibly predict the future in such a wildly changing cultural milieu.

I contend that the primary reason we have lost so many of the hearts and investment of our young when they leave the confines of the high school routine is that we have failed to provide them with the most vital resource they possessed in Christ: the God-given faith community. The leader of that small group of seniors, who happened to be me, was intent on fulfilling the call as a committed and faithful leader. While we practiced our faith together the way we had been taught—we attended church programs, sometimes took notes and discussed the sermons, and participated in the level and kind of Christian community that went beyond most of their peers—even our small little community did not seem to be enough. By the time the three students moved beyond high school, they slowly began to drift from their faith. As much as I tried to help them be faithful, "committed," and invested, what I had given them was not enough. They were products of traditional youth ministry, each a solid "student leader" and visible follower of Christ. Yet if I am honest, beyond me, they were not as deeply connected to the fullness of the body of Christ—even the one who grew up in the church—as they needed to be. Yes, there are no guarantees, and their story is not the story of all youth ministry products, but it is the story of most. When the youth ministry lights go dim and the faith journey is no longer programmatically handed to them, they are left on their own.

## The Historical Backdrop: Why We Are Where We Are

The youth ministry that now commonly functions as the model of Christian adults initiating relationships with young people so that they may come to know Jesus Christ, described by Mike Yaconelli in 2003 as an "experiment," has been more or less the same for the past fifty-plus years. While some argue that youth ministry started hundreds of years ago when people began to address the needs—both material and spiritual—of vulnerable young people, the way we have come to practice youth ministry around the world began in the twentieth century. The zeal and focus of parachurch movements during the late nineteenth and early twentieth centuries partnered with churches in reaching out to the young. Most of the young people involved were already identified with a congregation but benefited greatly from the generational focus of groups like Christian Endeavor. A greater recognition of the coming generational fissures was affecting not only advertising, education, and parenting but also religious communities. In the mid-twentieth century, missional parachurch groups like Young Life and later Youth for Christ generally focused more on all young people, not just those who were involved in a church. Throughout and following World War II, the drive to introduce the young to God through Jesus Christ by seeking them out where they lived and gathered, building welcoming relationships, and speaking the gospel to them in terms they could understand had become the basic methodology of the youth ministry "experiment." In the 1960s and 1970s, churches began to put more energy, staff, and money into the young, and through the influence of emerging leaders, books, training opportunities, and materials like Youth Specialties, what we now know as youth ministry took shape: a group of adults who were willing to invest in the lives of young people and introduce them to a relationship with Jesus.

In 1987, Mark H. Senter III and Warren S. Benson wrote one of the earliest textbooks for youth ministry. Up to this point there had been a handful of books that had helped define and ground the fledgling field of youth ministry in biblical and theological thought, but to many of the pioneering teachers in college and seminary youth ministry classes, *The Complete Book of Youth*

*Ministry* was the most comprehensive to date.[1] Benson and Senter, as Christian educators, were among the first to bring together in one volume a good number of the most prominent voices in what eventually came to be known as "academic" youth ministry.[2] In the first chapter—"A Theology of Youth Ministry"—as Benson makes the case for grounding the work of youth ministry within the rubric of theology, he lands on the work of Jim Rayburn, the founder of Young Life, and the theological impetus for seeing the incarnation as the "model for youth ministry."[3] Benson, citing his coeditor, Mark H. Senter III, offered three statements that define youth ministry.

1. "Youth Ministry begins when adults find a comfortable method of entering a student's world."
2. "Youth ministry happens as long as adults are able to use their student contacts to draw students into a maturing relationship with God through Jesus Christ."
3. "Youth ministry ceases whenever the adult-student relationship is broken or the outcome of that relationship ceases to move the student toward spiritual maturity."[4]

In many ways, *The Complete Book of Youth Ministry* broke new ground for the thinking and doing of youth ministry. In the late 1980s and early 1990s, as colleges and seminaries across North America and eventually around the world hired faculty and instituted classes and even some degree programs, the idea of youth ministry being on solid theological and pedagogical footing encouraged faculties and administrators, and vicariously churches and pastors, to embrace youth ministry as a worthy field of undergraduate and even graduate study (to say nothing of the potential for greatly increased enrollments).

Around this same time, Wayne Rice and Mike Yaconelli of Youth Specialties, and to a certain degree Thom and Joni Schultz at Group, provided a highly visible platform for writers and speakers to influence the shape, style, and structure of youth ministry. Through their seminars and conventions, and later in their publishing, the speakers and writers were also often the academic leaders of the youth ministry "experiment." A synergy developed around the pre-web, viral Yaconelli mantra "Jesus and kids; that's who we are, that's what we do" that gave youth ministry its philosophical core. Regardless of tradition, denomination, or organization, men and women who were tasked with overseeing a youth ministry program in their church, or who served as Young Life or Youth for Christ leaders, read the same books and articles, went to the same training events and conferences, and perpetuated this universal calling—roughly the same that Benson and Senter advocated: youth ministry begins when an adult "enters a student's world" and continues "as long as they are able to *use their student contacts to draw students*" into "maturing relationship with God" (italics mine).

For the past half-century, then, youth ministry has primarily focused on adults building relationships with teenagers for the purpose of helping "each and every young person grow personally and spiritually."[5] The expression, delivery, and style of this basic premise have been debated, nuanced, contextualized, and dissected over the years. At certain points in the youth ministry landscape, a book or leader would come along and propose a corrective to a perceived movement or trajectory, whether it was pragmatic (as with Mark DeVries's *Family-Based Youth Ministry* in 1994), strategic (Doug Fields's million-plus seller *Purpose Driven Youth Ministry* in 1998), or programmatic (Duffy Robbins's *Ministry of Nurture* in 1990).[6] In each of these and numerous other cases, and for the most part across traditions and denominations, the core has remained committed to individual young people being the recipients of a relational investment of a concerned adult, or group of concerned adults, for the purposes of the spiritual development of the adolescents' individual journeys. Again, as Peter Benson notes, youth ministry is adults making "contact" with young people and using "their student contacts to draw students into a maturing relationship with God through Jesus Christ."[7] Although he does not explicitly say this, it is clear that one could easily insert "draw students into a maturing *individual* relationship with God."

The common denominator from the very beginning—despite corrective movements, such as including a greater recognition of the parents' role in their kids' spiritual growth, the development of a comprehensive ministry strategy, and the need to recognize how deeply growing up in a fragmented culture has affected all young people[8]—has been youth ministry's focus on the *individual*. The seedbed of contemporary youth ministry, and where Young Life's Jim Rayburn developed much of his missional theology, was the "tent meeting" evangelism of the early twentieth century.[9] This movement defined evangelism as the church's job to share the "good news" with "outsiders" (Col. 4:5). To invite them to personally embrace the Christian faith became the garden youth ministry was planted and cultivated in. Much of the rhetoric summarizing the emphasis on an individual response to the gospel as the goal of contemporary discipleship has become the bumper sticker theology of youth ministry, regardless of tradition, from "Accept Jesus Christ as your personal Lord" (or sometimes "Savior") to "Become a Christian." By encouraging a personal decision to conversion,[10] followed by the amorphous "rededication," the next step for those who had at some point previously "accepted" Christ (usually at camp), youth ministry has been focused on the task of helping "committed"[11] kids to "grow" in their faith. What this means is difficult to precisely pin down, but essentially it is to encourage young Christ-followers to live their lives in a way that is a reflection of how a "Christian" in a given context looks, talks, thinks, and behaves. In youth ministry seminars, articles, and books, "discipleship" is described in the "doing" of faith: consistent Bible reading, regular prayer, active church life, response to social issues in light of their faith, involvement in some sort of "ministry" where they serve others, and the like.[12] Obviously, none of these is wrong or even negative, but are they enough? Or, more important, do they represent the fullness of the call of God in the Scriptures? Perhaps this is what Dallas Willard was describing when he decried the "gospel of sin management."[13]

For all of the good that youth ministry has done, for all of the lives that have been changed, we have moved into a "post-Christian" culture where the young have fewer relational resources than ever to navigate the complexities of entering interdependent adulthood, and the historic focus on faith as an individual responsibility has left countless young people with an inadequate understanding of the Christian faith. The danger of youth ministry exclusively dedicated to evangelizing and then personally "discipling" individuals during adolescence is that faith at its core can easily become so personal that both the daily walk and the lifelong journey as a Christian is all about and up to me. One may argue that this is not exclusively an issue in youth ministry but one found in the wider North American church, and contemporary youth ministry is no more or less culpable than the church at large. Certainly, the youth ministry models and practices focused on individual faith are a reflection of a greater individualism in society and also in the church. I contend, however, that the common complaint among youth ministers that "we want to teach our kids about community, but there is no community in our church, so we can't" has become an excuse that youth ministry leaders and practitioners can no longer tolerate. Even if adults in a given church flee intimate relationships, deny the Johannine mandate of "loving one another" (John 15:9–17), and demonstrate in their attitudes and behavior that while they may "love the kids" from a distance, they are at best afraid of them and at worst don't want them around, this is no excuse for us to perpetuate a gospel of individualistic faith.

## Family as Biblical Metaphor

New Testament writers, reinforcing who we are as followers of Jesus Christ post-Pentecost, typically rely on the term "assembly" of God's people (from the Greek word *ekklēsia*, translated "church" in most English Bibles). In describing what it means to relate to one another and function as God's assembly, two primary metaphors are used: we are the "body of Christ" and we are the "family of God." In 1 Corinthians 12 Paul uses the metaphor of the body to describe who we are in relationship to one another, especially between those who hold more prominent positions or roles and those who live on the periphery, and in contrast to who Jesus is as the "head." Using this metaphor, Paul is often misunderstood to be describing a categorically prescriptive list of the various "spiritual gifts" that God gives to his people. His argument, in fact, is much more concerned with the reality that Jesus has called us to be his "body" here on earth, even while he takes his place in the heavens as he reigns as Lord, and is therefore much more about unity and participation in the gathering of the assembly than about how one identifies and lives into his or her particular "gift."

There are two aspects to being the body of Christ in Paul. First, there is the call to the members of the body to function as partnering agents as we collaboratively participate in Jesus's work on earth bringing the kingdom to its ultimate end. We, as his body, are a primary means by which God has chosen to further his kingdom on earth.[14] The second aspect of living together as the body of Christ is that we are thereby intrinsically connected one to another, without regard to gifts, function, power, status, or *age*. Paul insists that this "body" is a whole thing—consistent with Hebraic holistic thought where, in contrast to the prevailing Platonic philosophy of the era, there is no separation in a "body": it is one thing.[15] This concept is central to Paul's understanding of the church: "There is neither Jew nor Gentile, neither slave nor free, nor is there male and female, for you are all one in Christ Jesus" (Gal. 3:28), to which we could safely include, "neither child nor adult." As Richard A. Gaillardetz notes, "Paul's theological reflections on the Christian community centered on the metaphor of the body. By speaking of the church as a body, Paul privileged the communal nature of Christian life, a spiritual coexistence, and the interdependence of all the members."[16] The New Testament is clear on this point: all people who belong to Christ belong to one another in the community, without reservation or qualification.

The second primary metaphor describing who we are as the gathered assembly of God's people is that we are the "family" of God. Throughout Scripture, God's people are referred to as his "children" (as in Deut. 14:1, "You are the children of the LORD your God").[17] Jesus not only refers to God in familial terms, but in the Lord's Prayer he directs his disciples to call on the Lord with the same level of intimacy, "Our Father, who art in heaven . . ." (Matt. 6:9 ASV). The Spirit also leads us into one of the most sacred of family relationships when we are able to cry out to our "Abba," essentially to call on our God in the most intimate of family terms (Rom. 8:15).[18] In John's Gospel, the incarnation is what makes possible our new familial relationship with God, and therefore with each other, by proclaiming that "to all who did receive him, to those who believed in his name, he gave the right to become children of God" (John 1:12). The New Testament writers apply this family metaphor, consistently encouraging believers to see one another as brothers and sisters. In Galatians 6:10, we are admonished to "do good to all people, especially to those who belong to the family of believers," and Hebrews 2:11 claims that Jesus "is not ashamed" to refer to his followers as his "brothers and sisters."

Jesus himself affirms how his incarnation establishes the newly ordained family of God when his mother and brothers come to "take charge" of him, and he responds with the rather stark and, in terms of the overemphasis that contemporary Christians place on the institution of the family, harsh question, "'Who is my mother, and who are my brothers?' Pointing to his disciples, he said, 'Here are my mother and my brothers. For whoever does the will of my Father in heaven is my brother and sister and mother'" (Matt. 12:48–50).

Ironically, the call to live as a family, while thoroughly biblical with profound theological implications, is rarely used in the development of a holistic ecclesiology. Yet, as we've demonstrated, the reality that God is our Father and we are his children, related not only as sons and daughters but as mutual siblings, is a crucial and illuminating picture for the church, especially in a world of increasing relational fragmentation and isolation. We regularly use words like "community" and "fellowship," yet these and other similar terms pale in comparison to the concept of a family. Dennis Guernsey, in one of the most insightful books on family ministry, *A New Design for Family Ministry*, bases his argument on this single principle.

> The church is a family of families. . . . The church of the first century were called to leave their earthly familial allegiances and to bond to one another as the new family of God. The revolutionary impact of the first-century church was their love for one another as Christ had commanded them. The need for the church in the twentieth century is to respond as they responded. We are the church and we are family. Let us get on with our business.[19]

## Adoption as Ministry Metaphor

If the church is to be, as Guernsey asserts, a "family of families," then the leadership in power must be proactive in relationally connecting all members of the community, especially anyone who is disenfranchised from the dominant segment of the congregation. The church has the obligation to not only program for this but take the proactive initiative to draw those who feel like outsiders into the center. To strengthen the family imagery for the body of Christ, the apostle Paul employed the term "adoption" to describe the familial privilege we have with God and one another in Christ.[20] The power of this term is that an adopted child, by definition, receives all of the rights and privileges of a "natural" child.[21] Although the church is not often described in family terms, the idea of all members of the body being mutually included and embraced by all is a powerful ministry image, especially as we fulfill our calling to care for those who feel they do not have much of a place or relational standing. The implications for adoption as the goal of ministry present a new way of thinking about the church for everyone—small children, the elderly, the homebound, those who are divorced, the disabled, and, of course, young people, both adolescents and emerging adults.

In terms of youth ministry, where for years the young not only have been seen as a separate population but programmatically arranged to maintain and even reinforce that separation, the only way the church can begin to realize its calling to live as a family is by literally adopting the young. *This is the theological and sociological rationale for youth ministry as adoption.* Youth ministry is, by definition, ministry to and for teenagers, typically middle and high school students aged eleven to eighteen, and it sometimes includes college ministries. As a group, this population rarely experiences their relationship with the dominant population of the church or society at large as something to which they belong. If the church is indeed intended to be a network of familial relationships, a "family of families," then the need for a comprehensive ministry strategy to make this happen trumps all other programmatic goals. If people do not know one another, if they do not feel cared for or necessary, and if they do not sense that the rest of the community values them, the church is simply not the church. The church must adjust its vision and structure to ensure that everyone in God's family experiences their faith as a vital member of God's household as expressed in the local faith community.

## Adoption as the Goal of Youth Ministry

Few would argue that growing up is easier today than it was for previous generations. David Elkind (*The Hurried Child*) and Robert Putnam (*Bowling Alone*) expose how our cultural commitment to "hurrying" children is a form of giving them everything they need except for what they need most:

adult support and authentic presence. While some systems and programs have sought to push against this isolating trend of abandonment, like the best of youth ministry, the societal forces have simply been too potent. One of the most visible outcomes of this increasing lack of social support and capital, according to many who study the state of the adolescent psyche, is the difficulty our young experience entering into healthy interdependent adulthood. Jeffrey J. Arnett and others have identified a whole new stage of development: emerging adulthood.[22] In every area of life, because there is so little available communal support, it is simply more difficult to grow up. This includes the area of faith development.

When it comes to the quest for a lifelong faith, with the best intentions we present a gospel where God loves them, but that same gospel comes without the long-term, broad-based familial support that they need to grow up into a healthy, mature, interdependent faith. For most, because of the individualistic and programmatic focus of youth ministry, their discipleship often becomes one more thing on the agenda. What we so often offer them is a solitary and individual trek that they are ultimately responsible to complete. In traditional youth ministry, we may use the rhetoric of community to describe our practices, and we believe that what we do actually is an expression of Christian community (although limited to peers and a handful of adults), but generally the best we offer is a shallow and generationally limited approximation of what the New Testament treats as normative. When even the most involved of our seniors graduate from the youth program, their impression of authentic biblical community is a weekly or at most biweekly event where they play the role of observer to a program that others plan and execute.

To know and be known, to intimately participate in a "family of families," is so foreign that few graduates of even the best youth ministry programs know how or even why to seek it when they leave. The result is that youth ministry creates spiritual orphans where, when the lights are dimmed and the next class arrives, all that the students have to hold on to is a vague sense of personal responsibility. It is no surprise, then, that so many young people no longer align with a church after they graduate.[23]

As we've noted, all of humanity was intended for familial community, to experience the *shalom* of God's reign as the Father's sons and daughters: "It is not good for the man to be alone" (Gen. 2:18). Yet somehow we have become so focused on the isolated responsibility of the self in relationship to God, and have so sanctified the "personal journey" of faith, that we have failed our young. Youth ministry, and the church itself, has effectively removed the primary resource that God has given his people for living the

life to which we are called: each other. We have left today's abandoned
adolescents as solitary spiritual nomads. For forty years of well-intentioned
youth ministry, we have ignored their need for a choir of saints in order
to grow up to maturity in Christ. If the gathering of God's people is not
a body, or a family of families, and is reduced to a friendly network of
individuals, it is *not* the way of Jesus, and we are not the church. When
we graduate a "solid," core member of our youth program, even one who
is a celebrated "student leader," who has been an evangelistic force in the
adolescent community, is well-grounded in biblical theology and doctrine,
*but has few or no familial relationships with God's people driving all of
this*, we have only brought that person halfway. We have, in essence, created
Christian "performers" who have learned that they are loved and blessed
when they "take a stand for God" or publicly pray. The issue isn't whether
a young person's faith is real; rather, it is whether the Christianity we have
handed our young disciples is deep and relationally embodied enough in
God's family for them to rely on it in the years to come.

When that young, energetic, and "passionate" disciple moves into her
mid-twenties and feels alone and isolated from her roots like so many of her
friends from "back then," who is there for her? Hopefully her parents—or
at least a parent—have been able to maintain some sort of bridge to faith,
but even in that rare case, who else? Where does she turn when she feels like
she has no one who is present who knows her, whom she can turn to when
confused or hurt or in need of grace? When that all-star "student leader"
eventually lands that first job, or gets married, and yet still gets to a place
where he wonders whether the Jesus he knew in high school has any idea
who he is or what his life is like now, where does he go? Who is there to
remind him of his gifts and calling and impact? The default answer from
traditional youth ministry is that our students have all that they need to live
into mature Christian faith by finding a college ministry, mentor, or church
where they can be nurtured. Many are beginning to recognize we have to
do more, to go deeper, like *Sticky Faith*, which encourages extending youth
ministry to a "4 + 1" model to help with the transition out of high school.[24]
This is a good first step, but is one more year of connection to a particular
ministry enough to provide them with the family God offers them? Without
an adoptive model of youth ministry, even those broader ministry strategies
focused on parents as disciplers and the most solid youth programs cannot
possibly provide the intrinsic participation in the whole of the family of God
that our young need to be convinced of their place and worth. It takes the
entire faith community, and the global church, to commit to the long-term
embrace of children, adolescents, emerging adults, and everyone else who

calls Christ Lord to provide the emotional and relational environment God has for all of us.

Clearly along the way there must be an internal, personal commitment to seek out support and invest in a Christ-centered community. Yet, when it takes ten to fifteen years longer to move into interdependency as an adult—and the adolescent/emerging adult journey is by definition a time of transition, self-focus, and vulnerability—the onus falls on the mature in the community to initiate sustaining structures that can envelop the young person *while they are within the relational cocoon of middle and high school.* They must be convinced when they leave home that their spiritual family, the family of God, is always there for them, regardless of where or how they live. Otherwise, as we maintain the ways we have been doing youth ministry for decades, some may flourish, but the majority are destined to hit that faith wall so many young adults describe. God, while very real in high school, becomes a distant, albeit warm memory from a bygone era.

## Youth Ministry as Adoption

What is the answer? The goal of youth ministry must shift away from segmenting young people off from everyone else to offering them a mutual, empowering, engaging, and supportive new family. We must abandon the notion that lifelong faith can be solidified by the time one is in high school and that external expressions of faith—especially emotional (i.e., "passionate") outbursts and measurable outcomes—do not predict the lifelong story, and we must purpose to collectively reengage and embrace our young as members of our own family. We must rethink youth ministry so as to literally *adopt* them into the family of the church. Honor their gifts and calling, yes. Celebrate practices, and acts of justice and mercy, and investment in others' lives and souls for the kingdom, certainly. But underneath and around all of these external effects and markers, we must commit to making sure every young person knows that they matter not only to God but to a large and diverse family because God *and his church* declare it so. To put it more clearly, *The goal of youth ministry as adoption is for every child, every adolescent, and every young adult to be so embraced by the community of faith that they know they always have a home, a people, and a place where they can discover who they are and how they are able to contribute.* In short, youth ministry is adopting young people into the family of God.

This definition, then, requires the community of God's people, the local church, to create a youth ministry marked by the following three distinctives.

### 1. Personal Response, While Important, Is Not the Point of Ministry.

The Bible is unequivocal in the call of individual people to "come" to God through Jesus Christ. This is described in a variety of ways, such as "receiving" (John 1:12), "acknowledging" (Matt. 10:32), accepting an "invitation" (Matt. 22:1–14), "repenting" (Mark 1:15; literally, to "turn around"), and "believing" (John 3:16; 6:28–30, from *pisteuō* or *pistis*, which is usually translated as "believe, trust, or faith"—see Gal. 5:5–6). The call for each human person is to an individual, willful assent to trust God in Jesus Christ. Theologian Louis Berkhof, summarizing the Reformers' description of "the crowning element of faith," noted the Latin word *fiducia*, or "volitional" faith, as the ultimate definition of the call of faith (a trust that is of the will, as opposed to *notitia*, intellectual assent, or *assensus*, emotional agreement).[25]

Yet biblically, even a willful assent to the gospel by individually "making a commitment" (which is often used as a synonym for "receiving" or "believing in" Christ) does not take into account that the act of trusting requires the step of aligning oneself with the mission of Jesus ("As the Father has sent me, I am sending you," John 20:21). This is where the concept of obedience is applied to faith. Jesus himself makes clear that the initial requirement to enter into the family of God is to trust (or "believe," *pisteuō* [Greek], *fiducia* [Latin]) when he told the crowds that "the work of God is this: to believe [trust] in the one he has sent" (John 6:29). For this belief to be actualized, however, there must be an initial step of obedience into the corporate call of faith. *Fiducia*, without stepping out into that faith by loving "one another," is not *fiducia*; at best it is *assensus* (emotional assent) and/or *notitia* (cognitive assent). The idea of "trust and obey" is usually packaged together, thus making saving faith conditional on obedience. But the biblical call is to willfully trust. Because of that trust, I therefore take the step of obedience, which begins with the call to "love one another." Our attitudes, lifestyle, and actions toward immersion in the family of faith demonstrate that we truly believe.

That step of obedience and submission to the Lordship of Jesus Christ, then, is first and foremost an alignment with a life that is forged in intimate familial relationships with one another in the body of Christ. All too often in our zeal to encourage young people to own their faith, we have not helped them to know that the first and constant step of faith is to "love one another," especially as this is applied to the entire family of God and not simply their small group or biological family. We regularly fail to lead them to the one reality, and one place, where God has supplied to find the encouragement, support, and familial grounding they need to foster and empower *fiducia*. All too often in youth ministry we forget to help them to see the plural "you" of the gospel call.

Thus, given the biblical mandate of loving one another, the point of youth ministry, and the essential corporate nature of living out faith, is to lead our young (and our old) to express and live out their place as God's children within God's family. We must not only model but teach that while personal faith is important, for that faith to take root, for us to be obedient and follow the call of the gospel, we must strive to establish their faith within the familial relationships of the body of Christ. This is not only their calling as believers; it is all of ours. This family of families is our grounding, our home, our destiny.

### 2. Youth Ministry Is an Important Beginning Point of Adoption.

The reason youth ministry developed was that young people were finding themselves increasingly alienated from dependable adult nurture and regular communal engagement, and they responded by grabbing onto one another as the only source of support and comfort they could count on (other than perhaps their family). It wasn't that the young left the church; the church left the young. A few adults saw this and responded by initiating relationships with the intent of helping the young to see God as their advocate, and to help them to make faith their own. For decades many kids have responded to this initiative we call youth ministry. In so many ways youth ministry is as healthy and externally thriving as it ever has been. Both parachurch and church-based ministries still see many teenagers come to sincere faith who are active in their communities and able to sustain that faith into their adulthood. A theology of adoption does not mean to say that youth ministry is broken. The way we have operationalized and delivered youth ministry as being primarily about individual faith and discipleship, however, has now caught up to us in today's atomized society. Finding oneself feeling isolated and alone is bad enough. When a young person moves beyond youth ministry with the idea that personal faith is all there is to the gospel, it is unconscionable. The fall shattered all of creation, and the consequential loneliness and isolation are the essence of the fallen human condition.

God is in the business of restoring that which was broken and bringing *shalom*—not just the absence of conflict but the sense of rightness and wholeness—to those who are lost ("For the Son of Man came to seek and to save the lost," Luke 19:10). It is not that youth ministry has failed, it is that it is not enough. Young people, like the rest of us, as members of the fallen race are at core lost and alone. Youth ministry still matters and is indeed a vital entry-level expression of Christ's love for children and adolescents. Adoption as the goal of youth ministry does not negate the important role of a targeted ministry that incorporates adventure, risk, mission and ministry opportunities, small groups, and the like. Youth ministry as adoption is best conceived as a bridge ministry intent on moving the young beyond peer-experienced faith by leading them into the welcoming arms of the adoptive family of faith. The goal of even the best and most thriving youth ministry must be a strategic commitment toward authentic, inclusive, and participatory adoption.

### 3. Adult Youth Ministry "Leaders" Are Adoption Guides.

In historical youth ministry, the work rises and falls on the shoulders of volunteers. Youth ministry has never been sustainable as solely the product of a gifted speaker or musician presenting a program from the front. Virtually every model and philosophy of youth ministry presupposes committed and qualified adult volunteers—even those who advocate "student leaders" to "lead" the ministry. There is almost always a recognition that it is a form of abandonment of the young when adults simply offer the programmatic scaffolding of ministry but remain disconnected and in the background. Adults are crucial players in any youth ministry.

The role of adults in youth ministry as adoption, however, must change from "discipling teenagers" to being agents in the adoptive process. In historical youth ministry models, adults usually function in roles such as small group leaders, "advisers," or quasi–life guides who help individuals—or in the case of small groups, a group of individuals—to "grow in their faith." For most adults, this lack of clarity to their purpose can be anywhere from confusing to frustrating. The ones who find satisfaction by simply being with teenagers and enjoy relationships with young, energetic disciples tend to stay involved in youth ministry for years. For those adults who are healthy and serve out of a mature faith and satisfying peer relationships, this is the best of contemporary youth ministry. But there are those adult leaders who clutch their role with young people tightly and use their "ministry" as a way to feed their own soul, perhaps in order to avoid the complexities of adult relationships or because they enjoy what kids give to them. In these circumstances, youth ministry can actually undermine healthy discipleship and will always hinder adoption, for those leaders will see their ministries being fulfilled in them. To strategically seek to "pass them off" to the larger family of the church can easily be seen as "losing my kids." Regardless of the motive, one leader, as good as he or she is, is simply not enough of an expression of the fullness of the body to launch a young person into reliance on and engagement with the family of God.

The adult role, then, whether paid staff or volunteer, is to be the relational and at times programmatic bridge into familial connection in the Christian community. When a small group leader, for example, discovers that a high school junior is a gifted audio technician, then that leader may use that knowledge to find a way to connect that junior to the group of people who are responsible for the worship sound production. The key to this strategy, however, is *not* to simply use a young person's skill or interest to connect them to a task. Rather, the tech team is tasked with *adopting* the teen as a member of the family of God. The junior thinks that he or she is there just to help run the audio mix, but the other adults realize that they are, and are even trained to be, literal adopters of that teenager. Spiritual practices (prayer, sharing, even a Bible study) then become a routine part of their work, and everyone welcomes the young person as if he or she were their little brother or sister, or "adopted" child.

If every adult volunteer and paid staff member has this goal in mind and is committed to *not only* developing the personal faith of the young people but *also* seeking adoption for each of them by connecting them to the broader body, they will experience a much more satisfying ministry experience. It is true that even without a clearly delineated commitment to adoption as the goal of youth ministry, some young people will find their way into a meaningful connection to the larger family of the church. A few teenagers, for example, who become preschool "teachers" during corporate worship or who play the bass in the "contemporary" service might find themselves to be organically embraced by caring adults. This does not, however, deny the strategic imperative to make this the goal of ministry for all young people, beginning with children and moving throughout the congregation (this same chapter, for example, could have been written for how a church ministers to senior adults or singles). Youth ministry as adoption seeks this for every young person.

Some churches have made great strides seeking to build relational bridges across generations by offering "intergenerational" programs, events, and opportunities (this, again, is a current outcome of the *Sticky Faith* movement). This is a good beginning or gateway strategy to move into the direction of adoption, but just because we program for diverse populations to meet and even get to know one another, this alone rarely translates into the same level of connection to create the long-term impact of familial adoption. Just as in a family, adoption is far more than just knowing and being around each other. Family cuts much deeper than building networks of mutual acquaintances.

Adoption, then, must be more than just allowing kids to be known or to serve or teach or sing; it is about them knowing that they are welcomed and embraced as *participants* in the family and that their voice and heart and perspective matter far more than their service or offering. For a worship leader to say to a singer, "You're great, we need you! Welcome!" is not adoption. For an elderly couple to regularly seek out and speak to an eighth grader they met at a mission day is not adoption. Even classic models of individual mentoring rarely have the staying power of the multiple and diverse relationships that come naturally with an adoption ministry strategy. When we offer our young people real, mutually participatory familial relationships that go beyond the single mentor, in line with the family and body metaphors especially found in the New Testament, the church becomes a more natural and wide-ranging environment best described as a *mentoring community*.

When a worship leader, elderly couple, pastor, or middle-aged divorcée begins to appropriately intentionalize familial relationships with appropriate safeguards and boundaries to protect them—when members of the church send out invitations to small group meals, invest in one another's activities, encourage others to participate in business, pastoral, or ministry decision-making networks, know one another's stories, and mutually pray for God's work in and through them—*this is adoption*.

# Responses to the Adoption View

✚ Greg Stier

I was pleasantly surprised at how many times I said "Amen!" in my soul as I read your chapter, Chap. You and I have "tangled" a bit in the past when it comes to youth ministry strategy, philosophy, and focus, but your chapter spoke to me personally, because I am the result of an "adoptive" approach to youth ministry.

Galatians 3:26 reminds us, "So in Christ Jesus you are all children of God through faith." The result of putting our faith in Christ alone based on his finished work on the cross is being adopted into the family of God. Ephesians 1:4–6 puts it this way, "For he chose us in him before the creation of the world to be holy and blameless in his sight. In love he predestined us for adoption to sonship through Jesus Christ, in accordance with his pleasure and will—to the praise of his glorious grace, which he has freely given us in the One he loves."

This "adoption to sonship" is more than a salvific reality that's true in heaven; it has powerful consequences on earth as well. Because God adopted me, I'm part of a family full of adopted brothers and sisters in Christ (aka "the church"). Chap, you did a phenomenal job of making a theological case for this in terms of how we view and do youth ministry.

Bravo!

Growing up, I never knew my biological father. He was in the army and abandoned me and my mom before I was even born. My mom was married four different times (that's how many old marriage certificates I found in her footlocker after she passed away, anyway). As a result, I never had a sense of being a part of a complete family as I was growing up, so coming to faith in Jesus and viewing God as my "Father" had a deep and meaningful impact on me.

Ten years ago, when my mom was dying of cancer in hospice, we had several significant conversations about how Jesus changed everything. She asked me, "Do you remember what you used to say when you were a kid and other kids would make fun of you for not having a daddy?" I didn't remember, so she reminded me, "You used to say 'God's my Daddy.'" I told my mom, "I don't remember saying that, but I remember feeling that from the time I put my faith in Jesus."

So when this youth ministry from the suburbs reached into the inner city where I lived to "adopt" me into their church, it was a game changer. Now, I wasn't just a kid adopted by a heavenly Father whom I would see someday; I had brothers and sisters to embrace me, train me, and unleash me.

Mark Schweitzer, Kenny, "Timo," "Yankee," and a host of other adults took me in and poured into my life. They were more than traditional youth leaders to me; they were, in your words, Chap, "adoption guides." They taught me the traditional youth ministry stuff, but much more. They helped me discover my spiritual gift, trained me to share my faith, and even taught me how to preach.

My youth leaders even set it up for me to preach in "big church" when I was twelve years old. I just about couldn't see over the large pulpit, but I preached my first sermon there. And I wasn't alone. Some of us teenagers were given opportunities to preach, but if you had musical skill, they put you in the band. Teenagers could lead Sunday school classes, teach in the children's ministries, be on service teams—just about anything and everything an adult could do.

Underneath it all pulsated a heart for adoption. We were a bunch of young people that the church took in, trained up, and plugged in as viable members of the body. Although it was a very "old school" church in many ways, it modeled adoption better than any youth ministry I have seen to date.

To this day, many of the adults who spoke into my life forty years ago still speak into my life today. Even when I left the church, I still felt it was a home base for me.

So, Chap, as I read your chapter, I was not thinking of a radical new paradigm; I was thinking of the philosophy of ministry that rescued me from the streets and formed the basis for what I do at Dare 2 Share today.

All that said, I would add three things.

### 1. The Mission of This Approach Must Be External, Not Just Internal.

First Peter 2:9 makes it clear that we've been chosen for a purpose: "But you are a chosen people, a royal priesthood, a holy nation, God's special possession, that you may declare the praises of him who called you out of darkness into his wonderful light." The purpose of our adoption is proclamation with our lives and our lips of the gospel of Jesus Christ.

A teenager who knows, owns, lives, and shares their faith has a much stronger likelihood of keeping their faith long term. In her book *Almost Christian*, based on the National Study of Youth and Religion, Kenda Creasy Dean identifies four marks of young people who are highly devoted to their faith traditions:

1. They confess their tradition's *creed*, or God-story.
2. They belong to a *community* that enacts the God-story.
3. They feel *called* by this story to contribute to a larger purpose.
4. They have *hope* for the future promised by this story.[1]

Note that community is only one component here. Teenagers who fully embrace Jesus's message grasp the reality that something intensely important is at stake in a larger story here—the souls of their friends. They understand the truth that they—they personally—have a role to play as Christ's ambassadors to a lost and hurting world. They truly believe Paul's words in 2 Corinthians 5:19–20 (NLT): "For God was in Christ, reconciling the world to himself, no longer counting people's sins against them. And he gave us this wonderful message of reconciliation. So we are Christ's ambassadors; God is making his appeal through us. We speak for Christ when we plead, 'Come back to God!'"

### 2. The Message for This Approach Must Be Grace-Based, Not Performance-Based.

Teenagers today are under huge pressures to perform for acceptance. From school, to sports, to relationships, they are used to having to do well before they can excel. It's with this as a backdrop that I cringed a bit when I read the words you wrote about the gospel we present to teenagers: "The idea of 'trust and obey' is usually packaged together, *thus making saving faith conditional on obedience*" (italics added).

This assertion unintentionally opens the door to a performance-based approach to Christianity as opposed to the grace-based approach that sets Christianity apart from every other religion.

For it is by grace you have been saved, through faith—and this is not from your-selves, it is the gift of God—not by works, so that no one can boast. (Eph. 2:8–9)

However, to the one who does not work but trusts God who justifies the ungodly, their faith is credited as righteousness. (Rom. 4:5)

He saved us, not because of righteous things we had done, but because of his mercy. He saved us through the washing of rebirth and renewal by the Holy Spirit. (Titus 3:5)

In one of my favorite books, *The Grace Awakening*, Chuck Swindoll writes these powerful words.

> I can tell you that as a sinner you need to have a stronger commitment to Christ demonstrated by the work you do in His behalf, before you can say you truly believe. My problem in doing so is this: A sinner cannot commit to anything. He or she is spiritually dead, remember? There is no capacity for commitment in an unregenerate heart. Becoming an obedient, submissive disciple of Christ *follows* believing in Christ. Works *follow* faith. Behavior *follows* belief. Fruit comes *after* the tree is well-rooted.[2]

Philip Yancey shares some profound words in *What's So Amazing about Grace?* "The world runs by ungrace. Everything depends on what I do. I have to make the shot. Jesus's kingdom calls us to another way, one that depends on not our performance but his own. We do not have to achieve but merely follow. He has already earned for us the costly victory of God's acceptance."[3]

Adding fine print to God's free gift of grace is not only dangerous theologi-cally (Gal. 1:8) but potentially damaging to teenagers psychologically, because it introduces them to a Christian version of religious performance-ism instead of the shocking, beautiful, and amazing message of God's grace.

This psychological damage was something I experienced personally as a teenager. The same church that reached my entire family with the good news of Jesus, and was so clear on the subject of salvation being a free gift of God's grace through faith alone, had a long legalistic list of "do's," "stops," and "starts" when it came to spiritual growth. This list became a frustrating replacement for a grace-based, Spirit-empowered approach.

This same church that transformed my entire family as a result of preach-ing justification by faith alone messed me (and a bunch of my teenage peers) up by preaching a sanctification of performance. I meet casualties of this mind-set to this day everywhere I go.

No, we are saved by grace and we grow by grace. And our obedience to Jesus is the exciting result of salvation, not the joy-quenching requirement for one to receive it.

The performance-based youth ministry has a checklist of things you must do in addition to trusting in Jesus to be saved. The grace-based youth ministry invites teenagers to receive the free gift of salvation by faith alone in Christ alone and then challenges them to live in radical obedience as a joyful response to this amazing gift.

Which kind of family would you rather be adopted into? I choose grace! And, Chap, I'm sure you do too!

### 3. The Mentors in This Approach Must Be Missional, Not Traditional.

Getting teenagers plugged into a church community is only a long-term solution if that community is both deep and wide. If the adults in that church family are not modeling the life of Christ (deep) and sharing the message of Jesus (wide), then all we have done with our teenagers is perpetuate another church-going narcissist who fills in blanks in sermon outlines, participates in meetings, and gives 10 percent of their income to God.

Traditionally, adults in the church don't have a kingdom-advancing focus. There's a natural propensity for church to become a comfortable, inwardly focused "social" hub, to the point that many adult Christians today have virtually *no* social relationships with nonbelievers. Yet how can we lovingly and relationally advance the gospel and plead with the lost on Christ's behalf when we don't know anyone who's lost?

To a significant extent, I believe the church's lack of missional focus is a major contributor to why young people are leaving the church—because it's become largely irrelevant in the world they inhabit.

But God calls all of us to more.

I'm convinced that our young people are our best hope for leading the way back to the early church's radical, revolutionary, world-transforming model of ministry. In *You Lost Me*, David Kinnaman notes that young people "are desperate for a new way to understand and experience the worthy risks of following Christ. Life without some sense of urgency—a life that is safe, incubated, insular, overprotected, consumptive—is not worth living. The next generation is aching for influence, for significance, for lives of meaning and impact . . . yet we have done all we can to lower the stakes for the newest real-life protagonists in God's grand, risky story."[4]

If the mentors in this adoptive approach to youth ministry are not seeking to model this missional lifestyle, then the family we are adopting them into is dysfunctional. And a dysfunctional spiritual family can be as damaging as a dysfunctional human family.

Of course, this doesn't mean that the mentors must be perfect at advancing God's kingdom forward. They just must authentically seek to attempt this way of living. Even if these mentors are "failing forward," teenagers will learn just as much from their honesty, failures, and frustrations as they will from their evangelistic successes.

We need to nurture the energy, passion, longing, idealism, and cause-focused drive of our young people to help call the church back to its mission. We need to mobilize them to inject a Gospel Advancing mindset into the adults in our lukewarm churches, transforming them from comfortable "social gatherings" into healthy, missional lighthouses that actively, intentionally, and continually reach out to the lost and hurting.

Chap, overall, this chapter on adoptive youth ministry is spot-on. It put words to something I have subconsciously felt for a long time, and I will be using many of your points as I train youth leaders across the nation. Thank you.

## ✚ Brian Cosby

Without question, Chap, you have given us a gift with your chapter on youth ministry *as adoption* into the family of faith. Thank you. I learned a lot, especially about current sociological trends, the historical development of youth ministry, and the precise failure of the church in building lasting, nurturing, and family-modeled relationships with teenagers. For the sake of organizing my response to your position, I'd like to offer what I see as some very positive aspects of your chapter and then some areas of disagreement and constructive criticism.

### Positives of the Adoption View

You describe well the typical story of church-going youth who end up leaving the church after high school. Unfortunately, this is the new normal for teenagers today, and you plot their journey as most reading this book would see it today. I've personally observed this "journey" for a number of teenagers, and it breaks my heart.

I also appreciate the historical and theological overview of how modern youth ministry began. Throughout its relatively brief history, the core of youth ministry has remained a "relational investment" (as you put it) of a concerned adult into teenagers' lives. However, in this type of relationship, it segregates the youth from the greater family—they are treated merely as a group of individuals rather than the biblical "body" of Christ and the "family" of God. Thus, as you rightly argue, we should not perpetuate a "gospel of individualistic faith." In some ways, what we see happening in the church is paradigmatic of the hyperindividualistic society at large.

I love your biblical exposition of the metaphors used of the church, namely, (1) being a body with many members functioning together, serving together, and using the gifts that God has given for the building up of the body; and (2) adoption into the family of God through faith. I like that you continue to use the image of a "family of families" to describe the church.

Thank you for making this careful distinction that even well-intentioned terms like "community" and "fellowship" pale in comparison to the idea of a *family*. The idea of the "family" naturally assumes commitment and the well-being of the other. What are the implications of church as family? They must know one another, forgive one another, care for one another, love one another, serve one another, and so on. These couldn't be more right on.

Finally, your analysis that most youth today think of Christian "community" as a weekly or biweekly meeting—thus rendering them as merely an *observer* in a program that others plan and execute—is a brilliant insight. I can see this perception all around my ministry circles. Youth ministry should move beyond a mere "private" or "personal" journey of faith. Indeed, if it doesn't, both the journey and the faith seem to evaporate. Adults of all ages should come alongside to adopt teenagers into this family as a "mentoring community," as you put it. Very well said.

### My Concerns with the Adoption View

While I certainly do appreciate certain elements of your position as seen in your chapter, I ultimately find it lacking for the following reasons.

1. Where's God in the salvation, development, and sanctification of youth? The family of faith is very important, but how should we understand God's design and active role in this model? I just didn't see an emphasis on God. You point out his design of the church as a family and body of Christ, but what about his ongoing work in that family? This one element has a huge implication on how we are to understand youth ministry (as I'll point out below).

2. You state, "I contend that the primary reason we have lost so many of the hearts and investment of our young when they leave the confines of the high school routine is that we have failed to provide them with the most vital resource they possessed in Christ: the God-given faith community." Similarly, you argue, "Youth ministry, and the church itself, has effectively removed the primary resource that God has given his people for living the life to which

we are called—each other." My question is simply this: Are other Christians the *primary* resource God has given his people to grow and mature in the faith? I think not.

While I agree that the family of God—the local church—is *one* of the means that God uses to grow his people, the *primary* means (as I see it) by which he sanctifies them is his Word, as Jesus contends (John 17:17). We must remember that the gospel is the power of God for salvation (Rom. 1:16), not people. It's nice to have adults "love on" and "invest in" the lives of teenagers, but this falls flat apart from the whole counsel of God. Thus, I would argue that your "reason" why so many have wandered from the faith would be a *secondary* reason, not a primary one (even if you have sociological data to back it up).

3. You say that the "first and constant step of faith is to 'love one another.'" While we are certainly called to love one another, this is but the *second* greatest commandment. Again, where is the love and affection for God? We shouldn't miss the first and greatest commandment: to love *God*! Would the love for God, because he first loved us, not ultimately be "the first and constant step of faith"? Our love for one another would be a natural outworking of our love for God and his love for us.

4. Thus, to be rather blunt, I see your model as incomplete and unbalanced. The church as family is one of the *several* means of grace that God has given us to grow and mature—at any age or life stage. Thus, I must disagree when you argue that "the goal of youth ministry must shift away from segmenting young people off from everyone else to offering them a mutual, empowering, engaging, and supportive new family." Rather, I see the goal of youth ministry as glorifying God by planting and watering the gospel through the means that God has already provided: his Word, prayer, sacrament, worship, service, and gospel community. Your model simply takes this last element as the foundation without giving balance to the others.

5. You say, with reference to the fall, "The consequential loneliness and isolation are the essence of the fallen human condition." What about sin? Certainly our sin has something to do with the fallen human condition. It is our sin that has led to our feeling lonely and isolated, not the other way around.

6. It would have helped to have a few more examples on *how* to "adopt" teens into family of the church. In other words, explain what it looks like for a youth worker to be a "bridge" into this family. You give a couple of quick examples, but it was still difficult to visualize this in an actual youth ministry context.

7. You talk about our "response" to the gospel call, our faith, and our obedience—and you even cite Louis Berkhof (love it!). But we must remember that all of this is from God. We were dead in sin (Eph. 2:1), not seeking God (Rom. 3:11), and unable to please him (Heb. 11:6). By his grace alone, he has

removed our hearts of stone and given us hearts to believe. Surely this must be emphasized in a discussion on the doctrine of salvation, even as presented in your chapter. What I keep coming back to, Chap, is a more active role of God in youths' lives. Where is the emphasis on his grace, his holiness, his righteousness, and his glory in youth ministry? I would categorize your model not as God-centered but as people-centered.

8. I think your entire push might be the exception to the rule of *parents* being specifically called and, therefore, specifically responsible to raise their children in the discipline and instruction of the Lord (cf. Eph. 6:4). *If* youth don't have Christian parents, then your model kicks into full gear. I typically tell people that we must continue to state the principle, even if there are a thousand "exceptions" to the rule.

Yes, older men should mentor younger men and older women should mentor younger women (cf. Titus 2, which you might have overlooked). However, the primary responsibility of a youth's discipleship and growth *in the community of faith* is his or her parents. Other concerned adults should come alongside, but your position needs to make a much more concentrated focus on the role of parents. Again, if no Christian parents are to be found, then "adopting" them would become absolutely necessary.

## ✚ Fernando Arzola

Chap's introductory story reflects the honest reality of many Christian teens—they were on fire for the Lord during adolescence and eventually disconnected from the church later. This is a common narrative throughout all denominations and traditions. And his thesis is correct when he writes, "I contend that the primary reason we have lost so many of the hearts and investment of our young when they leave the confines of the high school routine is that we have failed to provide them with the most vital resource they possessed in Christ: the God-given faith community."

It is sadly ironic that teens who have been nurtured in the faith within a church community would leave it and possibly not return to it in later years. This leads to a second irony—is it possible that parachurch ministries, a youth ministry pillar, may actually have contributed to the demise of the eventual teen-church connection?

The first part of Chap's chapter provides a helpful snapshot on the history of youth ministry. What this highlights, in addition to demonstrating the dedication and passion of many parachurch ministry founders and leaders, is that many of these were (and perhaps remain) insufficient in keeping teens connected with the church. One wonders, after all these years, whether these ministries, although important, would change their paradigm to reflect a more intentional connection with and toward churches rather than separate from them. This leads to the concern Chap raises that perhaps one-on-one evangelizing and discipling alone may ultimately lead to an individualized faith separate from the church community.

The "body of Christ" metaphor seems to be used today with more regularity than the "family of God." I wonder why. Is it perhaps that families are not as intact as they once were? Perhaps the diversity of the contemporary family unit may require a reenvisioning of what it has traditionally meant to be a "family of God"? Jesus's words in Matthew 12:48–50 are challenging ones indeed, for he underscores that the "family of God" is bigger, broader, and greater than blood relatives. Hence, Chap's recommendation for the "adoption" metaphor for ministry is apt. Not only is it a Pauline metaphor, but it seems to take into account the reality of contemporary diversity and the modern family. Not only is it appropriate theologically, but it is appropriate sociologically. Relationally, this also allows space for teens (and all of us) to experience an ecclesiological adoption option for those who do not feel connected with a local congregation. The arms of God are stretched wider and embrace more families than our often-myopic familial/denominational/traditional presumptions.

Chap also challenges our presumptions of "community." This is very important. We all use this term, but how do we understand it, particularly within the context of youth ministry? What do we mean by community? How broad and inclusive is our understanding of community? And does our community actually perpetuate an exclusivity that pushes teens further from the church, especially as they get older and reflect on their youth ministry experiences?

This is not unlike the "All Are Welcome" signs in front of churches where all are not really welcome. Teens are often expected to join the congregational parade where all walk in unison. So, yes, this is a community, but is this a community that expands the kingdom of God, or moves teens closer to Christ, or moves them toward justice and mercy? Or does it move them out of the church and nurture a pseudo-community marked by judgmentalism and limitations, where the saints are welcomed and sinners are dismissed? Being in community is both comforting and very difficult, as Dietrich Bonhoeffer affirms.

> Let him who cannot be alone beware of community. . . . Let him who is not in community beware of being alone. . . . Each by itself has profound perils and pitfalls. One who wants fellowship without solitude plunges into the void of words and feelings, and the one who seeks solitude without fellowship perishes in the abyss of vanity, self-infatuation and despair.[5]

In this rapidly mobile society, perhaps the expectation of teens return-ing to their "home" congregation may be an unrealistic and nostalgic no-tion. This does not mean, however, that teens-turned-adults may not have nurtured the spirit of Christian community in their hearts. Perhaps this is a lesson for youth ministers—it is a greater good to have teens return and join a church community rather than to expect teens to return to the com-munity of their adolescence. In other words, adoption by God supersedes attendance at a specific congregation—maybe even (dare I say it) beyond a specific denomination.

Chap's development of moving from assent to obedience and submission is helpful indeed. It is also very, very difficult. To affirm a christological concept is one thing; to submit to it is something totally different. "The idea of 'trust and obey' is usually packaged together, thus making saving faith conditional on obedience," he writes. I agree with him. This is why I am also grateful for God's grace, for I frequently fail to obey and submit. As Bonhoeffer also poignantly and directly explains,

> It may be that Christians, notwithstanding corporate worship, common prayer, and all their fellowship in service, may still be left to their loneliness. The final break-through to fellowship does not occur, because, though they have fel-lowship with one another as believers and as devout people, they do not have fellowship as the undevout, as sinners. The pious fellowship permits no one to be a sinner. So everybody must conceal his sin from himself and from the fellowship. We dare not be sinners. Many Christians are unthinkably horrified when a real sinner is suddenly discovered among the righteous. So we remain alone with our sin, living in lies and hypocrisy. The fact is that we *are* sinners![6]

This too is a message that teens need to hear—that we all need to hear. As the man said to Jesus, "I believe; help my unbelief!" (Mark 9:24 ESV). For me, the theology of adoption is also a way of exclaiming that you are welcome, even with your doubts, unbelief, and questioning. Bringing your heart and honest search for God in Christ is welcome in the beloved community.

"Adoption guides" is a helpful term and visual. Ultimately, the youth min-istry leadership must undergo an inner paradigm shift for the program shift to occur. Chap states that youth ministry requires a team of adult leaders, a helpful reminder for youth leaders who may tend to separate youth ministry from the larger church. Separation not only causes teens to miss out in nurtur-ing healthy relationships with adults, but it also places unnecessary burdens on the youth ministry leadership. It also allows for a broader contribution of ideas and, pragmatically speaking, creates a greater menu of programmatic options.

What I appreciate most about the adoption model is that it is thoughtful, reasonable, and honest. It presents a traditional theological concept in a different light. It recognizes the challenges of keeping teens connected with the church. It invites us to examine historical cycles (both in our local churches and in the youth ministry field) and suggests a perspective that encourages not only teen-church connection, but teen-God connection.

## ✚ Ron Hunter

Chap's work with Kara Powell in the *Sticky Faith* project brought significant insight to the youth ministry world. Both he and Kara have dedicated their lives to helping build lifelong faith into kids. What a privilege to share in this *Youth Ministry in the 21st Century* project with you! As I read your chapter, Chap, I could not help but ask the all-important question—why did you not publish your section as a standalone book? This material was academically researched, thoughtfully written, and can be practically applied. The section begins with a case study that could represent the typical participants of any youth group. A constant build toward the thesis of the chapter gives the reader some rich and insightful looks at the history of youth ministry while hinting at how the experiment derailed along the way. A person should buy this book if only for Chap's taxonomy and history of youth ministry.

Chap lists three statements made by Benson and Senter from 1987, and youth ministers sometimes take their cues from their first two statements: "Youth ministry begins when adults find a comfortable method of entering a student's world" in order to "draw the students into a maturing relationship with God through Jesus Christ." But I believe that guiding statements might be more effective and biblical if the word "parent" replaced or accompanied the word "adults."

While Benson, Senter, and Chap are not saying the goal stops at entering a student's world, I offer a word of caution for anyone reaching the youth with Christ without drawing youth to Christ. Youth pastors and parents should be concerned if the goal stops at "entering the student's world" even if the goal is to reach them where they are with the gospel. One can and should see the fallacy of entering or moving to where the lost person is and residing there, even as a believer. Jesus went to people to call people out of where they were. The goal should be to enter the student's world to draw the student to the body of Christ. Later in the chapter, Chap makes it clear that adoption draws the student in service and heart to the community of the church in ways that serve Christ. Thank you for starting with a carefully worded goal (Benson and Senter's) and continuing to build on it to make it better. Chap, you have a pleasant tendency to argue a point, creating desire on the reader's part to ask a specific question, which you immediately provide the answer for.

This chapter provides a clear, distinct goal of youth ministry, which is that every child, every adolescent, and every young adult be adopted into and embraced by the community of faith so that they may always have a home, a people, and a place where they can discover who they are and how they are able to contribute. The adoption of young people into the family of God may sound simple, but it will take some breaking of routines and changing of attitudes, not to mention a healthy number of involved adults. The effort to achieve adoption is worthwhile, and time will show the value of changing the orientation of youth ministry efforts.

Chap's section certainly reinforces the idea of adoption. He shows how the student cannot rely on the group for an individual relationship with God. But the young person likewise cannot pursue discipleship and the development of gifts on his or her own. Then he points out how the student's growth in discipleship cannot be all about the student or left exclusively as the student's responsibility. The need exists for the community of the church to adopt the teenagers into a loving and developing environment. People normally operate and function within a community. Christ paints the picture of both the body of Christ and the family of God, and Chap makes this a clear call to work within the wider church group and be less concerned with labels or even denominations. This community described by Chap as a "family of families" provides accountability, love, acceptance, affirmation, and service in affirming and loving ways. This adoption includes all ages and all parts of the church.

Chap identifies how the youth ministry that functions as a separate population of the church programmatically operates opposite of how a family should. Chap makes several valid points regarding the youth not existing in isolation within the church. Chap says, "For years the young were not only seen as a separate population but have been programmatically arranged to maintain and even reinforce that separation," and "this population rarely experiences their relationship with the dominant population of the church, or society at large, as being something to which they belong." As Chap describes the church as a network of family relationships, he calls for the interaction among the whole family. The perpetuation of isolating youth from a normal social framework that includes adults, according to Elkind and Arnett (both cited by Chap), fashions a protracted path to adulthood.

The section on the historical backdrop, or why we are where we are, talks about youth ministry as an experiment. This apt term describes how various leaders in the 1970s and '80s theorized, practiced, and led seminars about the experience. The people writing and speaking on the topic garnered large crowds of emerging youth leaders who similarly wanted to grow their youth ministry. Youth leaders should ask, "Am I growing a youth ministry, or am I growing youth within a youth ministry?" The problem with this experiment in the earlier days of youth ministry is that those who wrote the theory of how it should be done were not fully objective. Consumer Reports brings credibility by not selling what they advocate. Youth Specialties and Group, both operating within the early years of the experiment, provided solutions to youth ministries, and, like any of us publishers, they bragged about their products as the cure to the problem. A true experiment documents the failures of certain interventions until the numbers bear out the success of the correct intervention. Who could have been objective during this time? Seminary professors, youth pastors not promoting a book, or someone else? It can be problematic when the publishing world releases books about various ministry solutions with short-success track records. Advocating unproven theories and approaches with only short-term successes may produce unintended consequences.

Youth ministry has focused on the committed teenagers and how their faith can grow. Efforts to nurture growth tend to focus on performance goals like looks, conversation, behaviors, and attitudes. Chap follows this up with a long list of popular writings about actionable ways to grow a teen's faith, such as praying regularly, reading the Bible daily, investing in social issues, and using talents in ministry. Chap insightfully points out how the list fails to get to some heart-related issues. He suggests the need for experiencing the fullness of God without filling in the blanks, but, while an exhaustive list is not possible, he stopped short of naming more practices, such as apologetics, discipleship, and processing all decisions within a biblical worldview.

Chap, I looked for you to provide a clear definition for the word "discipleship." You discussed how others use it and provided a critique. I would like to have seen you present at least a paragraph describing a biblically healthy, long-term discipleship apart from the functional terms of adoption. You likewise introduce a new term, "post-Christian," and leave the reader hanging as to the intended usage of this word. Do you intend a left-leaning Christian worldview? You do, however, leave nothing to chance for the reader to grasp the words "community," "fellowship," "relationships," "collaboration," "assembly," *ekklēsia*, "church," and "family," which allows for the adoption of youth into this larger body—Christ's body. You emphasize a word powerfully with only italics, one that I hope readers do not overlook—you say, "The second aspect of living together as the body of Christ is that we are thereby intrinsically connected one to another, without regard to gifts, function, power, status, or *age*."

Chap's goal for adoption provides a solution for disenfranchised young adults who left high school and allowed life to swallow up their time without including a relationship with God. To be clear, the adoption approach is a viable solution along with other possibilities, some found in this book and others being accomplished by youth ministries today. The case study Chap used to launch the chapter shows the young adults placing emphasis on careers, being distracted by other things, or being loosely attached to the church community. Each of these separate issues points back to a flawed value system or lack of a Christian worldview.

The subsection about the family as a biblical metaphor should be required reading prior to the ordination of any minister. It is in this section, Chap, that you show the framework God established in both the Old and New Testaments, whereby he desired the family to be the platform for youth and children to love God and grow in their faith. Our chapters complement each other in ways that could easily be woven together for practical teaching and application. The idea of family or adoption is not an experiment but a principle commanded by God to perpetuate a faith legacy.

Close to the end of your section, Chap, you make this statement: "It wasn't that the young left the church; the church left the young." The alienation induced by the church coexisted with the desire to be separate from what the adults were doing. It could be argued that this estrangement occurred because adults did not wish to worship with their sons and daughters' style of worship. A little relinquishing of one's comfort could embrace the spiritual growth of one's child. I would rather be slightly uncomfortable with my child dedicated and following Christ than comfortable in a staunch position that infers that if they can't worship and read the Bible the way I do, they should go to hell. While no parent would ever say that out loud, I have witnessed parents who through their traditionalism and performance mentality live out that very position. The truth is, the adults willingly let the youth find their own place just far enough away from the adult congregation to not lose control. I would submit that this dysfunctional relationship enables a mutual separation of the youth and adults.

The adoption model works well as long as the worldview of the parent and the teen has been shaped toward this idea. A gap that catches many of our teenagers is the move to college. Teens, if they look for a church, will often look for one like the one back home. Even if the home church of the teen perfectly practices adoption, what happens when that young person moves away or goes off to college? They lose this community. The teen will have to find a new church that practices the adoption process and be able to feel the assimilation potential. However, if the teen has a D6 parent, the parent is always there to coach or consult with him or her regardless of geographical location or church orientation.

If the church functions as a family of families, the goal should be to strengthen the families, not just the youth. Chap, you rightly acknowledge this chapter could address the plight of anyone who feels disconnected from the body—young adults, senior adults, adults, and others. If you wrote a completely new book with each chapter focused on a separate age and asked each to practice adoption, the challenge of a community goal may be in continually focusing on addressing the needs of the siloed age groupings rather than the unit of the family as a whole. The family needs to function as a community if the church should function as a community. Why then should we teach independent ministry focus when familial interdependence is required?

Adoption, by its very nature, accepts a child exactly where he or she is and lovingly brings him or her into the family until, over time, the child not only bears the name but embodies the identity of the family. God the Father adopted us with all of our messiness. He patiently develops us and continues the process with love, righteousness, and lots of grace. Then God hears our voice, uses our gifts, and affirms our standing not because he needs us but because he loves us. What a model for us to use in his family of families.

## ✚ Chap Clark's Response

Before I respond to your helpful and honest comments to my article on adoption ministry as the theological grounding for any programmatic ministry, I want to first express my sincere gratitude. In general, this kind of process is always a bit frightening, for who seeks to invite public disagreement or critique? Yet each of you has been thoughtful and kind, even in those places and with those issues that you felt I could use some sharpening. These responses have been a gift.

I also want to thank each of you for the affirming and kind comments you made in your responses. It goes without saying that when a colleague makes mention in a positive way of something we have poured our hearts into, there is a deep sense of gratitude. I will specifically thank each of you for these comments personally, but for this final response I feel it is better to cut straight to the areas and issues where you either disagreed or offered me a nuance, caution, or question.

Greg mentioned that he and I have, over the years, had a more or less running clash of perspectives on certain aspects of youth ministry. One of the greatest joys of doing this project together was to have the chance, for all to see, to lay out where the Lord has led us in our vision and thinking side by side. We've also had a long-standing, albeit somewhat distant, deep respect and appreciation for one another. Both of these came out in our responses to each other. We still have deeply held convictions that are not completely in sync, as is evident, but we are, as we both suspected we would be if we gave ourselves the chance, very, very close in both history and outlook.

I so appreciate your reminder, Greg, that mission must be external and not internal. I am completely with you on this. But the route to get there, it seems to me, especially in a culture of abandonment and generational segmentation, needs to *begin* with an internal missional emphasis in order for us to be a healthy, unified vessel useful for the external mission of God. John 13–17 says very little about the external mission of the church but a great deal about our relationships with one another. If we fail to get our own internal "family" house in order, we have very little to offer the world as "sent ones" (John 20:21) who are called to be salt and light.

I am not sure that we actually disagree on your point regarding grace. I also understand the gospel to be firmly resting on God's mercy and grace, and therefore our response is simply to trust (*pisteuō*) in personified grace, Jesus Christ. This is the "work" God has for us (John 6:28–30; see also Gal. 5:1–6). Trust that is not expressed, or fleshed out, in a response of obedience, however, is not biblical faith. You cite Phil Yancey's *What's So Amazing about Grace?* (a book he wrote and freely talked through while we were in a small group together) to stress the central importance of grace, and I agree with both of you on this point. When you quote him saying, "We do not have to achieve but merely follow," he is saying what I attempted to say, that is, that our obedience is simply our "following" Jesus.

Last, your comment that mentors must be missional is a crucial element to the adoptive model. Without people who are both inwardly and externally missional, there is a theological disconnect and therefore brokenness in our life together. I agree. For the adoption view to have any impact not only in the lives of our kids but in us as well, people must be committed to how God has called us to live, both together and in our mission in the world that God loves.

Brian, to your thoughts, my initial response was simply "Wow!" Your list of eight areas of concern or disagreement was thorough, well stated, and fairly comprehensive (and I had no idea in seven thousand words I could elicit this much depth of response and conversation!). But in response to you, I will try and go point by point in bite-sized chunks, listing your point number alongside my response, trusting that this will not be our last shot at dialogue.

"Where is God?" (1) Great question, related as well to your question regarding the "greatest command" (3). Without the ability to really go after this here,

I fall to Jesus and Paul. Jesus does affirm that to "love God" is "the first and greatest commandment" (Matt. 22:37–38). He then says, as you well know, that "the second is like it," and "all the Law and the Prophets hang on these two commandments" (22:39–40). I can see how my view can look "people centered" (7) on the surface, and I wish I had somehow addressed this concern more up front. Yet, in addition to Jesus's equating how we treat others as "being like" how we love God, throughout Paul's letters he consistently calls Christ-followers to love one another as they live out their love for God. In Philippians 2, for example, he admonishes his flock to be "like-minded, having the same love, being one in spirit and of one mind" (v. 2). This may sound "people centered," but the Scriptures are consistent in the message that love for God is expressed in how authentically we love one another (1 John 4:20) and also the world ("Who is my neighbor?" Luke 10:29). By the way, you also made a good catch when you challenged my statement "*the* primary means by which God" (2). Before you wrote your response, I had already changed it to "*a* primary means by which God." Well done.

As you see in my chapter, I have no problem with the goal of youth ministry being to nurture the faith of the young (4). Where I do think I would like more conversation is how we do that with a population that is, by definition, in transition, in need of relational and emotional nurture, and who also does not readily receive adult leadership and teaching without first seeing how trustworthy that adult is. Discipleship is a lifelong process, and to take development seriously we must *first* embrace, encourage, listen to, and empower our young within appropriate developmental realities *before* we expect them to meaningfully respond to the "means of grace" in an adult-like way. Similarly, as to your comment regarding sin (5)—"our sin has led to our feeling lonely and isolated"—I agree. Yet the *consequence* of our sin, regardless, is this experience. That was my point. Yes, regardless of the theological tradition, human sin has consequences, and one of them is being, and therefore feeling, isolated.

Last, you wonder how we can actually pull the adoption model off (6) as you go back to Deuteronomy 6, affirming that "the primary responsibility" for discipleship of children is their parents (8; see my comments for Ron's D6 view on this). Ron, you also make this a staple argument (and, as an aside, I didn't quite "overlook" Titus 2; I simply chose not to use it, for lots of reasons I won't go into here). As much as I believe that parents who are sincerely walking with Christ are an important and often an effective discipling force and presence—and currently, from all indications, by far the most potent (see my and Kara Powell's comments on this in *Sticky Faith*)—I believe that particular text (Deut. 6), in light of the entire Scripture, is not meant to say that parents are "primary." Even the best parents fail, are inconsistent, and are wholly insecure when it comes to simply parenting, much less discipling, their kids today. The best parents need the church as *their* family to grow as followers of Christ, and *so do their kids!* As a father of three, I am so grateful for those Christian friends who poured into our kids' lives in partnership with us.

Fred, given your history and current work with college students, you have a unique take on how difficult the road from high school to adulthood is for so many. That you see the adoption model of ministry as both theological as well as sociological brings an added dimension to the need for the church to reinvest in our young in intimate familial relationships. With all the various expressions of family in today's society, and with even the best of these needing all the help they can get, your conviction regarding our role in the community of faith to be the refuge for all members is essential.

I agree with you, as well, that the move from trust to obedience and submission is difficult for all of us, especially if our relationships are not authentic and safe. For decades youth ministry has been based on a simple foundation: an adult committed to coming alongside a young person so that he or she has the opportunity to encounter and follow the living God in the person of the risen Jesus Christ. As Youth Specialties' Mike Yaconelli used to relentlessly hammer into us all, "Youth ministry is about Jesus and kids. That's it. That's all it is." But this approach has also been allowed to be reduced to one adult and one kid, whether a small group leader, a mentor, or a youth pastor who cares for "each one." Yes, at its most basic level, I believe youth ministry is as simple as Jesus and our young. But that does not excuse subjugating our young to thinking that their faith is up to them, that in the final analysis God expects them to go it alone, even with a mentor to help along the way. "This is my command: Love one another." Youth ministry is inviting our young into the calling, life, and work of the kingdom as members of the family of God. That's the essence and point of the adoption model of ministry.

# Fernando Arzola

# The Ecclesial View
# of Youth Ministry

et's be honest. Protestant youth ministry has all but deleted ecclesiology from its theological radar. It's not so much that ecclesiology has become unimportant; rather, it is nonexistent in contemporary youth ministry thought. Youth ministries focus primarily on discipleship and worship. Of course these are central aspects, but they are not the sole ones. And they did not appear out of thin air. Rather, they flow out of two thousand years of ecclesiological evolution, starting with the churches the apostles left behind. Furthermore, it is also important to teach Christian teens that ecclesiology preceded the biblical canon for over three hundred years. As long as youth ministries do not reclaim a historically orthodox understanding of ecclesiology, it will perpetuate the myopic and thin contemporary North American expressions of pop-worship and neo-discipleship based on mega-ministry personalities, cultural trends, and repackaged curriculums decided by a handful of publishers.

## Ecclesiological Resurgence

In recent years, there has been an increase in the scholarly examination of ecclesiology.[1] So why hasn't this occurred in youth ministry?[2] Not only do youth ministry programs and churches, and therefore youth ministry leaders and practitioners, tend to separate themselves from each other, but by default they often seem to facilitate a de facto congregational polity within a congregational polity. Nevertheless, in some circles at least, there has been a resurgence of interest in the writings of the church fathers and in reappropriating Christian orthodoxy.[3] The purpose of this chapter is to examine selected issues of ecclesiology, specifically the nature and authority of the church, and suggest practices that may help reappropriate a historically orthodox ecclesiology within a youth ministry context.

## Historically Orthodox Perspectives

The historically orthodox perspectives are gleaned from the works of Donald G. Bloesch, Thomas C. Oden, and Robert E. Webber. Bloesch reflects the Reformed tradition; Oden, the Methodist tradition; and Webber, the Anglican tradition.

Bloesch argues for the need to move toward a *catholic* evangelicalism.[4] This requires a threefold integration: (1) the need to reappraise biblical authority, (2) the need to recover evangelical distinctives, and (3) the need to recover catholic substance.[5] What is catholic substance? Let us explore what this means for us.

Oden is considered the founder of "paleo-orthodoxy," a theological viewpoint that calls on Christians to rely on the wisdom of the traditions of the historic church, especially the early church.[6]

Webber is considered the founder of the Ancient-Future movement, a theological viewpoint committed to connecting ancient Christian faith, worship, and spirituality with the postmodern and post-Christian world. Webber clarifies his position as follows.

> I have structured *Ancient-Future Faith* around the phenomenon of the origin of the Christian faith. I have not started . . . with the Scriptures. Rather, I begin with the work of Jesus Christ, the primordial event of the living, dying, rising, and coming again. . . .
>
> Not starting with the Bible does not represent a lower view of Scripture. . . . Instead, the Christocentric method acknowledges the place of the Scriptures in the early Christian tradition. In the early centuries Scripture was not separated from the church or from the development of classical Christian thought, but was inextricably linked with the whole phenomenon of the rise of Christianity. In modern times the act of lifting the Bible out of its phenomenological context of the work of the Holy Spirit in the church has resulted in making the Bible the object of rational criticism. In post-modern Christianity the authority of the Bible will be restored, not by more rational arguments, but by returning it to its rightful place in the development of the entire spectrum of Christian thought in the first six centuries of the church and by learning to read it canonically once again.[7]

The early Fathers can bring us back to what is common and help us get behind our various traditions, not in the sense that we deny our own tradition, but that we give priority to the common teaching of the church.[8]

## Reclaiming the Incarnational View of the Church

According to Webber, there are five stages or paradigms of the church throughout history. In the classical period, the ancient stage, the church was understood as the visible continuation of the presence of Christ in the world.[9] It was viewed as the sacrament of Christ. That is, the real presence of Christ is found in the church. "This incarnational view of the Church saw Jesus present in the assembled people, in the ministry of the bishop, presbyter, and deacon, in the word and song and at the Table. In this way, Christ continues to minister to his church and to dwell among his people."[10]

During the classic period, the threefold order of ministry (bishop, presbyter, and deacon) was developed. Their primary responsibility was to pass down the orthodox teachings of the faith, to shepherd the flock, and to appoint others to be faithful ministers in the church. By the end of the sixth century, as the church expanded, the bishop took over increasing responsibilities, and the unity of the church was based on the unity of the bishops. "Truth, it was argued, originated in the church with the apostles and was handed down in Scripture, summarized by the creeds and guarded and interpreted by the church."[11]

Roman Catholicism began to develop institutionally around the thirteenth century, the medieval stage. This is most dramatically seen in the role of the pope and the hierarchical/ecclesial concept of authority. The church was no longer a community of equals. The source of power was rooted in the clergy. Decisions filtered down to the laity, who passively obeyed. Canon law defined all of the church's actions, laws, and penalties. And during the last two centuries of the medieval era, the institutional church became morally and politically corrupt.[12]

The Reformation stage was a response to the corruptions in the church. Protestants turned away from the institutional church toward the gospel. As stated above, the Reformers identified the marks of the "true" church as a gathering of Christians where the Word of God is rightly preached and the sacraments rightly administered. During this stage, the threefold order of ministry was replaced by the presbyterian and congregational models of church government. The true church was found in the "invisible church," which existed in the mind of God. Luther called this "a spiritual, inner christendom."[13]

This led to a shift from the "visible" church to the "invisible" church, which dominated modern Protestant thought.[14] Consequently, this led to the rise of various denominations and independent church movements, and the emergence of the parachurch movement. During this modern stage, the church was viewed by Protestants as not having a divine presence but a divine *calling* to proclaim the gospel message. Coupled with the rise of individualism flowing from the Enlightenment, the emphasis was on the purity and work of the local church, not the corporate body.[15]

In today's postmodern stage, there seems to be a resurgence of interest in the visible church from the ancient times. With the increase of globalization, the universal interconnectedness of the internet, and the decline of denominational distinctions, the local church increasingly is connected to the global church.[16]

## Ecclesiological Problems Inherited from the Enlightenment

Two specific problems have evolved that have significantly, and negatively, impacted the Protestant church in general, and youth ministry in particular, in its understanding of ecclesiology. Both problems were inherited from the Enlightenment.

The first problem is the emphasis on *pragmatism*, which has resulted in an a-theological understanding of the church.[17] Many churches have developed such a strong pragmatic perspective that the understanding of the church as the body of Christ has been replaced with the model of an effective corporation. And many church and youth ministries have adopted business models as their ecclesiological template. The pastor/youth minister is viewed as a chief executive officer, and the laity functions under this managerial leadership.[18] The church has also been co-opted as a political power base. The goal of some of these Christian groups is to legislate morality.

This pragmatic approach in the church has resulted in what is called "leadership development," a model that is popular in Christian colleges and seminaries. Much of the curricula, books, and content are based on secular leadership models baptized and re-presented after a biblical cleansing. They may be connected with personalities and perspectives from the Scriptures, but they seldom examine the lives of Christian men and women throughout the ages.

The second problem is the emphasis on *individualism*, which has led to an ahistorical view of the church.[19] While certain denominations have an appreciation of church history, generally speaking, many leaders are either uninformed about church history prior to the Reformation or they intentionally reject church history prior to the Reformation. This radical individualism often leads church movements or fellowships to "start over again" instead of learning about church history. Webber wonders whether "Enlightenment rationalism has robbed the church of its mystical self concept, so that it is now regarded as little more than a human organization made up of individuals."[20] Is this not the reality of many youth ministries, which tend to focus on contemporary matters rather than understanding their place within the communion of saints?

## Recovering the Four Creedal Characteristics of the Church[21]

### The Church Is One

Christ founded only one church, and he intended for that church to be one. In John 17:20–21, Jesus implores the Father to protect the unity of the church when he prays, "I ask not only on behalf of these, but also on behalf of those who will believe in me through their word, that they may all be one. As you, Father, are in me and I am in you, may they also be in us, so that the world may believe that you have sent me" (NRSV). In Ephesians 4:1–6, Paul later adds,

> I therefore, the prisoner in the Lord, beg you to lead a life worthy of the calling to which you have been called, with all humility and gentleness, with patience, bearing with one another in love, making every effort to maintain the unity of the Spirit in the bond of peace. There is one body and one Spirit, just as you were called to the one hope of your calling, one Lord, one faith, one baptism, one God and Father of all, who is above all and through all and in all. (NRSV)

The early church understood this to mean the visible unity of the church. Any break with the church was taken as a serious breach against Christ's body.[22] The emphasis on the invisible church is often attributed to the historical and seemingly perpetual schismatic nature of Protestantism; that is, what is most important is that the local body of believers faithfully proclaim the Word of God and rightfully administer the sacraments. Connection to the broader church is secondary at best.

The historically orthodox perspective believes that one of the most important features toward reappropriating historic orthodoxy is to restore the four creedal characteristics of the church, encouraging churches to recover the ancient church's concern for the visible church as a constitutive balance to the invisible and spiritual emphasis of the church. "The unity of the church is to be found not in its rites or creeds but in its obedience to Jesus Christ, its one head and Lord."[23]

There will be struggles for the visible church, but the body can find strength and solace in the invisible graces that it enjoys. Oden writes,

> The same single body that struggles against the principalities and powers and that expects even more severe difficulties in the future, is at the same time already victorious in virtue of its being presently united with its head in the heavenly city, anticipating that completed joy in the Lord wherein all the faithful shall praise God together at the end of days.[24]

Historically orthodox Christians recognize that the church has unfolded in many cultures and, therefore, do not necessarily believe there is a single expression of the true church. Oden explains,

> The idolatrous over-evaluation of unity results in uniformity, a tyrannizing excess of superficially imposed unity. The under-evaluation or neglect of unity is divisiveness and egocentricity, imagining that one's own individualistic opinion is more important or more closely ordained of God than the received consensual tradition. The Spirit sustains the unity of the church by enjoying and enabling centered variety, not uniformity, and by seeking and praying for reconciliation whenever centrifugal forces become intense.[25]

The characteristic of unity is also a way toward finding a common ground with the various Christian families. "This perspective will allow us to see Catholic, Orthodox, and Protestant churches as various forms of the one true church—all based on apostolic teaching and authority, finding common ground in the faith expressed by classical Christianity."[26]

### The Church Is Holy

Holiness is unquestionably an important theological concept. However, for many, it is viewed primarily as a personal characteristic, not as an aspect for the whole church. In 1 Peter 1:13–16, the church, not individuals, are challenged to be holy as Christ is holy.

> Therefore prepare your minds for action; discipline yourselves; set all your hope on the grace that Jesus Christ will bring you when he is revealed. Like obedient children, do not be conformed to the desires that you formerly had in ignorance. Instead, as he who called you is holy, be holy yourselves in all your conduct; for it is written, "You shall be holy, for I am holy." (NRSV)

The church is holy because Christ is holy. While the church is a gathering of redeemed sinners, "Nevertheless, Christ through the Holy Spirit summons the church to holiness."[27] Oden adds to this paradox when he writes,

> As the body of Christ, the Church is necessarily holy, yet its holiness is enmeshed in continuing human imperfection and finitude until the end of history. The church is holy while not ceasing to be subject to the infirmities of the flesh that accompany all historical existence . . . the holiness of the church is best expressed in the imperfect or unfinished tense—that God is now sanctifying the church, now calling forth a *communio sanctorum*.[28]

While youth ministries should certainly continue encouraging individuals to live a life of holiness, they should also view the larger church as a holy body belonging to and made holy by Jesus Christ. Jesus called his disciples out of the world, understanding that they will remain in the world, and asked the Father to protect them from the evil one (John 17:6–18). Because they remain in the world, the church will always be close to sin and sinners. "The distinctive function of the church is to bring sinners to the way of holiness. This requires that the church should love at close quarters the sinners it is called to save, and to draw near precisely to the sinners it is called to redeem and sanctify."[29] "The church is holy because it is marked off from the world by the interior illumination and cleansing work of the Holy Spirit. Its holiness is anchored in its Lord, but it is reflected, sometimes only dimly, in the members of his mystical body."[30]

### The Church Is Catholic

For Protestants to self-identify as "catholic" does not come easily, and neither is it even comfortably discussed. Yet, because of the rich meaning and heritage of the term, "catholic" should be reclaimed by the entire church. Webber quotes Ignatius, who writes, "Wherever Jesus Christ is, there is the catholic church."[31] Following this logic, therefore, "the Church is catholic that has all the truth—Jesus Christ."[32] Oden agrees when he explains, "Wherever there is consent to apostolic teaching, there the whole church is becoming embodied."[33]

The term "catholic" also means "universal," again, underscoring the nature of the larger church. It is not bound to a particular place or time. Historically orthodox Christians call for an outward, global-looking congregation. "The church is rightly called catholic insofar as it does not cease to be universal as it becomes intensely local."[34]

Integrative use of both of these concepts helps to understand the call of the larger church toward doctrinal orthodoxy, that is, the universal church as a body that is faithfully rooted in the truth of Jesus Christ. "The church is universal not only in the sense that it is worldwide, but also in the sense that it is grounded in the universality of the atonement. The church is identical in that it always remains true to itself in history; the church is always to remain orthodox."[35]

Bloesch agrees, "When we confess the apostolicity of the church we acknowledge that the true church is founded on the apostles. The faith of the church must stand in continuity with their enduring witness."[36]

### The Church Is Apostolic

The church is not a philosophy-of-life group but a living body shaped by the apostolic teaching.[37] To understand the church as apostolic is to acknowledge its ancient roots. "Apostolicity indicates that the church is linked to and built on the past."[38]

How then should we understand apostolicity? I agree with Bloesch, who writes, "The real apostolic succession consists in a reaffirmation of the teaching and doctrine of the apostles in the history of the catholic church."[39] According to Oden, the primary task of apostolic succession is to remember and pass on the original teaching.

> The task of the apostolic successor is not to improve upon the message or embellish it or add to it one's own spin or personal tilt or idiosyncratic twist, but rather simply to remember and attest it accurately, credibly, intelligibly, contextually. To assist in correct remembering, the Holy Spirit has enabled the apostolic testimony to be written down in a canonically received body of writings consensually received as normative apostolic teaching.[40]

Here, therefore, we differentiate between apostolicity and the historical, linear episcopate. While many Christians may embrace the apostolic succession as the passing down of the orthodox teachings of the apostles, the linear, historical succession of the episcopacy is a concept that is considered secondary. Recovery of the characteristics of the church as one, holy, catholic, and apostolic may help many churches and youth ministries to look outside themselves, both individually and locally, and toward the larger, universal, and historical church.

## Reappropriating Historically Orthodox Youth Ministry Practices

### Practice 1: Reappropriating the Four Characteristics of the Church

As seen above, many Protestant traditions understand the marks of the church as the right preaching of the gospel and the right administration of the sacraments. This twofold concept was established by Martin Luther and John Calvin in response to their understanding of the Catholic Church's works-based sacramental economy. They argued that the works-oriented teachings on justification and the sacraments were both contrary to the proper understanding of the gospel and the sacraments.

For Protestants, they serve as contemporary pillars firmly rooting the church against the wave of pluralistic teachings from many mainline and liberal churches. Wayne Grudem elaborates on these two marks as expression of the true church as follows.

> Certainly if the Word of God is not being preached, but simply false doctrines or doctrines of men, then there is no true church. . . . When the preaching of a church conceals the gospel message of salvation by faith alone from its members, so that the gospel message is not clearly proclaimed, and has not been proclaimed for some time, the group meeting is not a church. . . . The right administration of the sacraments was probably stated in opposition to the Roman Catholic view that saving grace came through the sacraments and thereby the sacraments were made works by which we earned merit for salvation.[41]

However, the four creedal characteristics of the church, namely, one, holy, catholic, and apostolic, root the congregation beyond the Reformation to the early church. The two marks of the church stated above seem to be primarily concerned with issues of form; that is, right preaching and right sacramental administration, whereas the four characteristics of the church are more all-encompassing of the nature of the church.

"The church as one" encompasses Christ's founding of the church, the paradox of the visible/temporal and invisible/divine nature of the church, historical schisms, the body of Christ, transcultural diversity within the unity of the church, and Christian unity.

"The church as holy" encompasses corporate holiness in addition to individual holiness, the holiness of the church based on Christ's holiness, the struggles of the holy church vis-à-vis an unholy world, the closeness of the church with sin, the church as a community of redeemed sinners, and the nature of salvation.

"The church as catholic" encompasses the proclamation of gospel truth, teaching doctrinal orthodoxy, celebration of sacraments, the relationship between the universal church and the local church, global interconnectedness, transcending place and time, and the nature of the true church.

"The church as apostolic" encompasses acknowledging the ancient roots of the church, the relationship between the contemporary church and the early church, fidelity to apostolic teaching, honoring the history of the church, honoring the communion of saints, encouragement of a missional ethos, and the passing down of the rule of faith.

### Practice 2: Reappropriating an Incarnational/Visible Understanding of the Body of Christ

Webber provides a helpful five-stage/paradigmatic survey of church history. He begins with the ancient church, which emphasized the incarnational/visible understanding of the body of Christ. That is, the church was viewed as the sacrament of Christ; the real presence of Christ is found in the church. "This incarnational/visible concept of the church saw Jesus present in the assembled people, in the ministry of the bishop, presbyter, and deacon, in the Word and song and at the Table. In this way, Christ continues to minister to his church and to dwell among his people."[42]

The incarnational/visible understanding of the church also connects the youth ministry with the larger church, the body of Christ. While youth ministries may rightfully refer to themselves as the body of Christ, they can only be understood as a part of the greater body of Christ. A tendency for youth ministries is to isolate themselves from the larger church as if to imply they are "a" body of Christ unto themselves as opposed to being a part of "the" body of Christ. The Catholic Church teaches, "In Christian usage, the word 'church' designates the liturgical assembly, but also the local community or the whole community of believers. These three meanings are inseparable. The church is the people that God gathers in the whole world."[43] Individual congregations should never be regarded as a part or a component of the whole church. "The church is not a sum or composite of the individual local groups. Instead, the whole is found in each place."[44]

This nuance is significant. Lothar Coenen affirms Millard Erickson's insight about Paul's writing "to the church of God in Corinth" in 1 Corinthians 1:2, when he comments on this *ekklēsia* reference: "It is one throughout the whole world and yet it is at the same time fully present in every individual assembly."[45] The universal church is composed of all believers on earth and transcends geographical boundaries.

### Practice 3: Developing a More Formal Teaching of Ecclesiology

Traditional youth ministry tends to focus on the spiritual concerns of individuals. Discipleship is primarily Bible study and prayer. The theology and content of worship often emphasize a group of individuals rather than the gathering of the community. The popular usage of contemporary Christian music, for example, often reinforces the "personal relationship" between the believer and Christ but rarely addresses the communal aspect of the faith. Preaching generally addresses how to apply biblical principles into one's individual life. Happily, there has been a growing resurgence in fellowship (*koinōnia*) and service (*diakonia*). Yet, again, these are sometimes understood individualistically, as things that can help a person grow spiritually.

While helping teens to grow in spiritual maturity is a significant responsibility of the youth ministry, I suggest that a more formal teaching of ecclesiology is in order. A more formal teaching on "the church" will help youth ministries with both informational and formational issues. From the *informational* perspective, members of the church will become familiar with the early church; the development of church doctrine; the evolution of liturgy, worship, and the sacraments; the positive and negative contributions of the Reformation; the positive and negative contributions of the Counter-Reformation; the interaction and tension between the church and the world; the ecumenical movement; and the contemporary state of the church. Review of these issues will both create a more informed congregation and raise the corporate awareness of its place within the larger historical church.

From a *formational* perspective, youth members will be embedded within the body of Christ, root their faith back to the ancient church, participate in communion with the saints (both past and present), grow from the writings of Christian classics, recognize the relationship between personal holiness and corporate holiness found in Christ, and reestablish and reconnect the importance of their personal spiritual formation within the context of the local church and larger catholic church. Review of these issues, together with the above topics, will help counter the individualistic nature of Christian spirituality, and will nurture a faith grounded in the one, holy, catholic, and apostolic church.

The purpose of this chapter was to examine selected issues of ecclesiology, specifically the nature and authority of the church, and suggest practices that may help reappropriate a historic, orthodox ecclesiology within a youth ministry context.

# Responses to the Ecclesial View

+ **Greg Stier**

While I believe that reconnecting Christian teenagers to the four characteristic of the church as "one, holy, catholic, and apostolic" is a worthy goal, it is only part of the solution.

Yes, teenagers need to know they are part of a two-thousand-year-old mighty river of reformers and transformers. Yes, they need to understand and embrace the founding creeds and elemental orthodoxy based in the Bible and forged over countless centuries. Teenagers who have a connection to the church (both here and now, as well as there and then) rise up from the myopic "Jesus is my Santa Claus" philosophy of Americanized, individualistic Christianity that Fernando rightfully disparages.

If these worthy subjects are what drive a particular youth ministry program, the four attending teenagers will have a great time. Seriously, if the subject of ancient creeds and pre-Reformation ecclesiology dominates the discussion, then it will no longer be a discussion, but a monologue in a mostly empty youth room.

What made the true ancient church (the one in the book of Acts) exciting was not their commitment to developing, dissecting, and distributing creeds but their commitment to advance the gospel of Jesus Christ among their own members and also outwardly into their communities. Prayer fueled it, communion reemphasized it, teaching solidified it, fellowship rekindled it, and creed clarified and protected it.

The early believers had a connection with their history. After all, the New Testament is built on the Old Testament! But their connection to the past served to advance the gospel and deepen discipleship.

When this connection to the past becomes the point, then it misses the point. When one becomes overly obsessed with creeds and confessions rather than Christ and his cause, then what was meant to bring stability and depth can become an idol that distracts us from our Savior.

I couldn't agree more that we should "rely on the wisdom of the traditions of the historic church, especially of the early church"! Jesus's call to his followers to "Come, follow me . . . and I will send you out to fish for people" (Matt. 4:19) and Luke's recounting of the spiritual wildfire that spread through the book of Acts serve as our primers.

Nothing comes through clearer in the book of Acts than the Spirit-controlled, Gospel Advancing, life-transforming, unstoppable, missional impact of the early church. Was the early church perfect in holiness, unity, and theological purity? Certainly not—Paul's epistles testify to several cases of rampant sin on the loose or theological confusion in the ranks of several local church bodies. These early heresies forced the apostles to clarify their theology and start building their creeds. But their creeds were developed in the midst of launching and deepening a mission movement (Acts 15:1–33), not for the sake of just building a creed.

Jesus's missional call to advance the gospel echoes through the centuries and unites our students with Christians through the millennia who sacrificed all for the sake of Christ. Yes, we must connect them with a greater sense of the holy, catholic church, but we must engage them with Christ and his cause as we do!

## ✚ Brian Cosby

Fernando, as one who loves the significance of the local and universal church as well as its history, I really appreciated your insights and perspective. It was a breath of fresh air to read something that was appreciative of Christian heritage. For the sake of organizing my response to your position, I'd like to offer what I see as some very positive aspects of your chapter and then some areas of disagreement and constructive criticism.

### Positives of the Ecclesial View

I really appreciated your research and source provision. It helped me glean a variety of perspectives on the doctrine of the church as well as its impact on a youth ministry context.

Thank you for calling out the problem of pragmatism inherited from the Enlightenment. The question shouldn't be, as you comment, "What's most effective?" Youth ministries shouldn't take part in the ministry success game. This leads to an unhealthy focus on the three "B's": buildings, bodies, and budgets. This also leads youth pastors into one of two dead ends: pride (look how many I saved/got to come to youth group!) or despair (nobody came to my meeting . . . and nobody will come next week either). We should strive for ministry faithfulness rather than success. Besides, it's God who provides the growth anyway (1 Cor. 3:7)!

Thank you too for pointing out the problem of modern individualism that plagues the American church today. As you note, this has led to practically a complete lack of awareness of and appreciation for those who have gone before us. The great cloud of witnesses and the "hall of faith" that the writer of Hebrews presents should at least make us consider the importance of the communion of saints down through the ages and our place in that line. Our extreme individualism is, as Timothy George has called it, an *imperialism of the present*—where our narcissism and hubris is on open display. Certainly this cannot fit within a biblical model of youth ministry.

I also agree that youth ministers need to teach the history of the church rather than the seven keys to your best life now or how to claim health, wealth, and prosperity. In my book *God's Story: A Student's Guide to Church History* (Christian Focus, 2014), I outline this precise need to recover a historical perspective on the Christian church—yes, even from the prophets and apostles of old!

Thank you for pointing out the importance of the reality of the *visible* church. When we look through the pages of the New Testament, we see that there is order, structure, church discipline, church officers, and so on. There are church rolls and those who belong to the church at such and such place. This visible church is extended in thousands of bodies throughout the world as the visible church universal. Thank you for calling us to the ancient roots of the church, built on the foundation of the apostles and prophets, who—under the inspiration of the Holy Spirit—presented a faith that was once and for all delivered to the saints (Jude 3).

Finally, I love your remarks about the holiness of the church as an identity marker, though not to the exclusion of individual moral holiness. We tend to focus all of our attention on the latter, without much thought to the former. But both are needed and important, so thank you.

### My Concerns with the Ecclesial View

1. I would hold Donald Bloesch as "Reformed" somewhat loosely. He had a Reformed background and Reformed leanings, but to associate him with

Calvinism (as such) and orthodox Reformed theology *as a representative* of those traditions would be going a bit too far, even if he is often labeled with "neo-orthodoxy." The problem, historically speaking, lies in Bloesch's own definition of Reformed, which he borrowed from Karl Barth. Barth, for his part, would hardly fit modern evangelical Reformed orthodoxy.

2. In your discussion on the insights of the three theologians from whom you glean, I found myself not really sure what *your* view was. I understood your position as being somewhat of a blend of the three. Is that correct? Your chapter has little to do with youth ministry. Youth ministry is part of the one, holy, apostolic, and universal church, so maybe the reader should see youth ministry simply as part of the whole. The goal of youth ministry, therefore, is for us to see ourselves as part of that church. Is that right? Ultimately, I don't really see your position being a distinct youth ministry "model." I see it as something to *teach* the youth, but I'm not sure how foundational this is to a unique methodology.

3. You state that during the Reformation, "Protestants turned away from the institutional church and turned toward the gospel." This is not entirely accurate. Other than some who bought into what is called the Radical Reformation, most still held to some form of the church *as institution*. As an example, we see book 4 of Calvin's *Institutes* as almost entirely concerned with this issue. Yes, they decried the abuses of the institutional (Roman Catholic) church and the errors of its theology and "worldliness," but most still held to some institution of the church.

4. While I appreciate your call to unity in the church, we mustn't forget that we are to have unity *in the truth*. You sort of point this out—that we shouldn't opt for an "imposed" or forced unity—but in a culture where unity and tolerance are elevated, we need to be careful in distinguishing biblical unity from unity for unity's sake. From my perspective, Fernando, there are several large, self-professing "Christian" denominations and organizations that have abandoned the core tenets of the gospel, thereby rendering them antithetical to Christ (cf. Gal. 1:9). The biblical writers would not envision "unity" or catholicity with these kinds of groups.

5. You note (in citing Ignatius) that, "Wherever Jesus Christ is, there is the catholic church." But the Spirit of Christ is omnipresent—everywhere present. Indeed, this is one of God's attributes. I understand the push toward the church being "incarnational," but we need to better differentiate between divine omnipresence and the covenantal and salvific presence of Christ, which does reside in his holy and catholic church. Moreover, you reference his "real presence," which is often attributed to Christ's physical body and blood together with his spiritual presence (as seen in the doctrine of transubstantiation).

But Jesus ascended on high and is physically in heaven. He has gone away to prepare a place for us and will come again (John 14:3). His divine Spirit, however, is "with you always, to the very end of the age" (Matt. 28:20). In this way, he will never leave you nor forsake you (Heb. 13:5). Thus, while God is everywhere present, he is "with us" (as our *Immanuel*) in the church in a covenantal and salvific way.

6. I would disagree with your threefold office of bishop, presbytery/priest, and deacon. In particular, I take issue with the distinction between bishop and elder. I understand, of course, the Greek distinction between bishop (*episkopos*) and elder (*presbyteros*), but they refer to the same office. For example, in Acts 20:17, Paul "called the elders [*presbyterous*] of the church to come to him" (ESV). He then said to them, "Pay careful attention to yourselves and to all the flock, in which the Holy Spirit has made you overseers [*episkopous*]" (v. 28 ESV). In Titus 1:5, Paul instructs Titus to "appoint elders [*presbyterous*] in every town" (ESV) and gives him qualifications. Why? "For an overseer [*episkopon*], as God's steward, must be above reproach" (v. 7 ESV). Peter, too, equates the two. In 1 Peter 5:1–2, he exhorts "the elders [*presbyterous*]" to shepherd the flock by "exercising oversight [*episkopountes*]" (ESV). The two words simply describe two functions of the same office.

7. My final word of constructive criticism is that you offer very little biblical support for your approach to youth ministry. While the formal canon wasn't organized *as such* until the early fourth century, this doesn't negate the necessary centrality of the inspired text before then. Indeed, we have a faith that was once and for all delivered to the saints (Jude 3), recorded in the pages of Scripture. To persuasively demonstrate a unique and justifiable position on youth ministry, you need to present it from the Bible. Church history is wonderful—yes, even *before* the Reformation—but the church itself is built on the inspired testimony and instruction of the "apostles and prophets" (Eph. 2:20). While youth need to understand their heritage and history, God's Word is the means of grace by which they are saved and sanctified.

## ✚ Chap Clark

In reading Fernando Arzola's chapter on "reclaiming ecclesiology" I was reminded of how vital theological education and training is. For anyone venturing into a vocation of Christian service, regardless of the role, to build one's life and ministry on solid, historical, and biblically orthodox theology is crucial. In an age where many are disparaging the time, energy, and cost of a degree, to prepare for and lead ministry—*any* ministry—without a solid knowledge of our history, foundational orthodoxy, and how the Scriptures as theologically interpreted across time have shaped who and where we are today is dangerous at best. Fred, you remind us, relying on some of the most significant thinkers of the last several decades, that we do not "do" youth ministry in a historical or theological vacuum. We instead stand on the shoulders of the men and women who have gone before us. We in youth ministry, who visit schools and parks and Starbucks, who plan and implement programs and events that engage the hearts, minds, and souls of young people, and who carry the high responsibility of representing Jesus Christ and the kingdom to emerging generations, have much to learn about the theological foundations of our task and calling.

Thank you, Dr. Arzola, for bringing us back into a much-needed look at youth ministry through the lens of theology and history, and for showing how we in youth ministry can find ourselves within God's story since the beginning of all things.

As a practical theologian working in a seminary where we train, equip, counsel, and guide men and women for the manifold ministries of Christ and his church, I so deeply resonate with your focus on ecclesiology, or what you call "the nature and authority of the church." I wonder whether any readers, in trying to get a more careful handle on the definition of "ecclesiology," did what I did: went to their Mac "hourglass" in the upper-right-hand corner of the screen and typed in the word. When I did this, the first definition displayed on the Apple dictionary was this:

*ecclesiology* (noun) "the study of churches, esp. church building and decoration."

Perhaps this is an example of the problem. For years the "study of the church," as ecclesiology is typically labeled, has been extremely limited in its scope. It is no wonder that few seminary students, much less undergraduates, who study youth ministry are trained to see their calling firmly planted in the academic and liturgical bucket of "ecclesiology." I know of no systematic theology course or instructor, scholarly article, or academic theological textbook that even hints at youth ministry as a vital application (there are certainly some out there, but I have yet to run across them). Yet this is precisely what you have done in this chapter.

In your relatively mild but fair critique of the present state of youth ministry practice, you note that youth ministry programs "tend to separate themselves from the host congregation" and that "the understanding of the church as the body of Christ has been replaced with the model of an effective corporation. . . . Youth ministries have adopted business models as their ecclesiological template." I agree that when we build programs, hire staff, and spend money to approach a complex issue (like the perceived disinterest and distance of young people from the faith), we can easily slip into pragmatism driven by measurable outcomes (usually numbers) and superficial rubrics of success. Your critique of business models devoid of theological grounding (what you call "exegetical cleansing," a line I rather appreciate) is also worthy of consideration. I, for one, greatly appreciate secular research that *informs* our exegetical orthodoxy and interpretive decisions, yet I also agree that when we hand the entire enterprise of mission—in this case, youth ministry—to the philosophical and pragmatic trappings of the world, we are in danger of using the Bible to justify our convictions, structures, and strategies.

One of the most poignant points you make, which obviously resonates with my view as expressed in the adoptive model of ministry, is the undue emphasis on individualism not only in youth ministry but in the entire church. What I especially appreciate here is that your critique focuses on the tendency to ignore, or worse, rewrite history in order to maintain the American cultural mandate of personal independence. Like N. T. Wright,[1] the way you take on the tendency of some to operate as if the Reformation trumps the Scriptures provides the backdrop for your argument for youth ministry to reengage the nature of the biblical church instead of a "human organization": "[Evangelicals] are either uninformed about church history prior to the Reformation or they intentionally reject church history prior to the Reformation. The radical individualism [of evangelicalism] often leads church movements or fellowships to 'start over again' instead of learning about church history."

Last, your use of and commitment to Robert Webber's "four characteristics of the church," which we get from the ancient creeds of the church, lays a helpful foundation for youth ministry. Your argument, using Webber's four categories, invites us to refocus our work and missional structure and strategy on what God had in mind as revealed in Scripture for what it means to live and serve together as his "mystically" connected people. These four characteristics—unity, holiness, catholicity, and apostolicity—may not be common language or even thinking for most youth ministry people, but their theological power cannot be dismissed.

### Where I Would Like to See This Model Take Us

All that said—without reservation, and with full support for the basic concepts you detail—I wonder first *how* a frontline youth ministry leader, lay or ordained, paid or volunteer, might possibly implement what it is you are asking for. In other words, my greatest critique of this model is not in the

conceptual, theological, or historical framework you've laid out but in the
"What do I do with this?"

My thoughts are offered in the following three musings, and they are related to the four characteristics and suggestions for changes in youth ministry.
Ultimately, I attempt to wrestle with how these characteristics actually play
out in the practice of youth ministry.

### Unity: What Does It Mean in Youth Ministry?

My first big question relates to how you, using Oden, Bloesch, and Webber, make a great *theoretical* point that one of the most serious fallouts of
the Reformation is the "perpetual schismatic nature" of the contemporary
Protestant church (to leave aside for this response the wildly interesting "unity"
of the various subcommunities in the Roman Catholic world). Your diagnosis
of our almost-flippant disregard for the "visible" church has merit, but your
prescription for addressing this by "seeking unity" seems to be, at best, naively
asserting what a weak nanny might try with unruly children: "Just get along!"
Especially as the church wrestles with serious issues like scriptural authority,
denominational disintegration, and generationally focused churches growing by gathering the young from other, more established churches, to ask the
people on the lowest rung of the institutional ladder (the youth worker) to
"seek unity" *when many of those in power are committed to the exact opposite*
is fraught with communal danger, to say nothing of potential career suicide.

Perhaps you're calling for youth ministry to teach *away* from individualism and *toward* a Christian discipleship that is committed to honoring and
affirming the visible church. This, I agree, is noble and important. But I do
think that we need to be careful to help people in youth ministry to navigate
this with care and within the context of the larger system of the church.

### Holiness

I agree that there has been an unwarranted and unfortunate lack of emphasis
on the corporate calling to holiness as compared to the responsibility of the
individual to pursue holiness, or what may be more aptly termed *personal
piety*. Your note that this is to be a both/and as opposed to an either/or calling
is so important. I would like to go further than you and Webber at this point
by stating that the Spirit not only "summons the church to holiness" but also
empowers the church to holiness, and in so doing summons and empowers the
individual to holiness. In your chapter, while you do say that youth ministry
"should certainly continue encouraging individuals to live a life of holiness," I
would have liked to see how you would help people to actually do this without
shaming or moralizing. And with that, how do we *both* encourage personal

holiness *and* seek corporate holiness in a youth ministry context? And just who, then, makes up this corporate "holy body" you refer to? This is, in effect, where the youth ministry rubber meets the road. To "disciple" young people toward holiness, without shaming or violating Willard's "sin management" rebuke, while creating a vision and impetus for corporate holiness, is not only the central task of youth ministry—it *is* youth ministry. Help!

In youth ministry, holiness is not only often misunderstood but also rarely talked about. When it is talked about, it typically falls into the category of personal piety, or simply behaviors like drinking, doing drugs, or sex. This is where holiness becomes more about shaming young people into conformity—Dallas Willard's "gospel of sin management" refers to contemporary discipleship models that seek to change behavior without pointing to the call of Christ and the empowerment of the Spirit.[2] Our call, then, is to encourage young people to pursue, trust, and follow Christ, both personally and as members of the body of Christ. In so doing, holiness will be sowed from the inside out. This corporate commitment to pursuing holiness as a body should not, however, be limited to the youth group or a small group; it is most readily actualized in the greater family of God (and this is what my article on adoption is trying to say as well).

### CATHOLIC AND APOSTOLIC

This is where your article has the greatest potential for a new way of thinking about youth ministry, and, again, I wish you had been able to describe this in a more practical way. Perhaps it is time to move beyond our most common prototypical discipleship models of "Do this, but don't do that" shaming and behavior adjustment, or the "Go out there (*alone*) and be a world changer!" challenges. Helping to plant a young person's faith in the communal soil of ecclesial history provides them with a deep and sustainable faith to grow out of, regardless of the mode, philosophy, or methods we employ. Reinforcing historic and "passed on" faith to someone in the most transitional phase of life allows them to see themselves as carrying the torch handed to them by a long lineage of God's people. This is sure to strengthen their experience of faith by providing a depth and lasting meaning that individualism cannot.

In addition to the benefit of the longevity of the Christian faith, when that faith is proclaimed as catholic (as you, Fred, rightly define it as "universal" faith) and apostolic (as the succession of orthodox teaching and obedience to that teaching), the credibility of the heart of that message, the kingdom of God, takes on a new gravitas, thus enabling the youth ministry student or practitioner to both recognize and embrace the validity of that faith. In middle and even high school this may rarely be a pressing issue for most disciples, but once they hit college and beyond, the intellectual challenges alone may wreak havoc on the person whose faith is limited to following a prescribed list of behaviors, attitudes, and voting tendencies. They might lose steam for continually trying to live up to the "world changer" mantle. And this is certainly your point. To be convinced that the message of Jesus Christ and the kingdom of God can not only survive but truly interact with different viewpoints but have also stood the test of time across the centuries can produce the kind of inner confidence in a young person (or a youth group) that the gospel is authentic and true. In so doing, faith may indeed become rich and deep and real.

In closing, I would hope to see this ecclesiological framework and historical and theological environment and training be located within a familial framework I call adoptive ministry. To have solid historical understanding, to be taught the "four characteristics" of the church, and to know basic doctrines is indeed important. But to be trained in all of that, and even to be immersed in a community that celebrates these essentials, is not enough to sustain long-term faith in young people in a world devoid of social capital. Adoption, at the center of your article, could make what you have written all the more powerful.

## ✚ Ron Hunter

Thank you for your comments, Fernando. In response, because you spend most of your article on paleo-orthodoxy and only a small percentage applying it to youth ministry, most of my comments will deal with your suggestion of which orthodoxy youth ministry should embrace. You suggest some ideas that I can easily agree with, such as not treating ministry as a business model but instead as an ecclesiastical one, and that youth ministries should not always be isolated from the larger body. Also, youth and all other ages within the church should know about church history, doctrine, the implications of the Reformation, and the tension that exists between the church and the world. Some major early church core aspects we should never compromise include the virgin birth, bodily resurrection, the Trinity, and others. One cannot ignore history and the value that the early church fathers bring to our development of beliefs.

"Orthodoxy" means "correct belief." "Paleo" means "ancient." All advocates of orthodoxy, regardless of the prefix, believe they hold the correct position. The distinctive prefix differentiates one view from another. Paleo-orthodoxy attempts to reach back to a predenomination era, and as a result it creates its own distinct set of beliefs. It is ironic that distinct approaches to orthodoxy, like the paleo position, is how we arrived at so many denominations.

Reading Fernando is like reading Oden and Webber—mostly Webber. Some versions of paleo-orthodoxy stand in danger of shifting the focus from Scripture to the apostles and early church fathers as the orthodox standard of our faith. Throughout the New Testament, early church fathers, and the Reformation, the nuances, prefixes, and core beliefs became dividing lines. Even today within Christianity, mainline denominations cannot agree on core doctrines, such as inspiration, infallibility, and the authority of Scripture, that serve as our foundation of truth. Without foundational truth, the apologetic arguments quickly unravel. I would never want to step out in any apologetic argument without establishing first the premise of the inspiration, infallibility, and authority of God's Word as given through the original authors. As Stier notes in his chapter, young people will not risk their social standing without confidence in what they believe. One cannot and should not compromise on Scripture, even when lifting up other historical teachings.

Fernando says, "Furthermore, it is also important to teach Christian teens that ecclesiology preceded the canon for over three hundred years." The current church era owes a debt of gratitude to the early developers of ecclesiology. While the early church fathers carried on Christ's Great Commission similarly to the apostles, their teachings begin to splinter as well. One can read about Jerome and others who felt inferior as nonmartyrs and taught self-deprivation, mutilation, and isolation.[3] Many are thankful these teachings did not make the canon of Scripture. The early church fathers do not agree with one another, and they do not always agree with themselves. One must be careful looking back and idealizing an era. One should reach back to Scripture for principles but look forward in implementing them in today's culture. Even Christ's methods were criticized in light of ancient teachings.

It might be idealistic to suggest that going back to the early church fathers provides a consensus that results in truth. After Christ, differences developed as more of the early fathers championed various interpretations of truth. Maximus the Confessor is a good example of a church father who stood for the truth by standing against the prevailing consensus of the church leaders in his geographic area, a stand that cost him his life. Consensus on truth did not exist during the early church fathers, and it may be presumptuous to suggest that unanimity could be reached by going back to this era.

While Fernando asks the modern church to rally around some overgeneralizations, he also brings us to some great reminders. We should recognize and show appreciation for how paleo-orthodoxy warns the church and its youth about the dangers of forgetting our roots. In fact, we should listen as

Fernando cites Webber, who calls the body of Christ to the awareness of how in "the ancient stage, the church was understood as the visible continuation of the presence of Christ in the world." However, it needs to be stressed that many evangelicals who do not strictly fit within the paleo-orthodoxy renewal have not abandoned the richness of our history. The very activity of preaching Christ, yielding to his authority, and calling people to salvation through the cross by faith connects us to the church of the past.

Through this section Fernando makes some wise insights about how the church functions today. One of the greatest problems identified is the way churches and youth pastors tend to isolate the youth group from the main congregation. Many would agree the constant isolation can cause a lack of desire to reassimilate into the main congregation as the teenagers move into young adulthood. Young-adult ministries that continue the tangential contact of youth ministries are growing. Stuart Cummings-Bond illustrated this perfectly when describing it as the "one-eared Mickey Mouse" (see fig. 4.1 below). Youth ministries sit in the peripheral of the congregation due to the desire to find their own identity, and the adults feel more comfortable when the group they least identify with functions at some distance.

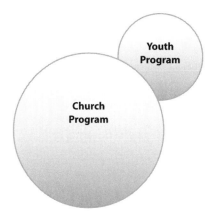

Figure 4.1. The one-eared Mickey Mouse[4]

Mark DeVries suggests that when adults and youth work together in mission and service, they tend to wind up spending time together outside a programmed context.[5] In addition, if a church never segregates by age group, all families will get to worship and interact together. The identity of totally separated youth groups can create a "cool versus the uncool" environment. This now causes churches to create the second ear to the Mickey Mouse— young-adult ministry—further separating and delaying the opportunities to create a church of all ages. In fairness to the youth and young adults, the self-centered preferences of the adults' traditional approach to worship often leave little room for including the youth and young adults. When the adults recognize the worship includes the youth and young adults, then maybe the way "we always did church" becomes less important than showing them how to have a relationship with the Heavenly Father, even if it is slightly different from their traditions. How quickly the modern church forgets that God is the God of Abraham, Isaac, and Jacob—not just Abraham. Thank you, Fernando, for pointing out how segregated the church can become if not intentional and inclusive.

Another insightful observation by Fernando shows how some churches tend to legislate morality today. While I agree with the statement, I disagree with which churches he assigns as doing this today. Fernando suggests that the churches that are run like a business have the goal of managing the actions of their members. Author and pastor Tim Kimmel has dedicated his life to family ministry, and he suggests the congregation or family without a grace-based approach places the youth and children in a performance mentality. Kimmel asks why we preach that "by grace through faith" allows us to be saved or become a Christ-follower, and then judge by performance as grace is left behind. Legalism is the by-product of the absence of grace and lack of the type of loving relationship that demonstrates what the Heavenly Father does for all his children.

I am grateful for how the paleo-orthodox position reminds Christians to recognize the church as a body. Christ works within and is represented by this body, and it should function as a whole rather than a collective group of individuals who are simply agreeable. Some religious leaders have been dismissive of the notion of the bride of Christ. This dangerous position ignores an important understanding given to us by our Heavenly Father, and it ignores the fact that we are called to look toward the day the church is wed to Christ at his return. Fernando's position reminds all of us to hold in high esteem Christ's bride, whom he loves and works within to accomplish his purpose.

Paleo-orthodoxy reminds us to seek truth over denominational labels and preconceived worldviews. Since Christ's resurrection, the body of Christ has been on a quest to define and explain truth as each generation creates a new banner, nuance, or even theological camp. Paleo-orthodoxy reminds us that it is more important to embrace Christian truth than it is to be labeled Baptist, Methodist, or Anglican. Correct teaching is even more important than the label "evangelical"! If the youth can catch the concept that we are a family of faith pursuing truth, they will be stronger.

## Fernando Arzola's Response

Thank you all for the thoughtful responses to my article. I will respond to you each individually.

Greg, I appreciate your honest reflections. Let me start by stating, however, that I think you too quickly dismiss the spirit of the chapter. The issue is not so much that teenagers "need to know" church history but that youth ministers should reflect on their own ecclesiological presuppositions and models. Being familiar with church history (including the history between the apostles and the Reformation) could prevent youth leaders from creating their own personal ecclesiologies based on their own personalities and temperaments. The overall purpose of the chapter is to examine an issue that I believe youth ministers, and the field of youth ministry, does not often address—ecclesiology. I reflect on the ancient practices as a template for self-reflection.

What will "drive" a youth ministry is not what I intended to address. This is secondary to me; otherwise, we fall into the same old "what programs will work this week/month/year" kind of exercises instead of examining the foundational presuppositions and theories from which the "drive" comes. My attempt was to focus more on the theory rather than the praxis.

Again, the chapter is not a curriculum to be used with teens. Rather, it serves as a theoretical and historical starting point encouraging youth leaders to reflect on their own youth ministry ecclesiologies. Sadly, I believe, most do not even think about it. They'll examine the usual (and important) issues of worship, discipleship, service, evangelism, and fellowship, but what about Christology, soteriology, ecclesiology, and so on? Perhaps a helpful place for youth workers to begin is to ask, "What ecclesiological theory/theology/paradigm am I using/nurturing/creating?"

You write, "When one becomes overly obsessed with creeds and confessions, rather that Christ and his cause, then what was meant to bring stability and depth can become an idol that distract us from our Savior." My response to this is, "Huh?" Again, the chapter is not meant to be a lesson curriculum. So let me push back. What a youth minister believes about Christ *is* his or her confession that is being passed on to teens. What a youth minister teaches teens about Christ *is* his or her creed that is being passed on to teens. I agree that any obsession is dysfunctional, but I think dismissing ecclesiological reflection is also unhelpful in developing a healthy youth ministry. Another question youth ministers might ask themselves is, "What traditions are being passed on in my youth ministry program?" Traditions are certainly being passed on. While I am not such a purist or so rigid as to define what this might look like, I do think that looking to the ancient teaching of the church can serve twenty-first-century youth ministry well.

Brian, thank you for the thoughtful response. I can see you took time to reflect on the chapter. For this, I am grateful. Let me jump right into the critiques.

I agree that Donald Bloesch may not necessarily be considered the most "classical" representative of the Reformed tradition. You write that "to associate him with Calvinism (as such) and orthodox Reformed theology *as a representative* of those traditions would be going a bit too far." Maybe. But I have also read enough traditional "Reformed" theologians who offer differing opinions on Reformed matters. So who's to say who is the best representative?

As it relates to this chapter, my perspectives were indeed a blend of Donald Bloesch, Robert Webber, and Thomas Oden. I certainly may not agree with each of them 100 percent, but they were selected for their ability to honor tradition and speak to its place in the contemporary church.

You are correct that I didn't specifically provide a youth ministry model. What I attempted to provide was a perspective that I believe is missing in youth ministry. The chapter, I hope, encourages youth ministry leaders to consider and reappropriate ancient practices within their youth ministry contexts. This is not significantly different from the traditional practices you suggest in your chapter. However, I am not limiting this to a Reformed model. How this might look within each context will vary.

The Reformed tradition has certainly held on to some of the more institutional marks/pillars. But, at least in my personal experience, particularly in the urban context, I still see that most youth ministries are focused primarily on the Bible and not on the traditions. I say this with no judgment, of course; I simply see it as limiting. Becoming familiar with and reappropriating some of the ancient Christian practices will, I believe, broaden and enrich youth ministries and reintegrate them more deeply into the church.

Your points about "unity in the church" and "unity in the truth" are well taken. And your concern about living in a culture where unity and tolerance are elevated above biblical unity "for unity's sake" is appreciated. I am committed to being kind and respectful (1 Pet. 3:15), but that does not mean that biblical unity is not vital. I don't mean to imply this necessarily reflects your opinion, so forgive my assumptions. But the fears you mention usually come from a conservative (or sometimes literal) interpretation of Scripture or tradition, or from a politically/socially right-of-center perspective that views a left-of-center perspective as necessarily "antithetical to Christ." In addition, would your critique not also apply possibly to those who interpret Scripture literally?

Furthermore, varying Christian traditions and denominations (Roman Catholic and Reformed, for example) may view each other's theological perspectives as contrary to unity, even if they agree on certain political/social matters. The biblical writers did not envision any of these types of divisions; therefore, to ask whether they envisioned unity with these groups is unhelpful.

I appreciate your insights regarding the distinctions among bishop, priest/presbytery, and deacon. (I would expect nothing less from a Reformed perspective!) This is a good time to remind all of us that the church existed prior to the biblical canon. Therefore, many of the traditions that were developed occurred prior to, or simultaneously with, the writings of the New Testament. We both addressed this, so I won't dwell on it. It is, however, also helpful to remember that the various Protestant interpretations developed fifteen hundred years after the birth of the church. Of course, this is not to minimize those perspectives, but simply to place the traditions in historical context. We may not necessarily agree with the Roman Catholic or Eastern Orthodox understanding of Scripture or tradition, but they provided the paradigm from which Protestantism based its reworked models.

Finally, Brian, you critique my perspective by saying it offers little biblical support. I would push back and say that just because something is extrabiblical does not mean it's unbiblical. Nevertheless, I agree that my perspective leans primarily on the traditions of the church, which flow from Scripture. That was the intention of the chapter. But doesn't this reinforce an implicit message? Yes, the Christian church must be rooted in the Holy Bible, but the Christian church is bigger than the Bible. While we should not base our ecclesiology on unbiblical teachings, let us also embrace the traditions of the church as part of the teaching ministry.

Thank you, Chap, for your kind words of introduction. I particularly appreciate your affirmation of the necessity of youth ministry to more intentionally connect with church history.

Often when I hear youth ministry leaders say, "We stand on the shoulders of men and women who have gone before us," they generally are referring to those in the brief history of youth ministry, or perhaps their own denominational leaders. Or, if they are more historically keen, they may go back as a far as the Reformers. Sadly, they rarely refer to standing on the shoulders of the apostles, the ancient fathers who led the worldwide expansion of the church, or the early church. This is why the reappropriation of the terms and concepts of catholicity and apostolicity are so important. And I am glad that you agree. These are phrases that are not comfortably said by our Protestant brethren, yet they should be reclaimed. As Ignatius writes, "Wherever Jesus Christ is, there is the catholic church."

Your highlighting that the definition of "ecclesiology" as "the study of churches" may be, in itself, a hindrance toward better understanding is right on. It sounds dry and academic. If we solely understand ecclesiology as an intellectual examination of a historical model, then this will perpetuate the problem. However, if we understand ecclesiology as a dynamic and living organism that serves as the backbone of our institutional and functional ministries, then it provides a very different understanding. I think Brian Cosby's chapter on youth ministry and the Reformed tradition underscores the interconnectedness between history, tradition, and contemporary youth ministry.

You state, "My greatest critique of this model is not in the conceptual, theological, or historical framework you've laid out, but in the 'What do I do with this?'" This made me smile. Although I offer some practices to help "reappropriate historically orthodox youth ministry practices," I agree that I really didn't present a youth ministry model. (By the way, your model is excellent, Chap.) My attempt here was to focus more on the theory rather than the praxis, to focus more on the "why" than on the "how." This book will provide several "how" models. First, I wanted to raise ecclesiological awareness; second, to examine ancient/classical ecclesiological perspectives; and third, to suggest that it behooves twenty-first-century youth ministries to reappropriate more intentional ecclesiological practices. As you know, whether we realize it or not, we all have ecclesiological presuppositions. My hope is to raise more intentional and conscious reflection.

My reflections on the visible and invisible church were precisely to critique the individualism that often occurs in many youth ministries. That is, the excessive focus on the visible in many Protestant denominations and traditions tends to reinforce an individualistic spirituality. (This, of course, is different from one's personal spirituality—a conversation for another day.) Recognizing the reality and place of the visible church helps one to better appreciate, I think, the interconnectedness between youth ministries and the church, both local and universal. I think awareness of the visible church is also significant within the context of social justice. If justice is viewed as an optional part of one's individual spirituality, then it remains only one item on a menu of individualistic options. If, however, it is understood as an aspect of the visible church, then we begin to understand peace and justice as a constitutive extension of the body of Christ—one that is as essential as baptism and the Lord's Supper.

Your insights on holiness are excellent, Chap. Much better than any efforts I could attempt. You are correct when you write, "The Spirit not only summons the church to holiness but also empowers the church to holiness."

I wish to underscore your emphasis that holiness, in certain church and ministry circles, is limited to certain behaviors as opposed to a deeper, conscious awareness of the Spirit in our lives. I affirm your concern that the church in general, and youth ministries in particular, should encourage holiness without shaming or moralizing. By focusing primarily on individualistic "holy behaviors," we begin to nurture an exclusivistic church of do-gooders instead of a safe and loving place for sinners.

Ron, thank you for your thoughtful and comprehensive response. I appreciate the fullness of your insights and affirmations on several of my points.

You are correct that most of the chapter focuses on the early church and ancient traditions. The overall purpose of the chapter was to use the early church as a template for examining ecclesiology, a topic that is rarely examined in youth ministry circles. You write, "Some versions of paleo-orthodoxy stand in danger of shifting the focus from Scripture to the apostles and early church fathers as the standard." Perhaps. But, the apostles and their followers were the writers and compilers of the Scriptures. And the writings of the early church fathers were the original commentaries on Scripture—and tradition. Should not those who lived among the apostles (or among the followers of the apostles) and who also participated in the establishing and expansion of the early church have an authoritative perspective on the ecclesiology of the church?

I agree when you write, "Without foundational truth, the apologetic arguments quickly unravel. I would never want to step out in any apologetic argument without establishing first the premise of the inspiration, infallibility, and authority of God's Word as given through the original authors." My response is, "Whose interpretation of foundational truth?" And what does inspiration, infallibility, and authority really mean? For example, I have a feeling we would hear many varying perspectives from the members of the Society of Biblical Literature.

I am not stating that youth ministries should "go back to the early fathers" in a literal sense. What "going back" might look like now in the contemporary reality is secondary. However, the ecclesiological pillars have served the church well for two millennia. Perhaps these should at least be reflected on by current youth ministries instead of too quickly trying to find "new" models of being church. It seems to me the emergent church has found a way to reflect on and incorporate the practices of the ancient church into its contemporary faith communities.

Also, you mention, "Consensus on truth did not exist during the early church fathers, and it may be presumptuous to suggest that unanimity could be reached by going back to this era." You are correct. Nevertheless, ecclesiologically speaking, I would give the ancient practices the benefit of the doubt, or at least a second look.

My one critique of your overall generous response is that you seem to reduce the totality of the chapter to "paleo-orthodoxy." I certainly refer to this, but my attempt was to remain faithful to and rooted in the orthodox faith of history.

# VIEW FIVE

## Ron Hunter

# The D6 View
# of Youth Ministry

outh ministers are superheroes. You show up for six different games on four sides of town, attend twelve graduations in one weekend, plan a summer's worth of activities on a week's worth of a budget, and yet maintain your own family dynamics. Most churches write an impossible job description. If your church does not actually write such a description, the parents have an unwritten one by which they judge you. Most youth ministers pull off the impossible. I am pretty sure some of you, especially the ones who lead my kids, hide a big "S" under your shirts. Many deserve that superhero title, but none of you aspired to be the lone guru working twenty-five hours a day and six months each summer.

The church, over time, has "siloed" the age groups by hiring gifted leaders over each ministry. The unintended consequences of such silos caused parents to leave most spiritual instruction to the church. Agricultural silos existed in various forms dating back thousands of years. They provide a place to store grain and keep individual types of grain protected. In current terms, silos describe a different phenomenon, that of an organization that completely segregates each department, creating barriers in communication and purpose. The Oxford English Dictionary describes the metaphor as a "system, process, department, etc. that operates in isolation from others."[1]

Silos represent isolation and prevent interaction. Looking past the agrarian era of our country, we see the development of the industrial age and what some have described as "McDonaldization." This term, first coined by George Ritzer,[2] describes a sociological process of logically examining every aspect of a task. Henry Ford, the pioneer of the assembly line, figured out that if he trained people for specific tasks, he could build cars faster and more efficiently than any other car maker. Ray Kroc used this principle of the assembly line to create identically prepared hamburgers in each of his restaurants.

The idea of finding the expert for each task rolled over into the church with the hiring of specialized staff members such as youth ministers, children's ministers, preschool ministers, and others. I know of several churches that have a minister of sports recreation. (I really missed that major in college!) None of these positions are wrong, unless the parents have delegated all their kids' spiritual development responsibility to these ministers. I know many youth and children's ministry leaders who feel like parents view them as the hired guns to clean up and fix what the parents took thirteen-plus years to engrain into their students' lives. We do not desire a silo of isolation or the McDonaldization of church ministry. D6 wants high-capacity and well-trained youth ministers to help, not replace, parents. Just as the Holy Spirit comes alongside to help, the youth minister can do the same with both students and parents. This view seeks partnership with all church leaders and all parents to prepare the next generation for life.

In this chapter, I will walk you through what D6 is and what D6 is not. D6 describes generational discipleship lived out through both the church and the home. I will share the genesis of the term "D6" and offer a brief biblical foundation of church and home interaction regarding generational discipleship from the Old and New Testaments. I will finish with five primary focal points for youth ministers who operate with a D6 philosophy. The purpose of this chapter is to share God's original plan for generational discipleship that includes both the church and the home. I will show the vital role youth ministry plays in both church and home discipleship.

## What D6 Is and What D6 Is Not

"D6" is short for Deuteronomy 6. The D6 approach involves integrating leadership from both church and home to disciple current and future generations. D6 views the church as the theological anchor, training ground, and resource center for discipleship. The church equips the parents to coach the kids. In addition to parents and teachers consistently teaching, modeling, and building relationships with the teens, the D6 model suggests that the youth ministry work closely with the other ministries to help the parents teach, model, and build relationships at church and in the home. The youth minister is restricted in the amount of time spent with the teen. In Deuteronomy 6, God commands the older generation of grandparents, parents, and the faith community as a whole to exercise generational discipleship by example and diligent instruction, and not to delegate this role to anyone else. We need the church and home to provide "echoing voices" to speak the truth into the lives of our kids. In the D6 model, parents learn from the church through sermons, small groups, Sunday school, and relationships so they in turn can provide consistency for the family when not at church.

Most parents seek the best for their teens. That's why they brought their teen to youth group. Parents hire tutors for the ACT test, sign their teen up for competitive teams to get the best coaching, and drive past two other schools to get to the one with higher tuition. Ironically, in the interest of seeking the best for their kids, parents often lose interaction with their kids and, as a result, lose influence. Most youth ministers recognize how much weight and spiritual responsibility parents place on their shoulders. D6 helps ministers recruit the parents to partner with them.

Some people may have the wrong idea about D6. D6 includes the home but does not exclude the church. The church creates a guiding, biblical direction and foundation on which the parents build. D6 does not suggest every age should be in one room for the teaching. D6 would not argue against this model, but it would not argue for it either. D6 finds value in placing parents with other parents whose oldest children are at similar seasons of life, thus allowing proper applications relevant to life. Parents seek answers to questions as their oldest navigates unknown phases. The church leadership and people within small groups provide insight, experience, and understanding. D6 does not devalue the church when emphasizing the role of parents but demonstrates a more scriptural approach when youth ministers partner with parents.

## The Genesis of D6

After pastoring for over a decade, it became obvious to me how heavily parents relied on the church to do all the work of discipling the family. Without strong discipleship among the parents and kids, each generation drifts further from a Christ-centered life. Children grow into unprepared teens and struggle to stay connected. As they grow older, the lack of a consistent Christ-centered relationship with their parents creates a convenient, easy out from church. The solution came when a friend reminded me of the logical progression—he said, "If you want to have a strong youth ministry, start building into the students' lives while they're in the children's ministry." This began my journey on what Randall House has called *generational discipleship*, where the church and home work toward a deliberate and strategic plan to change our culture by strengthening the family.

At Randall House, we recognized that the traditional Sunday school model alone was not enough. We dismantled the existing way of teaching only a single session once a week. We launched a teaching system that provides church and home components to connect and facilitate conversations around the weekly family themes. We put every age on the same page. In 2006, with the goal of trying to make the Pentateuch more attractive to today's culture, I came up with the abbreviation "D6." Three years later, a conference bearing the D6 name started. Now the term has been widely used by youth, children, and family ministries around the world. We developed the strategy for Randall House and D6 as "Building believers through church and home." This strategy suggests a two-part goal of evangelizing and discipling Christ-followers leveraged from two different vantage points—the church and home.

## The Biblical Foundation of D6

For ten years, I coached recreational soccer. It started when my kids began the sport around second grade. My son and daughter played right up through high school, and each served as the captain of their varsity team. Every year, I had first-time players on my roster. Both novice players and veterans of soccer need to work on basic drills like passing and dribbling when away from team practices. I assigned practical exercises for all the players to do at home. The players who rapidly progressed in skill and dexterity development, especially with the weak foot, revealed which parents worked with their kids and which ones did not. One other observation as a coach was this: every player wanted his or her parents to practice with them, and often those who had no one also had the worst attitudes. Parents' involvement makes a huge difference, no matter the quality of the coach or youth pastor.

Church leaders desperately want a better way to equip parents so they in turn can coach their own kids. The D6 philosophy comes from ancient roots found in Deuteronomy 6 in the way God instructed the Hebrew parents to be leaders in their kids' lives. From the very beginning, God wanted the tabernacle, and later the temple, to be the center of life around which people built their homes (or pitched their tents). This core passage of the Pentateuch shows parents how to let their love for God and his Word overflow into the lives of their kids and let a Christ-following relationship be caught and taught.

These are the commands, decrees and laws the LORD your God directed me to teach you to observe in the land that you are crossing the Jordan to possess, so that you, your children and their children after them may fear the LORD your God as long as you live by keeping all his decrees and commands that I give you, and so that you may enjoy long life. Hear, Israel, and be careful to obey so that it may go well with you and that you may increase greatly in a land flowing with milk and honey, just as the Lord, the God of your ancestors, promised you.

Hear, O Israel: The Lord our God, the Lord is one. Love the Lord your God with all your heart and with all your soul and with all your strength. These commandments that I give you today are to be on your hearts. Impress them on your children. Talk about them when you sit at home and when you walk along the road, when you lie down and when you get up. Tie them as symbols on your hands and bind them on your foreheads. Write them on the doorframes of your houses and on your gates. (6:1–9)

This passage shares God's *command*, not his suggestion. God's intent in this passage creates an educational process for families to disciple each generation. Deuteronomy 6 instructed the entire nation on how their faith and values were going to reach their great-grandchildren. The basics of this command tell us that we are to love God, love his Word, and teach our kids to do the same. The best lessons come from natural interactions during everyday life, much the way Jesus used parables to teach his disciples. Hebrew scholar Garnett Reid calls this "second generation nurturing."[3] Deuteronomy 6, and D6, asks parents to look for teachable moments throughout the day allowing for their Christ-following relationship to be caught and taught.

The New Testament quotes Deuteronomy, Psalms, and Isaiah more than any other books from the Old Testament.[4] Taking the entire Old Testament Law and Prophets, Jesus quoted from the twin pillars of Deuteronomy 6:5 and Leviticus 19:18 and summarized them into two commands with a single sentence, found in Matthew 22:37–40.[5] To limit Deuteronomy as outdated or to simply relegate it to ancient Israel would be to miss how often Jesus, Paul, and the New Testament quoted from this foundational book and this passage.

The New Testament sister passage to Deuteronomy 6, Ephesians 6, finds parallel admonitions by Paul. Paul begins this chapter by providing additional commentary from the commandment to honor your father and mother. In recalling the Decalogue so familiar to the New Testament believers, Paul noted that the command to obey your parents requires a reciprocal relationship. Parents expect honor, respect, and obedience from children. Paul reminded parents, specifically dads, that to receive honor one must likewise be careful not to agitate or anger your kids but positively nurture a relationship. Tim Kimmel, the well-known author of grace-based parenting, defines grace as "God's love showing itself in relational determination,"[6] and we in youth and family ministry should teach parents how to intentionally build relationships filled with grace with their kids. Dads provide a model for kids, who often derive their view of the Heavenly Father by what they know and experience with their earthly father. Deuteronomy 6 and Ephesians 6 expect dads and moms to build healthy relationships with their children and teens.

The Ephesians passage highlights key issues for the home, as Paul teaches the New Testament believer a type of household code of conduct where the relational connections emanate from emotional connections and anger issues push kids farther from the parents and from the Heavenly Father.[7] Paul spoke of anger and discouraging kids in Ephesians 4:29 and Colossians 3:20–21. Parents should recognize the Heavenly Father loans their children to them for a season, and like a steward, they must increase their children's healthy sense of self and their actual worth as valued by God. Parents cannot go about this process alone but will need the help of the church, specifically some godly individuals such as youth ministers, grandparents, aunts and uncles, and other special people who can reinforce biblical teachings and godly relationships.

The Shema is named so from the Hebrew word for *summons*—"Hear, O Israel," come listen to the Word of God. The commands were both propositional in that they affirmed who God is, and personal in how each generation was to be committed to him.[8] Deuteronomy speaks to parents in a similar manner that Proverbs 1:8 speaks to the children. Both passages emphasize an instructional relationship. All teachers can be knowledgeable, but what makes one or two of them the most memorable to us are the relationship connections that inspired us to want to learn. This demonstrates what Deuteronomy and Ephesians teach about how instruction and influence come from our closest connections, who believe in us and help connect the lesson with everyday life.

Throughout Scripture, God the Father consistently refers to believers as his children. You cannot limit D6 to a cultural setting found only among the Israelites and only in the Old Testament. The model of the family shows up everywhere in Scripture, both Old and New Testaments. God calls us his children, he is the Father, the church is the bride of Christ, and he adopted us into his family. Relationships become the structure on which instruction, discipleship, and growth can occur. Our Father follows the same admonition he gives us as he seeks a close relationship with his children, whom he does not agitate or anger but seeks to rescue and redeem. Without a relationship, one limits one's potential influence and teaching. Each of the three Synoptic Gospels tells of Jesus quoting the Shema, but Mark uses the word *ek* (the Greek preposition "with"). This would translate as "with all your heart," which suggests we should pursue God with our entire being—with our heart, soul, mind, and strength.[9] One can find generational discipleship addressed by numerous writers throughout the Bible. Even Christ reminded the disciples of the value of allowing for time with the children in the midst of a busy day of ministry.

Never underestimate the influence of the previous generation. Genesis 18:19 calls us to instruct our kids and model the Lord's ways. Exodus 12:26–27 and 13:14–15 suggest parents can use how God interacted in our lives to build in our kids trust in him for their future. Seven hundred years later, in Isaiah 38:19, God says the same is true. Going forward nearly another eight hundred years, Paul (2 Tim. 1:3–5) reaches back to the faith of Timothy's grandparents when instructing him on how his ancestral testimony continues. The D6 influence is not limited to the Old Testament. Parents, because of their persuading connection with their teens, possess a powerful influence. I pastored in my home state for eleven years and moved away when our oldest was just five. Today, both of our kids cheer passionately for the team within that state and against their home-state rival. Do they remember the team from the state of their birth? No, they adopted and cheer for the team Mom and Dad support. Sounds a lot like Daniel, Shadrach, Meshach, and Abednego, who cheered for the God of their parents even when living in a foreign land. This describes the power of generational discipleship.

Paul connected the reputation of the teacher to the validity of the teaching in 2 Timothy 3:14–17. This key passage teaches inspiration, but pay close attention to the surrounding verses as well. Paul tells Timothy how from early childhood he had been well instructed and prepared to represent the teachings of Scripture. Paul even points out to Timothy the godly genealogy of his mom and grandmother, who shaped his early life. I detest reading the genealogies. I use a phone app that reads Scripture to me daily, but hearing the genealogies makes them no more palatable. However, genealogies show trends, trajectories, and outliers. People's inclusion in a genealogy shows the power of generational affects and effects. God uses people to influence culture and to create lasting cultural change.

Christ-likeness should be rooted within the values of families and passed along within the threads of generations, as noted through all of Scripture. Just as Paul acknowledged the influence of Timothy's grandmother, mother, and now Timothy himself, we find notable groupings of three generations in the Bible causing both positive and negative influences. The most famous may very well be Abraham, Isaac, and Jacob. Observe David, Solomon, and Rehoboam as each slid further from God because of each dad's influence. Did you ever notice Noah's father, Lamech, his father, Methuselah, and the godly influence of his great-grandfather, Enoch? Soon after the death of Moses, Joshua spoke to and challenged the nation of Israel through his own commitment, "But as for me and my house, we will serve the Lord" (Josh. 24:15 KJV). Sadly, a little later in that same chapter (24:31), it is reported that the first generation served God, but the second generation only knew about God—a very different description from experiencing God. This second generation led to Judges 2:10 (ESV): "There arose another generation after them who did not know the Lord or the work that he had done for Israel." Bruce Wilkinson expands on the influence of three generations, showing how the first chair reflects an intimate relation with God, the second knowing about God, and the third not knowing him.[10] Psalm 145:4 shows how "one generation shall commend your works to another, and shall declare your mighty acts" (ESV). Biblically, the word "commending" shows a transfer, as when Christ said, "Father, into thy hands I commend my spirit" (Luke 23:46 KJV), or when Paul wrote his epistles, commending them to the church. The idea of sharing your relationship with God with your kids requires more than telling your kids; it entails a transfer. The relationship passes from one generation to another, helping them fall in love with Christ.

How do you get parents to break the cycle of not being the spiritual coach for their kids? Nehemiah speaks of how parents can redeem a failed example. In chapter 8, the celebration commences over the completion of the wall. During the week of festivities, Ezra and the people gather on the first day to hear the Word read. The spiritual leaders lead in worship and read the Book of the Law, explaining it and helping the people to understand Scripture (v. 8). This sermon leads to events the next day (v. 13), where small groups are further studying the Scripture and happen on a forgotten holiday—the Feast of Tents, or Tabernacles. The dads ask the priests to explain the meaning of the festival. Following God's instructions for teaching the Feast of the Tabernacles, or Tents, dads set up tents, bring their families into the shelters, and teach the provision and protection of God. From the initial assembly and reading of the Word to a week later when they gather again for Ezra to read and explain the Scripture, the parents teach their kids what they have learned. This is a great model of how a family interacts during a week within the D6 model, as it starts with the family in church listening to the Word, and then parents teaching their kids during the week until they come back the next week. Before Nehemiah 8, three-plus generations of dads and moms had failed to teach their kids the Word, but this generation changed the future of their families.

After the fall of Israel and Judah, after seventy years of captivity (about three generations), Nehemiah describes God renewing his model from Deuteronomy 6 at the end of the Old Testament era. Then, like an exclamation point, God closes the Old Testament with this verse: "And he will turn the hearts of fathers to their children and the hearts of children to their fathers, lest I come and strike the land with a decree of utter destruction" (Mal. 4:6

ESV). The New Testament opens with the other bookend verse, Luke 1:17 (KJV): "And he shall go before him . . . to turn the hearts of the fathers to the children, and the disobedient to the wisdom of the just; to make ready a people prepared for the Lord." The principles of generational discipleship appear consistently throughout Scripture for all people and apply to us today even if we have, like the generations of Nehemiah, forgotten to be the spiritual leaders of our kids.

## The Role of a D6 Youth Pastor

### Be a Transformational Leader

Every staff position within the church requires an intentional style of leadership. Like other fields, youth ministry continues to demand more from those who hold this position. One can lead without defining leadership, but the style determines his or her definition. James McGregor Burns, a seminal writer on leadership, defines leadership as "leaders inducing followers to act for certain goals that represent the values and motivations—the wants and needs, the aspirations and expectations *of both leaders and followers*" (emphasis added).[11] So, who are the leaders and followers as they relate to youth ministry? The obvious first pair shows the youth minister as the leader and the students as the followers. Parents and their teens are the second pair of leaders and followers. Notice the definition aims to raise the values and motivations of both leader and follower, indicating more than expecting a certain behavior. The goal raises the aspirations, the beliefs, and the attitudes of both groups, and does not focus on behavior compliance. In other words, dangling a carrot has little lasting healthy effect on teaching the right mind-set for life. Transformational leadership, leadership that encourages and enables life transformation, invests in followers to teach them how to want to make solid decisions on their own.

Burns's definition of leadership is helpful, but what does the Bible say about leading in the role of youth ministers? The Bible provides no explicit description for the specific role of the youth pastor but does implicitly describe what a pastor should be and do. Youth pastors lead and shepherd the youth group and, with the D6 model, influence the parents as well. Look at what God expects from leaders within the local church. Paul gives the benchmark for ministers from both aspects of being and doing. In 1 Timothy 3:1–3, Paul talks to a rising church leader about the importance of *being* the right kind of leader. Paul describes church leaders primarily through words of inner discipleship, where the character of the person must be intact before even considering actionable items. In this simple but profound passage, often used at ordination services, Paul tells ministers what to be and then what to do.

Look at the tremendous context laid by Paul in Ephesians as he builds toward a culminating point. Then consider the detail of Ephesians 4:11–16 (NLT).

> Now these are the gifts Christ gave to the church: the apostles, the prophets, the evangelists, and the pastors and teachers. Their responsibility is to equip God's people to do his work and build up the church, the body of Christ. This will continue until we all come to such unity in our faith and knowledge of God's Son that we will be mature in the Lord, measuring up to the full and complete standard of Christ.
>
> Then we will no longer be immature like children. We won't be tossed and blown about by every wind of new teaching. We will not be influenced when people try to trick us with lies so clever they sound like the truth. Instead, we will speak the truth in love, growing in every way more and more like Christ, who is the head of his body, the church. He makes the whole body fit together perfectly. As each part does its own special work, it helps the other parts grow, so that the whole body is healthy and growing and full of love.

Few teachers or pastors deal with Ephesians 4 within the whole framework of the book to show progression and purpose. Sermons or lessons bring out the spiritual gifts, equipping, and spiritual maturity—all of which are true—but each contributes to a bigger design for the family. Paul started with ministry leaders equipping. This role reads a lot like a coach today. Notice the spectrum of growth here as the coach takes a novice believer from the basics to an advanced, mature Christ-follower. Read the passage again, but this time through the lens of a coach. The minister (youth minister, senior pastor, family minister) builds up each believer and teaches him or her how to defend the foundational truths. Love surrounds the teaching and delivery of truth. Ministers model to parents the way to teach truth. In Ephesians 4, Christ is the head of the body, but in Ephesians 5 husbands and dads are told to follow the Heavenly Father's example (as noted in verse one) to lead the home by coaching the family with sacrificial love, teaching, care, and selfless provision. Notice the progression and intent from chapter 4. Leaders equip the Christ-follower toward maturity in order for him or her to stay unselfishly loving and giving to their mate as seen in chapter 5. In chapter 6, fathers (implied parents) teach kids the Word without pushing them away in agitation. The chapter ends with the armor of God. If Dad and Mom wear it properly, the kids will desire to put it on as well. Follow the family progression of Ephesians by first equipping individuals, making marriages stronger, and then empowering parents to teach their kids through authentic relationships. This will result in strong warriors for Christ.

Leaders who implement a transformational style of leadership understand the value of helping followers become stronger. Building on Burns's work,[12] Bass and Riggio say transformational leaders "are those who stimulate and inspire followers to both achieve extraordinary outcomes and, in the process, develop their own leadership capacities."[13] Some leaders like being the super-hero, but most would love to share the responsibility by empowering people toward greater maturity and capacity on their own. To create a D6 culture, youth leaders invest in the future of teens and help develop parents to share in the spiritual development of their kids.

### Build a Strategic Philosophy

Many leaders falsely believe the next program will be the answer, or spend enormous efforts creating the most unique ministry with a catchy name. "If you build it, they will come" works in movies, but build people and they will grow works in churches. Some helpful questions youth pastors can ask themselves are the following: What is my philosophy? Can I describe the underlying foundation for why each age-group ministry within the church exists and how each should function as an on-ramp to the next? Can I discuss what should be taught at each spiritual life stage and who should lead the students? Can I biblically articulate a philosophy of youth ministry that is not isolated to just youth ministry?

Youth ministers need to recognize the difference between their programs and their philosophy. Programs are not bad. Leaders must see programs as a tactical way to accomplish a bigger strategy. But never confuse a tactic (method) for a strategy (principled plan). A leader who only operates tactically (program driven) without an underlying strategy frequently appears busy but often changes directions and programs. Leaders who adopt programs as strategy create chaos and lack clarity because programs can only be a tactic. Leaders need to define their philosophy by creating a principled plan or a strategy that may include one or more programs to help accomplish the bigger philosophical objective.

Real revolution occurs when leaders focus on a philosophy of influencing people rather than behavior. Ministry staffs typically implement programs to boost numbers. Leaders use training to boost people. Which one will last? We need to invest in the development of people, not programs. Programs help people act differently more than helping them form new convictions of thought. People sign up for programs, but they live out their convictions. Just like Paul taught Timothy what to *be* before teaching him what to *do*, leaders today teach people to think differently before asking them to act differently. Watch any leader who effected cultural change, and you will see someone who taught people to think differently by investing in the layers of people around them. Martin Luther King Jr., Gandhi, William Carey, Winston Churchill, King Henry V, Lincoln, Washington, Billy Graham, and the apostle Paul all invested heavily in people close to them while also challenging people through writings, speeches, or sermons to think differently by examining the possibilities of being part of something exceptional. Each of these leaders had a goal in mind but knew that for the results to last, everyone had to buy into and believe in the direction—the cause—and be able to defend it in order to achieve it.

If transformational leaders bring revolution, then spiritual revolution can only occur by pointing students to Christ, the greatest transformational leader. Youth live with unanswered questions. When youth leaders help them work through Christ's answers, they strengthen the young person, prepare them for better decision making, and realign their priorities. When the youth see the youth leader, they should see Christ, and the leader should help the parents discover the transformational change that occurs with following Jesus.

Programs make parents feel good because their teens "look the part" while in the program. Never confuse conformity with commitment! Students can temporarily conform to a program without ever changing their hearts. Programs work like youth camp; when camp is over, so are many of the commitments, because camp was more about the place, the activities, and the experience. When all the activities are gone, the student is left with, well, her- or himself. If you do not teach youth how to handle life away from camp, then when they find themselves in their Babylon, they will fall to peer pressure and bow down to any big item that comes along. Programs meant to encourage and maintain faith can feel a lot like commitments at camp that are powerful in the moment but can be hollow over time. In addition, they do little to create an inner infrastructure away from church to enable the student to stand up and defend his or her faith.

### *Build a Team Approach among Staff and with Volunteers*

Guiding philosophies become stronger when adopted by every staff leader. What if the school kindergarten teacher ignored typical learning fundamentals like the basic social skills, counting, phonics, and recognition of sets? Would this make it easier or harder for the first-grade teacher? What if all elementary school teachers decided to ignore core learning for their grade? Every teacher should prepare the student for the material taught in the next grade. One leads to the other. In church, the nursery ministry should be the gateway for preparation for life, and each stage of youth ministry along the way should collaboratively prepare the student for the day they leave. Harvard's president in 1909, Dr. Charles William Eliot, suggested that every person could obtain the necessary knowledge of a liberal arts college education by reading fifteen minutes a day from books that could sit on a five-foot-wide shelf. A publisher challenged Dr. Eliot, and he compiled a comprehensive and extraordinary library of fifty-one volumes known as the *Harvard Classics*. Instead of a five-foot-shelf strategy, develop a five-age strategy (nursery, preschool, children, youth, and young adult) that intentionally includes working with the other staff members on developing and handing off a very prepared student. Again, some helpful questions that youth pastors can ask are, What is my comprehensive strategy that connects every age ministry within my church? Have I ever had the strategic conversation with the other ministry leaders?

The youth minister works with youth. The children's minister works with children. The preschool minister works with preschoolers. One could easily suggest every staff member of church forms a team, but do they share the same playbook? Or does each ministry have its own? If they share the same jersey, then the children's ministry can be viewed like a farm league that feeds the future team members of the youth ministry. If the children's minister worked hard to prepare the children to become teenagers and worked in coordination with the youth minister, imagine the spiritual superstars that could emerge. Just as one expects the steps on a set of stairs to be connected so that each leads to the next, each age should connect to the other with intentionality. Youth pastors can influence the youth before they reach the youth ministry and after they leave.

The staff-coordinated strategy should include helping parents develop as spiritual coaches. The youth minister works with teens but also with the student's dad or mom, and ideally both. Few teens today have the ideal family, which increases the need to help moms understand and fill the gap felt when kids don't have a father figure. The inverse, dads raising kids, presents similar challenges. If the youth pastor does not know how to help, then he or she needs to bring someone in to speak to the parents. Youth pastors only get the students for one to two hours a week—then they need Dad or Mom helping them to reinforce what they are trying to teach each week. Youth pastors need to get dads and moms engaging in spiritual conversations with their teens by teaching them how to ask the right questions and how to show unconditional love. Parents should know that not every conversation needs to be critical, contain biblical lectures, or even be serious. Who better to teach a parent how to connect with teens than a teen pastor? When pastors accomplish this, they become the students' and parents' hero.

Imagine if every age-group ministry leader worked with the target group (youth ministers with youth) and the secondary target group (the parents). This secondary group requires adding more time and energy to an already overwhelming schedule. But when a number of the parents of a group start to understand the Deuteronomy 6 (D6) role they play and partner with the pastor, the pastor's efforts to grow the youth will be exponentially more effective.

### Teach Students

Youth pastors teach the students vital concepts, character building, biblical values, and how to use their God-given talents in life. Planning how to build into a student's life takes time. Imagine if every parent collaborated with the pastor to build the same principles into the students through life as it happens. That sounds very much like Deuteronomy 6, or D6; when they lie down or get up, when they leave the house, when they are in the SUV, when they are on the way to soccer practice, or when they are pulling into the drive-through.

Youth leaders engage teens with depth and practical ways to live out their faith. The most powerful teaching includes how to study their Bibles, how to defend their faith, and ways to apply the gospel to social issues. In the youth's senior year, youth pastors should assess what the students have not been taught and then incorporate those lessons into their ministry strategy.

To teach the students further, leaders can enlist the help of dads and moms to keep their weekly lesson alive in conversations at home. They can get every age on the same page and allow parents to walk with their teens and partner with the leaders. Timothy Paul Jones provides some practical assessments to help triage and plan on how to equip parents in his *Family Ministry Field Guide*.[14]

Including parents can be simple. Our youth pastor sends a weekly email to all the students' parents. He includes a short paragraph about his message and gives the parents a couple of key talking points or questions to keep that message in the front of the minds of the students. This creates a parenting partnership and a consistent message for the teens. He also includes announcements of coming events to keep parents in the loop—so that they are not hearing the night before, "Mom, I need $20 for . . ." He can send his lessons as podcasts to parents. Picture the future in eight years when the teens carry with them a lifelong biblical foundation because parents partnered with preschool, children's, and youth ministers to coach their kids at home.

### Coach Parents to Be Coaches

Think about constantly running around a track, lap after lap after lap. You run some good laps, and you feel tired in some, but you never stop. Sometimes your run slows to a walk. Now imagine someone walking or running beside you to encourage you. They make each lap more doable. For teens, that person running beside them is their youth minister. Youth ministers provide an encouraging word, a listening ear, and timely insight. The problem comes from how little time one can spend running beside each teenager. The whole youth group interacts between one and three hours a week. One-on-one time is limited, unless there is a crisis. Evaluate the maximum amount of time a youth minister gets to run beside a young person on a standard 440-yard track. If she consents to the max of three hours each week and another thirty minutes in texts and social media, then she gets the equivalent of running beside the student for only nine yards. The remaining 431 yards of the student's week is run alone. Parents spend a lot of those 431 yards with those kids. They are in the position to reinforce what the pastor is teaching and building into their teenager.

If pastors position themselves as cooler than mom or dad, they undermine the home. If their attitude shows youth ministry is cooler than adult church, they erode the church's creditability and desirability. If they make youth ministry the ultimate ministry, the student has little to look forward to, and they create an off-ramp for the student before adulthood. The best recruiter the older congregation has is the youth pastor. A healthy approach helps students embrace and desire the next age level by preparing the students to contribute at each level. Preschoolers look forward to children's ministry, and children cannot wait to be in youth ministry. If youth ministers are not narcissistic, they make adult ministry attractive by connecting the relationships of the students' parents to one another. Youth leaders should help students love and respect their parents. They do not need to work hard to get the students to like them; the real work comes in engaging the parents to connect with their kids.

By investing in the parents as well as the teens, youth pastors help both groups thrive as they live out their faith in any environment. The Barna Group asserts the power of the impact of parents who model what the church teaches by connecting with their kids' everyday lives.[15] Schoolteachers meet with parents to show them how to help their student at home. Most parents thrive at helping their kids when given a model, some talking points, and confidence, knowing it is okay not to get it right the first time. Youth pastors should start with high expectations and inform the parents during the new members' class that they are the primary faith influencers.[16]

Parents feel overwhelmed, especially if they are new believers, with too much coming at them all at once. If each ministry teaches different topics and operates independently, then how can a parent keep up or feel competent to connect with their kids? Look in the floorboard or seatback pockets of the family vehicle, and you will find enough take-home papers to start your own recycling plant. Instead, youth pastors can provide a curriculum choice where every class studies the same theme, equipping parents while their kids are learning the same valuable lesson at home as at church. This enables the coaching conversations to take place at home. Good churches teach marriage topics, such as how to have financial peace, how to parent in a world of change, and how to communicate to your spouse; great churches teach the parents how to teach these principles to their teens. "Parents have an amazing opportunity and responsibility to take the unique temperament of each child and overlay it with the character of God by instilling habits and disciplines that will keep them connected to Christ."[17] Most moms and dads want to look competent in front of their kids. Parents cannot fake giving their kids biblical insights—so many do not try. It is not that parents do not want to lead their kids in faith values, but that no one ever showed them how.

Most of us have a similar story from our own experience that illustrates this point. When I taught my son golf, he was in third grade and started with a five iron and a putter I cut down to two feet. We both played on regular courses. I would tee off at the regular men's tee (whether 300 or 500 yards), and he hit from the hundred-yard marker. This allowed him to develop his swing with a similar number of swings per hole. As he grew stronger and older, he moved back to the 150, and eventually to the regular tees with Dad. By observing and playing together, he honed his skills. I still paid a pro to give him lessons, but his practice time came under my direction. Youth ministers are the pros, but playing time occurs with dads and moms. Parents can reinforce the minister's teaching when they are taught the same material and connect it to their teen's everyday life.

D6 knows no time limit, no cultural boundary, and no geographical preference. Generational discipleship passages show the value of the church equipping people, making marriages stronger, and helping parents spiritually coach and guide their kids. When all the ministries of the church find ways to strengthen parents to help their kids, every generation wins, and our culture will see the difference. D6 represents God's original plan for how to nurture a Christ-follower generationally from birth throughout the circle of life.

# Responses to the D6 View

✚ Greg Stier

I fully agree that Christian parents carry the primary responsibility for the spiritual development of their children. Youth leaders must do all they can to nurture and equip parents for that role. I love the view of youth leaders as "coaches" who engage, equip, and encourage parents to play the primary role of spiritual discipler in the lives of their own children.

But the challenge of this approach is that we are living in a culture where intact families, led by godly fathers and loving mothers, are a minority. To put it bluntly, the D6 approach only works when Mom and Dad are fully committed to these principles. Sadly, most of them are not.

The family landscape in America no longer looks like *Leave It to Beaver*. According to the Pew Research Center, among those under age thirty, more than half (52 percent) have at least one step relative;[1] in 2011, unmarried mothers accounted for 41 percent of births.[2] The statistics within the church today largely reflect the broader culture. Consider this disheartening headline from a 2014 Baylor University press release: "Evangelicals Have Higher-than-Average Divorce Rates, according to a Report Compiled by Baylor for the Council on Contemporary Families." Researchers found that evangelical Christians are more likely to be divorced than Americans who claim no religion.[3]

Of course, broken homes and struggling families are more than statistics for me. I was raised in a fatherless home by a godless mother. Were it not for the youth leaders at a local church who invested in me, I would be another spiritual statistic. Many of the teenagers attending youth groups today are being raised in families who fall short of the D6 norm. Maybe the dad is a deadbeat. Maybe the mom is emotionally dysfunctional. Or worse yet, maybe they are both rule-driven legalists who force-feed Christianity into the souls of their teenagers. These types of parents shatter the picture-perfect postcard that Christians want to print. The reality is much messier.

Of course, we need to change the picture. We need to build dads into godly dads, and moms into powerful examples for their children (and D6 is doing a great job of this). But as we do, we need youth ministries that run triage for the growing percentage of teenagers who don't have a dad who will mentor them or a mom who will disciple them. Another element that's missing from this approach is the Gospel Advancing thrust that will equip moms, dads, youth leaders, church leaders, and teenagers alike for the messiness of making disciples. If we are not careful, the D6 approach could unintentionally become a holy huddle of Bible-bubbled Christians who are so sheltered from the world that they are completely irrelevant when it comes to changing society.

The primary directive of Jesus for all of his followers is to "make disciples of all nations" (Matt. 28:19). This takes proximity. It takes getting our teenagers into the grit and grime of relationships with the lost (classmates, teammates, neighbors, and so on) and "coaching" them to engage in gospel conversations. If we really want our teenagers to be like Jesus, then we need to get them out of the huddle and into the game. We need to help them put their theology to the test by equipping them to engage the lost in the conversation that matters most.

Ideally, D6 parents would exemplify this lifestyle of evangelism for their own kids. And D6 youth leaders would invest in the fatherless or motherless or the have-both-parents-but-still-aren't-getting-it teenagers. When this happens, the discipleship will be both deep and wide. Parents and youth leaders alike will be working together to raise up young disciples who live and give the gospel.

## ✚ Brian Cosby

Ron, your D6 approach is very commendable. For the sake of organizing my response to your position, I'd like to offer what I see as some very positive aspects of your chapter and then some areas of disagreement and constructive criticism.

### Positives of the D6 View

You accurately portray the typical contemporary youth ministry scene, the craziness and impossible demands of a youth pastor's schedule, and the lack of spiritual "success" in the outcome. Your answer to this dilemma is simple and biblical: the church and home should work together as complementary institutions in the work of generational discipleship. I wholeheartedly agree.

I hear the age-segregation problem called many things today, but I've never heard the term "silo" being applied to it. It works. While assembly lines and fast-food restaurants produce specialized "professionals," they aren't taught to integrate their work into the whole. The same problem, as you note, exists in the church.

I love your call for youth pastors to help and equip parents, not replace them. I also like how you give some examples of how you see this happening at youth group and with announcements, seminars, and podcasts. This "partnership," as you call it, between the church and home is needed more than ever.

You also did a good job at your exposition of a number of passages, especially Deuteronomy 6 and Ephesians 6. You rightly state that even though Deuteronomy was written a long time ago and in a very different culture from our own, it is still just as relevant for us today. Thank you for showing how the New Testament writers (and Jesus) even affirmed the instruction of Deuteronomy to illustrate this. Deuteronomy 6 isn't just specific to the culture of its time period; it is *trans*cultural and *trans*generational.

I like the fact that you are careful to have the youth pastor not undermine the authority or "coolness" of the parents. Rather, they are to teach youth to love and respect—"honor"—their parents.

Probably the most poignant part of your argument is your simple question, What is the biblical foundation for the age-segregated model that we see so often in youth ministries today? I asked the same question last summer to a group of youth ministry professors at a seminary in Mexico. Silence. Thanks for this wonderful chapter.

### My Concerns with the D6 View

However (you knew this was coming!), I see some troubling aspects of your position. You may affirm what I'm about to point out, but I didn't see them in your chapter.

1. In a chapter decrying age-segregated modern youth ministry programs, I would have expected to also see some biblical foundation for the position of "youth pastor." You rightly ask the question for the biblical foundation for age segregation, but what about for the actual staff position itself?

You state, "The Bible provides no explicit description for the specific role of the youth pastor but does implicitly describe what a pastor should be and do." Are there not actual and biblical differences between a youth minister (who isn't found in Scripture) and a pastor (who is found in Scripture)? Similarly, what about the connection with the perpetual offices of elder and deacon? You mention, in general terms, "church leaders" throughout, but how can the youth pastor actually come alongside the specific callings of these perpetual officers?

While I actually agree with you that the position of "youth pastor" may be appropriate—with a number of qualifications—providing the biblical support for this would have made your position stronger, given your desire to see biblical support for other aspects of youth ministry.

2. You give some background into the age segregation that we see today, but you miss two other important parts: (1) the impact of human secularism and evolutionary theory on age segregation, and (2) the bigger aspect of how nearly 90 percent of *Christian* parents send their children to age-segregated schools. If age segregation is what you make it to be, and the impact of parents to be what it should be, then I would somehow dovetail your position into the bigger picture of how most of the teenager's week is spent with same-peer, age-segregated relationships. How can the church and home stand in *contrast* to this overwhelming cultural influence? Overall, it would have been nice to see your position placed in the larger context of our culture, which devalues children. Fewer people are having children because they are an "inconvenience," as they say, not a blessing from the Lord.

3. My biggest problem with your chapter, Ron, is that I kept asking, "Where is God in all of this?" God seems to be demoted to a sort of computer software program running in the background, or a deistic god watching how things play out. He's certainly not presented as the almighty and gracious One saving and sanctifying his people through the means of church and home generational discipleship. In other words, the emphasis is on the working operations of people to achieve an outcome, not God.

Your discussion of the complementary institutions of the church and home are excellent, except that God is almost left entirely out of the picture. It almost seems as if you are saying that if you just exert enough hard work—a splash of church and a dash of family—then you will have the desired outcome of long-term, sustainable, and obedient generational discipleship. All this happens, however, while God is in the background. The emphasis is on "building people" through church and home (as you point out), but the Scriptures teach that it is *God* who gives the growth (1 Cor. 3:7).

4. Another missing part is this: What makes up the actual discipleship in home and church? It's nice to have "teachable moments" (as you call them), but does God simply use teachable moments, or does he use his appointed

means of saving and growing people in the faith—his Word, prayer, worship, service, the local church, and so on? You see, it's what we do *with* those teachable moments. With such an emphasis on generational discipleship, the actual elements of this discipleship were noticeably absent.

Similarly, what does it look like—day in and day out—to lead your family in the home? Do you have a scheduled "family worship"? What do you use to disciple your children? Is D6 curriculum the only option? Some practical suggestions on this would have been helpful.

5. While I love the fact that you specifically mention the (oftentimes neglected) role of fathers, where is the biblical support for the father being his family's "coach"? You use this term frequently to describe his role, but where do you find that in the Bible? I kept envisioning a big guy with a whistle making his kids do Bible push-ups while yelling, "Jesus loves you." Why not simply use "father" and describe his role using Scripture? I found your use of "coach" a little distracting and perhaps out of accord with the view of the role of the father. Let's simply state that fathers train, equip, teach, lead, pray for and with, and read to and with their children rather than constantly use "coaching" for the primary role.

6. You didn't mention anything about God's covenant with us as his children. You write as someone who believes in covenant theology (i.e., continuity of Old and New Testaments, emphasis on raising children in the nurture and admonition of the Lord, etc.), but the real context is one of a *covenant* relationship between God and his people. His promise is for you and for your children after you (Acts 2:39). In fact, the context of Deuteronomy 6 is one of covenant (Deut. 5), with the stipulations extending into the Deuteronomy 6 passage. It also recounts God's redeeming work as the basis of God's commands. God works in us to will and to work for his good pleasure (Phil. 2:13). God works in us that which is pleasing in his sight (Heb. 13:21). This ongoing aspect of *God's* work was absent in your discussion of youth ministry. While parents and the church should together work to accomplish generational discipleship, this is ultimately about God.

7. Finally, you noted several times the youth pastor being the "hero" of the teen and parent. While I like youth pastors, we shouldn't forget the truer and greater Hero, God himself. Yes, youth pastors do lots of great things (by God's grace), but youth pastors don't save souls. They don't sanctify sinners. They are merely arrows pointing youth to the God who saves and sanctifies.

I want to again commend you for persuasively arguing for the complementary partnership between the church and home. That message needs to be heard more than ever. I also commend your criticism of church "gimmicks" and how this isn't the model we see presented in the pages of Scripture. But I would argue for a youth ministry position that takes into account more of the centrality of our Triune God: his sovereignty, his grace, his holiness, and his glory. He has established means of grace by which he will build his church. That said, thanks for an interesting chapter.

## ✚ Chap Clark

When we set out to put together this book, and when Ron Hunter, the founder and creator of D6, agreed to participate, I have to admit I was a bit curious. I haven't known Ron except for his work and reputation (which is stellar on both counts). I had heard of D6 and Ron Hunter for years, but until this project, I had not had the opportunity to interact with him. My curiosity focused first on his vision for the D6 movement and his take on its wildfire growth. (D6 has gone way beyond Ron, as the term itself has become its own brand.) My even greater curiosity was to see how Ron would line up philosophically and programmatically to those who disparage youth ministry altogether, like the people behind the *Divided* movie, who claim to have data to support their view that youth groups are driving Christian teens to abandon faith.[4] This numerically tiny but vocal movement with a large media presence is a fringe group that, while having a few good things to say to the church, has made life difficult for some youth ministry practitioners by dismissing all the good that youth ministry does well.

As with each chapter in this book, Ron's chapter, and our interactions as authors, has not only pleasantly settled my curiosity but has helped me become a huge fan of both Ron personally and the D6 movement. Ron, your chapter (as with the others in this book) is great: thoughtful, well resourced, and critically insightful, with an appropriate measure of grace. There are many points where I agree with you and where I resonate with your take on the historical issues that help to define and drive the D6 model. There are also, naturally, a few places where I wonder if there should be some fine-tuning of your perspective as recorded here. I will, therefore, respond in that order.

### *Where I Appreciate the D6 Perspective*

The way you frame the church and the relationship between parents and a church youth staff is theologically solid for your perspective. The phrase "D6 views the church as the theological anchor, training ground, and resource center for discipleship" is a concise and articulate description of the scriptural call to mutual nurture of the young. Your critique regarding church departments slipping toward being "silos of isolation" is, to me, both historically accurate and an important insight for today. Your qualifier, right off the bat, that D6 "includes the home but does not exclude the church" was especially refreshing in a world where the programs and staff of churches are under attack by some who passionately advocate for the family over youth ministry (e.g., the NCFIC and *Divided*). I also enjoyed your comparing ministry, presumably for children and also adolescents, to coaching soccer. The need to move the church to work with parents, supporting one another and being in relationship with one another in the interests of their children, is clear throughout your article. There is so much good in how you conceive of the D6 ministry model and strategy.

I have to say, before I get into the specific way you employ Scripture to support and define the D6 model, I also deeply appreciate your commitment to making sure that whatever it is you say and promote is true to and grounded on the Bible. I too believe that all theology, and therefore all ministry practice, must be carefully and fully rooted in revelation. When deciding on any course of action, behavior, or attitude, at the core of the deliberation process—whether it is for a philosophy or strategy of ministry, or in how we treat a child, a parent, or a senior adult—is a robust and historically sound hermeneutic. I can see that is where you are also coming from. This, then, opens the door to some questions I have regarding implementing the D6 model as described here.

### Where I Wonder whether Some Fine-Tuning Is in Order

First, in keeping with the soccer metaphor you use (and I too was a soccer coach for a brief period—don't ask!), I so agree with these lines: "Every player wanted his or her parents to practice with them. . . . Parents' involvement makes a huge difference, no matter the quality of the coach." This was my experience as well. What unsettled me at that point, however, and what is also the most pronounced programmatic issue I struggle with in the D6 model you espouse, is the line in the middle of those two: "often those who had no one also had the worst attitudes." Without pausing to reflect on the implications of this statement, you jump right into diagnosis, stating, "Church leaders desperately want a better way to equip parents so they can in turn coach their own kids." Apparently, then, your diagnosis of *why* some kids "have no one" is solely because their parents have not been "equipped." On many levels, this quick, offhand diagnosis and prescription is hard for me.

Like every one of us writing in this book, I have spent my years trying to care for kids in the name of Christ. Like every long-term youth worker, I have logged countless hours in relationships and conversations with teenagers and young adults: meals, camps, football practices, walks, drives, snacks, meetings—the gamut. In addition, I have used my academic training and the gracious Fuller Seminary sabbatical policy to study them—not just some of them, but every demographic our team and I could uncover—in the interests of understanding them so that we can care for and guide them more faithfully. That said, Ron, I am convinced that many if not most kids "have no one" *not* because a parent has not been "equipped to coach" but because there simply is no one. I am not only talking about overtly broken families, but this is also the case in so many "healthy" families, "intact" families, suburban, wealthy, and heavily resourced families *in addition to* the hundreds of thousands of families and parents in the United States who do not have the material means to be available to be their kids' "coaches." For these families, and there are many, many of them, the D6 model as described can become one more source of discouragement because they simply don't have the ability (or sometimes, yes, the willingness) to pull it off.

Second, the place where I get tripped up by some who base their ministry strategy on Deuteronomy 6 is in their theological method and use of the Bible. As I've said, I'm grateful for the way you describe the dance between discipleship in the home and in the church. Your strategy statement, "Building believers through church and home," states this twofold partnership. In Deuteronomy 6, especially vv. 4–7, from which you took the name of the model, there is exegetical evidence that to the Hebrew people, the Shema is not limited to parents but also includes the entire community, a both/and instead of either/or training in faith. You seek throughout the article to take this balance seriously. Yet, in actual practice—and what I'm about to say is less about your description in the chapter and more concerning others who take this idea to almost totally exclude the role of the community of adults in the church, staff or lay—this sometimes is a passage used to defend familial isolationism in the name of "biblical discipleship." I believe that is not your desire or intent in this chapter, but the potential is there for those who, for whatever reason, do not come to grips with the interconnectedness of the church/home partnership.

This, then, leads me to my third question, and it combines the first two. In your chapter, as you begin to talk about "being a transformational leader," you ask, "Who are the leaders and followers as they relate to youth ministry?" Your answer is that the "obvious first pair shows the youth pastor as the leader and the students as the followers. Parents and their teens are the second pair of leaders and followers." And later you say "youth pastors lead and shepherd the youth group." I find this to miss one of the more fundamental theological axioms of the post-Pentecost era, the role of the people in the family of faith in mutual nurture, mentoring, or discipleship. The three most pointed gift passages—1 Corinthians 12, Romans 12, and Ephesians 4—all are primarily concerned with unity in the church in the midst of various gifts and roles. They are *descriptive*, not *prescriptive* (even though most people get that one turned around and go through life looking for their "gift," when in reality these texts teach that *each person* is a called and gifted contributor to the health and growth of the whole). The point in these three passages, affirmed from the upper-room discourse in John 13–17 and throughout the New Testament, is that God's people are called to unity, to love and serve one another (Gal. 5:13), and to be a "chosen people" (1 Pet. 2:9). Ephesians 4:12 entreats leaders to "equip [God's] people for works of service." There seems to be overwhelming evidence that the role of leadership is to call every member of the body to participate in nurture and service to the entire family of God and to also, both individually and corporately, participate in the work of the kingdom of God.[5] The leader, then, in youth ministry and *every* ministry, is not the "staff" person but the people who call that church their home.

The reason this is so important in light of the D6 model of youth ministry is that the formula cannot be the "youth pastor as leader" and "parents as leaders" in partnership but rather the church as leader. *Everyone* is a partner in the discipleship, nurture, training, and sending ministry of the body to any person, including the young. As best as I understand the work of the Spirit in and through us as the body of Christ, and therefore D6 in particular, we all are, and must see one another as, members of the one body, the one family, the one people of God. This is God's design, to empower and equip us, by the Spirit in and through us, as we teach and serve one another. Parents, then, are obviously of supreme importance and influence, but they are not alone. And just because someone is uniquely trained, gifted, and possibly even paid does not mean they are the sole representative of the body of Christ to that child, adolescent, or family. We are the people of God. We pass on his truth and message and light. That is the message of the Scriptures. That is the point of D6.

In sum, I agree with and appreciate the goal and heart of the D6 movement, especially as you describe it here, Ron, with two vital caveats: the church must strategically commit to coming alongside and caring for the child or adolescent (and their family) whose parents are not able or willing to be a ministry partner, and the community of faith (not just the staff or leadership) must function as nurturing partners with parents.

## ✛ Fernando Arzola

Ron hits the nail on the head when he describes some of the unrealistic expectations placed on youth ministers. Many churches do write impossible job
descriptions. And often parents expect youth ministers to undo years of stuff
ingrained in the lives of their children—an unfair and unrealistic burden on
youth workers. This also lets parents "off the hook" as it relates to the spiritual development of their teens.

I am happy to see that D6 recognizes that the church is the anchor for youth
discipleship. At the end of the day, it is the local church that births, baptizes,
confirms, celebrates communion, marries, welcomes back, and buries. Parachurch ministries support churches but do not replace them.

D6 is also realistic. The youth minister can only do so much work with
teens. Therefore, the training of parents, guardians, grandparents, and the
faith community also empowers the gathering community. It takes a Christian
village to raise up Christian teens. But its emphasis on parents/guardians is
refreshing in an American youth ministry culture that at times tends to overemphasize youth strategies/programming that separates teens from adults
and the youth ministry from the congregation. By doing this, teens are not
adequately connected with the body of Christ. And if they leave the church,
when they return, they will not have strong relationships with members. This
reinforces what the Catholic Church popularly and correctly emphasizes, that
parents/guardians are the primary catechists. Furthermore, its developmental
sensitivity demonstrates age-appropriate awareness.

Ron also appropriately underscores the importance of children's ministry
and its necessary bridge to youth ministry. This expands the traditional youth
ministry paradigm from an isolated program to a more developmentally appropriate spiritual formation continuum. The use of the term "generational
discipleship" is quite apropos as it demonstrates both age development and
involvement of the broader faith community. More specifically, incorporating
the home with the church presents a more rich and expansive education process.
It may take more work, as it seems easier to focus solely on a "closed" youth
ministry model; however, in the long run, it will nurture a more spiritually
formed teen—and family.

By focusing on Deuteronomy 6, D6 is rooted in a biblical educational pattern that emphasizes a broader generational involvement. Ron's argument
to not dismiss Deuteronomy as being outdated or limited to ancient Israel
is valid. It is often quoted by Jesus, Paul, and the New Testament. He does
an excellent job in making this case. The biblical examples he provides are
various and rich educational models, both from the Old Testament and New

Testament. I particularly appreciate Ron's insights (and honesty) about biblical genealogies. They do demonstrate generational trajectories. His statement about Christ-likeness is especially apt: "Christ-likeness should be rooted within the values of families and passed along within the threads of generations, as noted through all Scripture."

Ron then spends a considerable amount on the role of the D6 youth pastor. In the section titled "Be a Transformational Leader," he presents James McGregor Burns's leadership definition and Paul's leadership expectation in Ephesians. While these are certainly leadership models and insights, I'm not sure what "transformational" leadership really is. I would have welcomed a more explicit and in-depth definition. The term "transformation" is as popular and vague as the word "purpose." What makes this leadership any more transformational than any other leadership model?

In "Build a Strategic Philosophy," I agree that youth ministry leaders need to spend significant time on developing an appropriate philosophy and underlying foundations. And this insight resonates with me: "Real revolution occurs when leaders focus on a philosophy of influencing people rather than behavior." This feels important, loving, and nonjudgmental. It focuses on people, not their behavior. Unfortunately, too many of our youth ministries and churches focus on behavior instead of people. Ron also challenges us when he states that youth should see Christ in us. Not an easy task.

As a religious educator, I was happy to see the "Build a Team Approach" section. Ron's suggestion that various leaders (preschool, children, and youth) work together and "share the same playbook" is in keeping with the Christian education tradition. In fact, much of the D6 model seems to me to be rooted less in the youth ministry and more in Christian education. (I say this as a good thing!)

He argues the most powerful teaching to youth includes studying the Bible, defending their faith, and taking the gospel to social issues. While there is certainly a place for apologetics, I am less concerned about students defending their faith and more concerned about them deepening and growing in their faith. I am always concerned about nurturing young zealots who are more energetic about defending their beliefs than growing in their faith. My experience is that this tends to develop argumentative, dogmatic teens rather than humble followers of Christ.

Ron's insight to youth leaders that if they "position themselves as cooler than mom or dad, they undermine the home" is right on point again. Youth leaders should position themselves as encouraging and supporting parents. This will be a challenge for younger youth workers who are trying to be relevant with teens. It is more important, I believe, to be authentic. Teens are looking for honest role models who respect them. Youth workers also have to earn the respect of parents/guardians. This does not occur overnight but through a long process of relationship building. The more support youth workers get from parents, the more support they will get for the ministry.

Overall, I think the D6 view is very helpful. However, the strongest area of critique I have is what to do with teens with no parents or an uninvolved home. While no program is necessarily applicable in all churches, I'm having a difficult time seeing the D6 paradigm applied in churches that have little parental involvement. This has certainly been my experience in many inner-city youth ministries. Here is where the D6 model seems to fall short. The heart of the program is parent/home driven. While this may work well in those congregations with greater resources and possibly a greater percentage of intact families or even those with greater parental involvement, what would this look like in poorer congregations?

## ✚ Ron Hunter's Response

None of us has found the exclusive way to minister to youth. All of the proposed models have merit. Young ministers today who wish to effectively lead will need a layered approach, utilizing bits of each of the methods listed in this book. Knowing we must be adaptive in our approach, I trust in God's foreknowledge. He knew the dysfunction and divorce that the New Testament and our current culture would face when he commanded us to work within a generational construct. The churches to whom Paul wrote faced an equal amount of sin and brokenness to that we face today, yet he did not relieve dads or moms of their spiritual coaching duty, as evidenced most pointedly in Ephesians 5–6. Still today, parents remain the primary influencers in the lives of youth, both in positive and negative ways. Ministry leaders cannot overlook the power of parental influence on a youth's worldview. To ignore proven principles will handicap potential outcomes.

The biggest criticism for D6 comes from the perspective that suggests it is designed for ideal homes that contain involved dads and moms who are both present and care about their kids. The idea that we get to start with the end in mind (a perfect set of concerned parents) is as contradictory as Jesus coming to seek and save those who are already saved. Parents are not always present. Some kids have one parent. Even when a teen has one or both parents, it does not mean either of them will participate in teaching biblical principles. We do need the adoption approach and Gospel Advancing approach along with parts of the others. Kids often have two homes and very mixed messages speaking into their world—if parents are speaking at all. I know—I came from a broken home as well. My parents divorced when I was fourteen. Let's look at some of the criticism and some counterpoints to consider.

Chap and Greg quickly point out that "most" kids are from broken homes and cite Pew Research that "among those under age 30, more than half (52%) has at least one step relative." Look at the reverse of the 52 percent and notice the 48 percent who need help to not become like the 52 percent. If we concentrate on simultaneously helping the 48 percent grow stronger in their marriage and parenting skills, they will have a positive influence on reducing the 52 percent statistic. While we cannot overlook ministering to those who have no parent present, the biggest asset the kids and youth ministry leaders have is getting parents to become more involved in their kids' lives. Greg noted that 41 percent of births occur among unwed mothers—my response is that 100 percent of the 41 percent of moms need our help to be involved, and most are willing to listen even if out of desperation. D6 fits the half that has parents, and the other half need what Chap describes in the adopted model of D6 dads and moms. We can still help spiritually abandoned kids find their way to significance when we invest in them, even when their parents do not. Ministry is messy; God never suggested a clean or easy way to connect with hurting people. However, the newest studies by Shaunti Feldhahn, a Harvard-trained researcher, in her recent book *The Good News about Marriage: Debunking Discouraging Myths about Marriage and Divorce* indicates the divorce rate is significantly lower than the often-quoted 50 percent. Kids of divorce still exist, as do the absentee dads and moms—even in church—but there is no better place to improve the trends.

I agree with Chap that when parents are absent, the community of the church must come around the teen to provide influence. However, the moms and dads who fill the gap at church must be careful not to use the adoption terminology at the risk of offending the unchurched parents who may take offense to this as an affront to their parenting. You still need to mentor and be there for them, but also look for a chance to connect with and, hopefully, one day hand off that responsibility to the student's parent.

Cosby, the presence of God is firmly established in the primary text of Deuteronomy 6. The first three verses tell us that we (parents, grandparents, and adults) are to (1) love God, (2) love his Word, and (3) teach our kids to do the same. I spent more time with my article trying to help people get past the current routines and practices of our day. I made some basic assumptions that God, his Son, his Word, and the work of the Holy Spirit were nonnegotiables, and I assume their presence. If God is absent from my chapter, it was not intentional. I argued for a very different paradigm than youth ministry as it has been conducted in its own separate world. I showed the value of youth ministry in collaboration with children and young adult ministry to prevent losing the teens in between each transition from one age group to the other. When each ministry operates in its own "silo," the emphasis on its own world makes others less attractive unless you build a long-term plan of discipleship that includes the input of every age-ministry leader. You are correct, without the centrality of God and his Word, nothing else we do will matter.

I use the term "coach" to describe the training and equipping role of the parents of teens. The coaching metaphor gives the title "father" an active description that everyone can visualize. As many of you suggested, a large number of kids do not have a positive mental image of what a father should do. The word "coach" implies training, practicing, putting them out on the field of life, and bringing them back to the sidelines for pep talks, new plays, and even first aid. Coaching is not controlling or hovering over teenagers. The term "coach" was meant to complement the role of dads of teenagers, which is different from dads of children or even adult kids. Each stage requires parenting adaptation as our kids grow from a very dependent stage to becoming independent, just as God designed.

The idea that this is not what the church looks like is flawed. While you correctly claim that the majority of homes are broken, the number you quoted is 52 percent. That is hardly a landslide, and to ignore the other half, which is far from an insignificant minority, would be negligent. One can look at the shift in the medical world to an emphasis on wellness care and see the benefits of emphasizing annual physicals and blood work. Physicians place a significant value on prenatal care for expecting moms. Why don't physicians and insurance companies just wait and treat the sick and hurting? The wellness care, screenings, and prenatal care have *significantly* reduced late-stage terminal diagnoses, infant mortality, and general health problems of involved people. Has cancer been eradicated? No—oncologists still treat cancer patients, but with early treatments the prognoses for many have been more positive today than even ten years ago. Ministry could learn from the medical field and provide preventative ministry. Is there a learning curve to get men to get an annual physical? Yes, and so there is in getting that same dad involved in his son or daughter's spiritual values and biblical worldview. It will take a generation of work to turn this around, but God gave us the method in his Deuteronomy 6 commands, which show up throughout Scripture. Youth ministry leaders should not position themselves to minister exclusively to broken families. That approach creates a reactive ministry rather than a strategic one that helps prevent such statistics.

D6 youth ministry works with the children's minister and the young-adult ministry, and hopefully has someone coordinating all generations of collaborative discipleship. A youth minister who wants to make ministry more effective in the long run will take the time to enlist available parents and seek to cultivate others to help with kids who don't have involved parents. D6 ministers can envision teaching youth to be the parent described in Deuteronomy 6 and Ephesians 6, and work to help their parents model it.

# Afterword

## Where from Here?

This is a book looking at the church's mission to the young through the eyes and convictions of five youth ministry leaders. Each has a proven and extensive track record. Many follow the writings, teaching, and thinking of every one of them. And each one believes, at the end of the day, that his perspective is the most significant and helpful way to think about youth ministry. The point of the book is not to determine who is "right" but to give each one a voice and then have a conversation.

As I said in the introduction, the goal has been to get the youth ministry world to think deeply about what it means and looks like to care for and nurture the life and faith of those who have not quite entered into the peer-driven status of adulthood. We hope that we have opportunities to offer this conversation live at conferences in the future, and we are planning on trying to do just that. We also have given each author some space at youthministry.fuller.edu to make their case. Yet our greatest hope is that people will be less committed to a single "view," program, or philosophy of ministry, and, in communion with their own church or ministry "family," more open to God leading as they design their ministry perspective and strategy. What should be evident at this point is that we all believe that everyone is "right," as our "views" are more about emphasis than disagreement.

If you as the reader—or class, or church, or organization—would like to get more information from any of our authors or even bring them to your church (via the web or live), each one has made it his life's vocation to serve the church. Their websites are included with their bios at the beginning of the book and on the website. However you use this material or engage in this conversation, we all hope and pray that our thoughts will spur you on to faithfully pursue Jesus Christ and the kingdom of God. Thank you for joining in the exchange.

# Notes

## Introduction

1. See Christian Smith and Melinda Lundquist Denton, *Soul Searching: The Religious and Spiritual Lives of American Teenagers* (Oxford: Oxford University Press, 2009).

2. Chap Clark, *Hurt 2.0: Inside the World of Today's Teenagers* (Grand Rapids: Baker Academic, 2011).

3. See the writings of Daniel Siegel, especially *Brainstorm: The Power and Purpose of the Teenage Brain* (New York: Tarcher, 2014). For "social capital," the concept of the kind and quality of social support networks that we all need to grow up, see the work of sociologist Robert Putnam, especially his seminal work, *Bowling Alone: The Collapse and Revival of American Community* (New York: Touchstone, 2001).

4. To see more of Kara Powell and the Fuller Youth Institute's work, see www.fulleryouthinstitute.org.

5. Greg Stier, one of the authors of this book, actually wrote me early on in the process to ask why Doug was excluded. He initially felt like we were leaving out arguably the most important voice.

## View One: Greg Stier

1. Ray Vander Laan, "Age of the Disciples," *Follow the Rabbi*, That The World May Know Ministries, Holland, MI, http://www.followtherabbi.com/guide/detail/jesus-authority-and-disciples.

2. Greg Stier, *Nine Evangelism Insights That Will Transform Your Ministry* (Arvada, CO: Dare 2 Share Ministries), 24.

3. David Kinnaman, *You Lost Me* (Grand Rapids: Baker Books, 2011), 23.

4. Timothy Keller, tweet on @timkellernyc, July 29, 2013.

5. Lewis A. Drummond, "The Secrets of Spurgeon's Preaching," Christian History and Biography, *Christianity Today*, January 1, 1991, http://www.ctlibrary.com/ch/1991/issue29/2914.html.

6. David Hertweck, "The Sucker's Choice: Is It Either/Or . . . or . . . Both/And?," *Doug Fields: Marriage, Family, Youth Ministry, Leadership* (blog), August 31, 2012, http://www.dougfields.com/posts/the-suckers-choice-is-it-eitheror-or-bothand/.

7. "Minority Rules: Scientists Discover Tipping Point for the Spread of Ideas," *RPI News*, Rensselaer, July 25, 2011, http://news.rpi.edu/update.do?artcenterkey=2902.

### View One Responses

1. I know that you hold to the notion that Jesus called teenagers as his disciples, and you cite a source for this; however, I cannot find any theological or published peer-reviewed commentary that supports this view. After much study and reflection, I simply believe that it is not true that the disciples were youth, although some may have been young adults, and to make the comparison between today's complex adolescent journey and young adults in Jesus's time is unsupportable. It is, however, for the purposes of this chapter, not worth debating.

2. For more on this, see the work of Denise Clark Pope (*Doing School: How We Are Creating a Generation of Stressed-Out, Materialistic, and Miseducated Students* [New Haven: Yale University Press, 2003]), Madeline Levine (*The Price of Privilege* [New York: Harper Perennial, 2008]), Brené Brown (*Men, Women, and Worthiness: The Experience of Shame and the Power of Being Enough* [Louisville, CO: Sounds True, 2012]), and Chap Clark (*Hurt 2.0: Inside the World of Today's Teenagers* [Grand Rapids: Baker Academic, 2011]).

3. I generally appreciate Tim Keller, but the comment you cite, "Get them in places where they have to rely on God," is fraught with danger when referring to teenagers and needs nuancing, especially as you apply it. "Relying on God" surely has a wide variety of applications for the often difficult and painful reality of the adolescent journey (from getting through a messy parental breakup to struggles with addiction or loneliness). I believe that we must take great care when we call kids to "risk" for God.

4. N. T. Wright, *Surprised by Hope: Rethinking Heaven, the Resurrection, and the Mission of the Church* (San Francisco: HarperOne, 2008), 267.

5. Fernando Arzola Jr., *Toward a Prophetic Youth Ministry: Theory and Praxis in Urban Context* (Downers Grove, IL: InterVarsity, 2008).

6. Mike King, *Presence-Centered Youth Ministry* (Downers Grove, IL: InterVarsity, 2006). Robert E. Webber, *Ancient-Future Evangelism: Making Your Church a Faith-Forming Community* (Grand Rapids: Baker Books, 2003).

7. Brennan Manning, *All Is Grace* (Colorado Springs: David C. Cook, 2011).

### View Two: Brian Cosby

1. "Moralistic therapeutic deism" has captured some of this sentiment as a description of American religion among teenagers. See Christian Smith and Melinda Lundquist Denton, *Soul Searching: The Religious and Spiritual Lives of American Teenagers* (New York: Oxford University Press, 2005).

2. See the classic book by Marshall Shelley, *Well-Intentioned Dragons: Ministering to Problem People in the Church* (Minneapolis: Bethany House, 1994).

3. For a summary of Reformed theology, see Brian H. Cosby, *Rebels Rescued: A Student's Guide to Reformed Theology* (Ross-Shire, UK: Christian Focus, 2012). I note ten doctrines that summarize the distinctives of Reformed theology: (1) *sola Scriptura*, (2) *sola fide*, (3) *sola gratia*, (4) *solus Christus*, (5) *soli Deo gloria*, (6) total depravity, (7) unconditional election, (8) limited atonement, (9) irresistible grace, and (10) perseverance of the saints. From their confessions and catechisms, most Presbyterian, historically Baptist, Anglican,

Episcopal, and Lutheran denominations would affirm most if not all of the above theological distinctions. However, most Methodists, Pentecostals, and self-proclaiming Free-Will Baptists would obviously *not* affirm a number of these distinctives.

4. I should note that while the idea of "covenant" is also central to a consistently Reformed approach, it is beyond the scope and purpose of this brief overview to demonstrate its role in shaping the church, family, and youth ministry.

5. Wayne Rice, *Reinventing Youth Ministry (Again): From Bells and Whistles to Flesh and Blood* (Downers Grove, IL: InterVarsity, 2010).

6. I applaud the efforts of ministries and organizations toward this end. See the National Center for Family-Integrated Churches (ncfic.org) and Mark DeVries, *Family-Based Youth Ministry*, 2nd ed. (Downers Grove, IL: InterVarsity, 2004).

7. These purposes are evangelism, worship, fellowship, discipleship, and ministry. Doug Fields, *Purpose Driven Youth Ministry* (Grand Rapids: Zondervan, 1998), 43–54.

8. These statistics are often cited in books and articles and seem to slightly change due to the demographic sampled, year (or years) surveyed, and how the surveyors interpret "commitment" or "faith" in the first place. Additionally, many also report that a number of those who leave the church rejoin the church after several years, even though these statistics range by denominational affiliation. See Barna Group, LifeWay Research, Fuller Youth Institute, Pew Research, and a number of denominational studies. See also Kara E. Powell, Brad M. Griffin, and Cheryl A. Crawford, *Sticky Faith: Practical Ideas to Nurture Long-Term Faith in Teenagers* (Grand Rapids: Zondervan, 2011) for a breakdown of many of these statistics.

9. See Ken Ham and Britt Beemer, *Already Gone: Why Your Kids Will Quit Church and What You Can Do to Stop It* (Green Forest, AR: New Leaf, 2009).

10. For a fuller treatment on entertainment in youth ministry, see Brian H. Cosby, *Giving Up Gimmicks: Reclaiming Youth Ministry from an Entertainment Culture* (Phillipsburg, NJ: P&R, 2012).

11. Janie B. Cheaney, "Despising Our Youth," in *World*, September 25, 2010, 24.

12. Ravi Zacharias, tweet on @ravizacharias, July 18, 2013.

13. See Brian H. Cosby, "MTD: Not Just a Problem of Youth Ministry," *Gospel Coalition*, April 9, 2012, http://www.thegospelcoalition.org/article/mtd-not-just-a-problem-with-youth-ministry.

14. Kenda Creasy Dean, *Almost Christian: What the Faith of Our Teenagers Is Telling the American Church* (New York: Oxford University Press, 2010), 3–4.

15. Ibid., 10.

16. Powell, Griffin, and Crawford, *Sticky Faith*, 141.

17. This statistic is frequently cited, including in Gary A. Goreham, "Denominational Comparison of Rural Youth Ministry Programs," *Review of Religious Research* 45, no. 4 (June 2004): 346–48.

18. Kent and Barbara Hughes, *Liberating Ministry from the Success Syndrome* (Wheaton: Crossway, 2008). I am fully aware of Timothy Keller's plea for "fruitfulness," a third way between success- and faithfulness-oriented ministries (see Timothy Keller, *Center Church: Doing Balanced, Gospel-Centered Ministry in Your City* [Grand Rapids: Zondervan, 2012], 13–16). But his "fruitfulness" approach looks remarkably similar to a success-driven approach, functionally.

19. Robert L. Reymond, *A New Systematic Theology of the Christian Faith*, 2nd ed. (Nashville: Thomas Nelson, 1998), 913.

20. Literally, "by the work performed."

21. Hughes Oliphant Old, *Worship: Reformed according to Scripture* (Louisville: Westminster John Knox, 2002), 74.

22. "How Teenagers' Faith Practices Are Changing," Barna Group, July 12, 2010, https://www.barna.org/barna-update/millennials/403-how-teenagers-faith-practices-are-changing.

23. "Sacrament" comes from the Latin translation of the Greek word that means "mystery" and has historically been used to describe these two ordinances. "Lord's Supper" is the phrase Paul used to describe this sacrament (1 Cor. 11:20).

24. John Calvin, *Institutes of the Christian Religion*, ed. John T. McNeill, trans. Ford Lewis Battles (Philadelphia: Westminster, 1960), 4.14.1.

25. Ibid.

26. "Report Examines the State of Mainline Protestant Churches," Barna Group, December 2009. https://www.barna.org/barna-update/leadership/323-report-examines-the-state-of-mainline-protestant-churches.

27. We do not resacrifice Jesus all over again, as he was sacrificed once (cf. Heb. 7:27). Thus, we don't have an "altar" but a "table."

28. The phrase "fencing the table" is used by some as a way to describe the process of examining the biblical warnings given about how we approach the Lord's Supper. These include warnings for the unbeliever and the unrepentant (cf. 1 Cor. 11:27–29).

29. Joel R. Beeke, *Puritan Reformed Spirituality: A Practical Theological Study from Our Reformed and Puritan Heritage* (Darlington, UK: Evangelical Press, 2006), 8.

30. Ibid., 410.

31. J. C. Ryle, *Practical Religion* (Edinburgh: Banner of Truth Trust, 1998), 441.

32. Jon D. Payne, *In the Splendor of Holiness: Rediscovering the Beauty of Reformed Worship for the 21st Century* (White Hall, WV: Tolle Lege, 2008), 15.

**View Two Responses**

1. See the Pew study for a balanced report on this and other religious trends in American culture: "'Nones' on the Rise," Pew Research Religion and Public Life Project, October 9, 2012, http://www.pewforum.org/2012/10/09/nones-on-the-rise.

2. Daniel Siegel, *Brainstorm: The Power and Purpose of the Teenage Brain* (New York: Tarcher, 2014).

3. This is the thrust of my work on *Hurt: Inside the World of Today's Teenagers* (Grand Rapids: Baker Academic, 2004) and *Hurt 2.0* (Grand Rapids: Baker Academic, 2011).

4. Theresa O'Keefe, "Growing Up Alone: The New Normal of Isolation in Adolescents," *Journal of Youth Ministry Educators* (Fall 2014).

5. Henri J. M. Nouwen, *A Cry for Mercy: Prayers for the Genesee* (Garden City, NY: Doubleday, 1981), Monday, February 19.

6. Thomas C. Oden, *Life in the Spirit*, vol. 3, *Systematic Theology* (San Francisco: Harper & Row, 1992), 300.

7. Resources and studies include Jeremy Weber, "New Research Suggests Calvinists Tied with Arminians in SBC," Gleanings, *Christianity Today*, June 19, 2012, http://www.christianitytoday.com/gleanings/2012/june/new-research-suggests-calvinists-tied-with-arminians-in-sbc.html; Russ Rankin, "SBC Pastors Polled on Calvinism and Its Effect," *Lifeway*, http://www.lifeway.com/Article/research-sbc-pastors-polled-on-calvinism-affect-on-convention; "Is There a 'Reformed' Movement in American

Churches?," Barna Group, November 15, 2010, https://www.barna.org/barna-update/faith
-spirituality/447-reformed-movement-in-american-churches.

### View Three: Chap Clark

1. Mark H. Senter III and Warren S. Benson, *The Complete Book of Youth Ministry* (Chicago: Moody, 1987).

2. To many in what has become the academic guild for youth ministry scholarship in the United States, the Association of Youth Ministry Educators, or AYME, I am certain that this statement will elicit at least a question if not a severely negative response. My intent was to quickly bring new students into the dialogue of historic grounding of youth ministry, not to be as historically precise as I would be otherwise. I ask my thoughtful colleagues to forgive me for this reduction in the service of brevity.

3. Warren S. Benson, "A Theology of Youth Ministry," in Benson and Senter, *Complete Book*, 19. In attempting to make the case for youth ministry to be seen as a theological discipline, he "academically located" youth ministry practice in "the constructs of educational philosophy," where some academics see youth ministry today. In contrast, many, perhaps most, youth ministry academics see it as an expression of practical theology, or perhaps, as I do, theology and culture. This is a long-standing debate in the world of academic youth ministry preparation.

4. Ibid., 26–28.

5. "What Is Youth Ministry?," Youthpastor.com, http://www.youthpastor.com/Youth_Ministry/.

6. Mark DeVries, *Family-Based Youth Ministry* (Downers Grove, IL: InterVarsity, 1994); Doug Fields, *Purpose Driven Youth Ministry* (Grand Rapids: Zondervan, 1998); and Duffy Robbins, *Ministry of Nurture* (Grand Rapids: Zondervan, 1990).

7. Benson, "Theology of Youth Ministry," 16.

8. For the family movement, Mark DeVries's *Family-Based Youth Ministry* is credited with raising awareness in the broader youth ministry community. Wayne Rice, Jim Burns, Duffy Robbins, and especially Doug Fields provided the programmatic framework; Rich Van Pelt, Walt Mueller, Marv Penner, and Chap Clark, in his *Hurt: Inside the World of Today's Teenagers*, raised the awareness of how culture affects our young.

9. See Jim Rayburn, *The Diaries of Jim Rayburn* (Houston: Whitecaps Media, 2008); Jim Rayburn, *Dance, Children, Dance: The Story of Jim Rayburn, Founder of Young Life* (Wheaton: Tyndale House, 1984); and Char Meredith, *It's a Sin to Bore a Kid: The Story of Young Life* (Waco: Word, 1978).

10. To be fair, certain traditions prefer to see youth ministry as "evangelization," where baptized and/or "confirmed" young people, while being found in standing as a member of the faith community, nonetheless need the impetus of youth ministry to come to see their faith as important. These communities typically chafe at the notion of "conversion" while functionally tending to call for a similar personal response.

11. The most prominent example is Doug Fields's *Purpose Driven Youth Ministry*, where those who have "accepted Christ" move from the "crowd" to the "congregation," with the hopes of eventually becoming "committed" and, ultimately, moving into leadership as "core" members. See the writings of every major youth ministry author over the past forty years, from Larry Richards to Mark Senter, Jim Burns to Duffy Robbins.

12. In academic studies of faith, most notably the "Faith Maturity Scale" (P. L. Benson, M. J. Donahue, and J. A. Erickson, "The Faith Maturity Scale: Conceptualization,

Measurement, and Empirical Validation," *Research in the Social Scientific Study of Religion* 5 [1993]: 1–26), lists that allow us to measure mature faith generally focus analysis on activity and external involvement.

13. Dallas Willard, *The Divine Conspiracy: Rediscovering Our Hidden Life in God* (San Francisco: HarperSanFrancisco, 1997), 40.

14. This is one of N. T. Wright's staple arguments. For an example, see *Evil and the Justice of God* (Downers Grove, IL: InterVarsity, 2013).

15. For a comprehensive understanding of this distinction, see George Eldon Ladd, *The Pattern of New Testament Truth* (Grand Rapids: Eerdmans, 1968), 13–40.

16. Richard A. Gaillardetz, *Ecclesiology for a Global Church: A People Called and Sent* (Maryknoll, NY: Orbis, 2010), 20.

17. See also Isa. 63:16; Hosea 11:1–4; Rom. 8:15–17; Gal. 4:4–7; and Eph. 1:5.

18. "The Aramaic word 'Abba' is thought to be a very intimate term for 'Father' suggesting that those who use it to refer to God enjoy a close relationship with him. Jesus Christ uses the term as a consequence of his natural sonship of God; believers may use it as a consequence of their adopted sonship of God through faith." "Abba," Martin H. Manser, *Dictionary of Bible Themes: The Accessible and Comprehensive Tool for Topical Studies* (London: Martin Manser), 81. It should be noted that marriage is also an "intimate and sacred of family relationships," as we are referred to as the "bride of Christ." While this is familial as well, because marriage is a covenant entered into by choice and being adopted as a child is not, there seems to be a unique significance to this use of the term "child of God."

19. Dennis B. Guernsey, *A New Design for Family Ministry* (Elgin, IL: David C. Cook, 1982), 100, 112.

20. *Huiothesia*; see Rom. 8:15, 23; 9:4; Gal. 4:5; Eph. 1:5. A. C. Myers writes, "It is a spiritual adoption which replaces the natural familial relationship with God that had been forfeited through the fall" ("Adoption," *The Eerdmans Bible Dictionary* [Grand Rapids: Eerdmans, 1987], 82).

21. For a theological definition of "adoption," see Michael Braeutigam, "Adopted by the Triune God: The Doctrine of Adoption from a Trinitarian Perspective," *Scottish Bulletin of Evangelical Theology* 27, no. 2 (Autumn 2009): 164; and s.v. "5206: *huiothesia*," Bible Hub, http://biblehub.com/greek/5206.htm.

22. While extended adolescence and the lack of social capital is a major conceptual factor in understanding the psychosocial need for adoption as the theological goal of youth ministry, there is not adequate space to go into depth. See the work of David Elkind for some of the early cultural factors leading to where we are today, Robert Putnam for the need for and dissolution of social capital, J. J. Arnett for understanding emerging adulthood, Daniel Siegel for the way the teenage brain now develops, and Chap Clark for a holistic integration of all of these and other sources that have led to what I have called "systemic abandonment."

23. There is widespread agreement that the church is facing a crisis with young people. See Kara E. Powell and Chap Clark, *Sticky Faith* (Grand Rapids: Zondervan, 2011), 153. The numbers vary from study to study, but one of the most robust, Fuller Seminary's College Transition Project and the Fuller Youth Institute, estimates that nearly 50 percent of active and involved high school seniors leave behind their faith within a year or two of graduation. The research can be accessed at www.fulleryouthinstitute.org.

24. See www.stickyfaith.org for this and other research-based suggestions for developing faith after high school.

25. Louis Berkhof, *Systematic Theology* (Grand Rapids: Eerdmans, 1939), 503–7: "This third element consists in a personal trust in Christ as Saviour and Lord, including the surrender of the soul as guilty and defiled to Christ, and a recognition and appropriation of Christ as the source of pardon and of spiritual life" (505).

### View Three Responses

1. Kenda Creasy Dean, *Almost Christian* (New York: Oxford University Press, 2010), 49.
2. Charles R. Swindoll, *The Grace Awakening* (Dallas: Word, 1990), 22–23.
3. Philip Yancey, *What's So Amazing about Grace?* (Grand Rapids: Zondervan, 1997), 72.
4. David Kinnaman and Aly Hawkins, *You Lost Me* (Grand Rapids: Baker Books, 2011), 106.
5. Dietrich Bonhoeffer, *Life Together: The Classic Exploration of Faith in Community* (1939; San Francisco: HarperOne, 1978), 77–78.
6. Ibid., 110.

### View Four: Fernando Arzola

1. Everett Ferguson, *The Church of Christ: A Biblical Ecclesiology for Today* (Grand Rapids: Eerdmans, 1997); Miroslav Volf, *After Our Likeness: The Church as the Image of the Trinity* (Grand Rapids: Eerdmans, 1997); Crain Van Gelder, *The Essence of the Church: A Community Created by the Spirit* (Grand Rapids: Baker Books, 2000); Veli-Matti Kärkkäinen, *An Introduction to Ecclesiology: Ecumenical, Historical and Global Perspectives* (Downers Grove, IL: InterVarsity, 2002); Donald Bloesch, *The Church: Sacraments, Worship, Ministry, Mission* (Downers Grove, IL: InterVarsity, 2002); John Stackhouse, ed., *Evangelical Ecclesiology: Reality or Illusion?* (Grand Rapids: Baker Academic, 2003); Reinhard Hütter, *Bound to Be Free: Evangelical Catholic Engagements in Ecclesiology, Ethics and Ecumenism* (Grand Rapids: Eerdmans, 2004).

2. Brian Cosby's chapter in this book is a rare and thoughtful examination of youth ministry from the Reformed tradition.

3. Several books written in this area include James S. Cutsinger, ed., *Reclaiming the Great Tradition: Evangelicals, Catholics and Orthodox in Dialogue* (Downers Grove, IL: InterVarsity, 1997); Christopher A. Hall, *Reading Scripture with the Church Fathers* (Downers Grove, IL: InterVarsity, 1998); Christopher A. Hall, *Learning Theology with the Church Fathers* (Downers Grove, IL: InterVarsity, 2002); Thomas C. Oden, *The Rebirth of Orthodoxy: Signs of New Life in Christianity* (New York: HarperCollins, 2003); Thomas C. Oden and Christopher A. Hall, eds., *Ancient Christian Commentary on Scripture*, vols. 1–28 (Downers Grove, IL: InterVarsity, 1998–2006); Kenneth Tanner and Christopher A. Hall, eds., *Ancient and Postmodern Christianity: Paleo-Orthodoxy in the 21st Century* (Downers Grove, IL: InterVarsity, 2002); D. H. Williams, *Evangelicals and Tradition: The Formative Influence of the Early Church* (Grand Rapids: Baker Academic, 2005); D. H. Williams, *Retrieving the Tradition and Renewing Evangelicalism: A Primer for Suspicious Protestants* (Grand Rapids: Eerdmans, 1999); Robert Webber and Donald Bloesch, *The Orthodox Evangelicals: Who They Are and What They Are Saying* (Nashville: Thomas Nelson, 1978); Robert E. Webber, *Evangelicals on the Canterbury Trail* (Harrisburg, PA: Morehouse, 1989); Robert E. Webber, *Ancient-Future Faith* (Grand Rapids: Baker, 1999); Daniel H. Williams, *Evangelicals and Tradition: The Formative Influence of the Early Church* (Grand Rapids: Baker Academic, 2005).

4. The terms "catholic" and "evangelicalism" are used in a historically broad sense, not specifically referring to the Roman Catholic Church or the evangelical church per se.

5. Donald G. Bloesch, *Essentials of Evangelical Theology* (Peabody, MA: Hendrickson, 1978, 2006), 1:283.

6. For further reading on paleo-orthodoxy from leading evangelical scholars, see Tanner and Hall, *Ancient and Postmodern Christianity*.

7. Webber, *Ancient-Future Faith*, 30–31.

8. Ibid., 89.

9. Ibid., 73.

10. Ibid.

11. Ibid., 74.

12. Ibid.

13. H. T. Kerr, *A Compend of Luther's Theology* (Philadelphia: Westminster, 1943), 125–26.

14. Ibid.

15. Ibid.

16. Ibid., 75.

17. Ibid.

18. Ibid.

19. Ibid.

20. Ibid., 76.

21. These characteristics are found in both the Apostles' and the Nicene creeds.

22. Ibid., 84.

23. Ibid., 100.

24. Thomas C. Oden, *Life in the Spirit*, vol. 3, *Systematic Theology* (San Francisco: Harper & Row, 1992), 306.

25. Ibid., 307–8.

26. Webber, *Ancient-Future Faith*, 85.

27. Ibid.

28. Oden, *Life in the Spirit*, 316.

29. Ibid., 319.

30. Bloesch, *The Church*, 100.

31. Webber, *Ancient-Future Faith*, 86.

32. Ibid.

33. Oden, *Life in the Spirit*, 338.

34. Ibid., 340.

35. Webber, *Ancient-Future Faith*, 87.

36. Bloesch, *The Church*, 102.

37. Oden, *Life in the Spirit*, 349.

38. Webber, *Ancient-Future Faith*, 87.

39. Bloesch, *The Church*, 103.

40. Oden, *Life in the Spirit*, 352.

41. Wayne Grudem, *Systematic Theology: An Introduction to Biblical Doctrine* (Grand Rapids: Zondervan, 1995), 866.

42. Webber, *Ancient-Future Faith*, 73.

43. *Catechism of the Catholic Church*, para. 752.

44. Millard J. Erickson, *Christian Theology* (Grand Rapids: Baker Academic, 1998), 1043.

45. Lothar Coenen, "Church," in *The New International Dictionary of New Testament Theology*, ed. Colin Brown (Grand Rapids: Zondervan, 1975), 1:291.

### View Four Responses

1. For a concise apologetic of Wright's position regarding the Reformers and Paul, see http://ntwrightpage.com/Wright_New_Perspectives.htm.

2. Dallas Willard, *The Divine Conspiracy* (New York: HarperCollins, 1998), 41.

3. H. Waddell, *The Desert Fathers* (London: Constable, 1987), http://www.christianethics today.com/cetart/index.cfm?fuseaction=Articles.main&ArtID=240.

4. Stuart Cummings-Bond, "The One-Eared Mickey Mouse," *Youthworker* (Fall 1989): 76.

5. Mark DeVries, *Family-Based Youth Ministry* (Downers Grove, IL: InterVarsity, 2004).

### View Five: Ron Hunter

1. Pocket Oxford English Dictionary, 10th ed., s.v. "silo."

2. G. Ritzer, *The McDonaldization of Society*, 20th anniversary ed. (Thousand Oaks, CA: SAGE, 2013).

3. G. Reid, *Deuteronomy 6 in 3D* (Nashville: Randall House, 2010), 19.

4. J. C. VanderKam, *The Dead Sea Scrolls Today* (Grand Rapids: Eerdmans, 1994).

5. See D. L. Christensen, *Deuteronomy 1:1–21:9*, 2nd rev. ed. (Nashville: Thomas Nelson, 2001); and E. J. Woods, *Deuteronomy: An Introduction and Commentary* (Downers Grove, IL: IVP Academic, 2011).

6. T. Kimmel, *Connecting Church and Home: A Grace-Based Partnership* (Nashville: Randall House, 2013), 39.

7. A. T. Lincoln, *Ephesians* (Dallas: Word, 1990).

8. C. J. H. Wright, *Deuteronomy* (Peabody, MA: Hendrickson, 1996).

9. E. H. Merrill, *Deuteronomy*, vol. 4 (Nashville: B&H, 1994).

10. B. Wilkinson, *Experiencing Spiritual Breakthroughs* (Colorado Springs: Multnomah, 1999).

11. J. M. Burns, *Leadership* (New York: Harper & Row, 1978), 19.

12. Ibid.

13. B. M. Bass and R. E. Riggio, *Transformational Leadership*, 2nd ed. (Mahwah, NJ: L. Erlbaum Associates, 2006), 3.

14. T. P. Jones, *Family Ministry Field Guide* (Indianapolis: Wesleyan, 2011).

15. G. Barna, *Revolutionary Parenting: What the Research Shows Really Works* (Carol Stream, IL: BarnaBooks, 2007).

16. B. Haynes, *Shift: What It Takes to Finally Reach Families Today* (Loveland, CO: Group, 2009).

17. M. Holmen, *Faith Begins at Home* (Ventura, CA: Regal, 2005), 99.

### View Five Responses

1. "A Portrait of Stepfamilies," Pew Research Center Social & Demographic Trends, January 13, 2011, http://www.pewsocialtrends.org/2011/01/13/a-portrait-of-stepfamilies/.

2. "Five Facts about the Modern American Family," Pew Research Center, April 30, 2014, http://www.pewresearch.org/fact-tank/2014/04/30/5-facts-about-the-modern-american -family/.

3. "Evangelicals Have Higher-than-Average Divorce Rates, According to a Report Compiled by Baylor for the Council on Contemporary Families," Baylor Media Communications, February 5, 2014, http://www.baylor.edu/mediacommunications/news.php ?action=story&story=137892.

4. To read more on this, I suggest both the description and defense of the research and perspective of the National Center for Family-Integrated Churches (http://www.charisma news.com/us/41465-youth-groups-driving-christian-teens-to-abandon-faith; see also www .NCFIC.org) and also the blog/critique of the research from *Christianity Today* (http:// www.christianitytoday.com/edstetzer/2014/may/are-youth-groups-bad.html). You may also watch the movie for free at https://ncfic.org/resources/view/divided-the-movie.

5. The book of Acts opens with the risen Jesus proclaiming one thing, the kingdom of God (Acts 1:3), and closes with the apostle Paul in house arrest, as he "proclaimed the kingdom of God and taught about the Lord Jesus Christ" (Acts 28:30–31).

# Index

adolescents
  building trust with, 58–59
  contextualizing for, 57, 67–68
  desires of, 40
  holistic approach to, 25–26
  need for adult support and presence, 83–85
  from single-parent homes, 163–64
  training and guidance for, 22–23
adoption, 81–90
altar calls, 27, 59
apostolic teaching, 120, 135
Arnett, Jeffrey, 83, 186n22
authenticity, 13, 83, 96, 134, 157, 173

baptism, 47–48
Beeke, Joel, 51
Benson, Warren, 76–78, 102, 185n3
Berkhof, Louis, 86, 98, 187n25
Bloesch, Donald, 114, 120, 127–28, 139
Bonhoeffer, Dietrich, 100
Burns, James McGregor, 155, 173

Calvin, John, 47, 121
Cheaney, Janie, 39
Christian Endeavor, 76
Christian fellowship/community, 27, 51–52,
    75–76, 93, 100
church
  age segregation in, 147–48, 165–66
  creedal characteristics of, 117–23
  family model of, 21, 79–81, 97, 100, 103, 105
  incarnational view of, 115–16
  membership in, 47–48
  unity in, 117–18, 128, 132, 139–40
  visible/invisible, 115–17, 127, 141
Coenen, Lothar, 122
college, 39, 84, 105, 134, 186n23
conversion, 185n10
covenant theology, 167, 183n4
creation, 37
creeds, 93
Cummings-Bond, Stuart, 136

Dean, Kenda Creasy, 40, 65, 93
denominations, 55
developmental stages, 14
DeVries, Mark, 78, 136, 185n8
discipleship, 5, 11, 23, 27, 29–30, 78–79, 104,
    108, 122, 171
doctrinal orthodoxy, 119–20

early church, 123, 125, 135, 142
ecclesiology, 113–23
Elkind, David, 82, 186n22
Enlightenment, 116–17, 126
entertainment, 39–41, 60, 63
Erickson, Millard, 122
evangelicalism, 114–15, 188n4
evangelism, 5, 7–10, 53–54

faith
  and action, 9, 28–29
  call of, 86
  as individualistic, 78–79, 83, 87, 97, 127, 141
  and obedience, 94–95, 101
  and repentance, 48

and success, 41–42, 64–65
and works, 121
family worship, 167
fasting, 46
Feldhahn, Shaunti, 175
Fields, Doug, xiv–xvi, 39, 78, 185n11
Francis of Assisi, 27

Gaillardetz, Richard, 80
generational discipleship, 148–62
God
  adoption of, 21, 81–90
  as Father, 152–53, 186n18
  glory of, 20
  love of, 98, 107–8
  role in evangelism, 19
  sovereignty of, of 37
gospel, 10–11, 23–24, 27
Gospel Advancing Ministry, 4–15
gospel-motivated service, 49–50, 61, 68
grace, 43, 52, 59–60, 93–95, 98–99, 107,
  151–52
Great Commission, 5, 21, 30
Grudem, Wayne, 121
Guernsey, Dennis, 81

Hertweck, David, 10
holiness, 118–19, 123, 127, 132–33, 141–42
Holy Spirit, 51, 119
Hughes, Kent and Barbara, 41–42

incarnation, 77, 81

Jesus
  church as the body of, 52, 80–81, 122
  finding identity in, 24, 51
  obedience and submission to, 86–87, 117
  real presence of, 115
  as a youth leader, 3–4, 18, 25, 182n1
Jones, Timothy Paul, 160
justification, 94, 121

Keller, Tim, 8, 182n3
Kimmel, Tim, 137, 151
King, Mike, 26
Kinnaman, David, 45, 95

leadership
  development of, 116, 155–57, 173
  motives and insecurities in, 23
  philosophy of influencing, 157–58
London Baptist Confession of Faith, 43

Lord's Supper, 47–49, 61, 184n23, 184n28
Luther, Martin, 115, 121

means of grace, 42–49, 56–57, 60
mentors, 6, 21, 95–96, 99, 107
mission trips, 50

Nouwen, Henri, 60–61

Oden, Thomas, 61, 114, 118–20, 135
Old, Hughes Oliphant, 44
orthodoxy, 114–15, 134–37

parachurch ministries, 50–51, 61, 64, 99–100
parents
  as coaches, 13–14, 29, 105–6, 148–62
  responsibility of, 20, 38–39, 65, 99, 108–9
Payne, Jon, 52
personal conviction, 23
post-Christian culture, 79–80
Powell, Kara, xiv–xvi, 102
pragmatism, 116
prayer, 12, 22, 45–46, 60, 122
preaching, 44, 67, 123
Putnam, Robert, 82, 186n22

Randall House, 149–50
Rayburn, Jim, 77–78
Reformation, 115–16, 123, 128
Reformed theology, 56, 182n3
Reformed youth ministries, 38–52
regeneration, 20
Reid, Garnett, 151
Reymond, Robert, 43
Rice, Wayne, 38, 65, 77
Ritzer, George, 147
Robbins, Duffy, 78
Roman Catholicism, 115
Ryle, J. C., 52

sacraments, 47–49, 120–21, 184n23
salvation, 9, 37, 51, 70, 94–99, 136
sanctification, 94, 97–98
Schultz, Thom and Joni, 77
Scripture
  and sanctification, 98
  sufficiency of, 63
  and Word-infused youth ministry, 43–45
Senter, Mark, 76–77, 102
Siegel, Daniel, 186n22
sin, 19, 43, 98
Smith, Christian, 69

social awareness, 27
social capital, 22, 186n22
social justice, 8, 12, 23–24, 28
spiritual disciplines, 26–27
spiritual gifts, 80
spiritual growth, 104
spiritual orphans, 83
Spurgeon, Charles, 10
storytelling, 9–10
Swindoll, Chuck, 94

temple tax, 3–4

Webber, Robert, 26–27, 114–15, 117, 119, 122, 131, 135
Westminster Larger Catechism, 42–43

Wilkinson, Bruce, 154
Willard, Dallas, 79, 133
worship, 20, 122–23
Wright, N. T., 24, 58, 131

Yaconelli, Mike, 73–74, 77, 109
Yancey, Philip, 94, 107
Young Life, 76
Youth for Christ, 76
youth pastors
  isolation of, 136
  legitimacy of, 38
  responsibilities of, 44, 47, 62–65, 116, 155–62
  working with other pastors, 20, 28

Zacharias, Ravi, 39–40, 68

**FULLER THEOLOGICAL SEMINARY,**
in partnership with
**BAKER ACADEMIC,**
has created a website dedicated to this book at
**YOUTHMINISTRY.FULLER.EDU**

• • •

This site will provide supplemental content for *Youth Ministry in the 21st Century: Five Views*, as well as author interviews introducing and describing their various perspectives, conversations among the authors, and a variety of other resources—video and print—that extend the conversation found in this book.

The website features more about each author, including contact information. We encourage professors and leaders who would like to have their students or others dialogue with one or more of the authors to invite them to participate in a video chat through this website.

In the future this website will host conversations related to Chap Clark's forthcoming book *Adoptive Youth Ministry: Integrating Emerging Generations into the Family of Faith* (also from Baker Academic) as well as other books, people, and topics that move the faithful to think differently about youth ministry.